The Business of Factoring

A Guide to Factoring and Invoice Discounting

David Hawkins

McGRAW-HILL BOOK COMPANY

London · New York · St Louis · San Francisco · Auckland · Bogotá
Caracas · Lisbon · Madrid · Mexico · Milan · Montreal · New Delhi
Panama · Paris · San Juan · São Paulo · Singapore · Sydney · Tokyo
Toronto

Published by
McGRAW-HILL Book Company Europe
Shoppenhangers Road, Maidenhead, Berkshire, England SL6 2QL
Telephone 0628 23432
Fax 0628 770224

British Library Cataloguing in Publication Data

Hawkins, David
Business of factoring: Guide to Factoring and Invoice Discounting
I. Title
658.15
ISBN 0-07-707476-9

Library of Congress Cataloging-in-Publication Data

Hawkins, David,
The business of factoring: a guide to factoring and
invoice discounting / David Hawkins.
    p.   cm.
Includes index.
ISBN 0-07-707476-9 :
1. Factoring (Finance)   I. Title.
HG3752.3.H38   1983
658.15-dc20   92-43383

Copyright © 1993 McGraw-Hill International (UK) Limited. All rights reserved. No part of this publication may be reproduced, stored in a retrieval system, or transmitted, in any form or by any means, electronic, mechanical, photocopying, recording, or otherwise, without the prior permission of McGraw-Hill International (UK) Limited.

1234 CUP 9543

Typeset by Computape (Pickering) Ltd, North Yorkshire,
and printed and bound in Great Britain at the University Press, Cambridge.

Contents

Foreword	vii
1. Factoring and invoice discounting	1
What is factoring?	1
Invoice discounting	2
Who are the factors?	3
Who are the clients?	4
Some general themes	4
2. An industry in the making	7
Early days	7
Back to Europe	9
The industry today	10
3. The services	18
Trade credit and factoring	18
The full factoring service	19
Credit control and advice	22
Collection	24
Full factoring—who needs it?	27
Recourse factoring	29
Invoice discounting	32
Management buy-outs	34
Agency or bulk factoring	35
Maturity factoring	36
Export factoring	37
The costs	37
Is factoring expensive?	40
4. Risks, security and law	45
Customer risk	45
Client risk	47
Financial weakness	53
Who *cannot* factor?	55
Reservation of title	58
The factor's security	59
5. Accounts and accounting	67
Sales ledger accounting	67
Client accounting and payment availability	69
Client's audited accounts	73

CONTENTS

6. Some cases in point — **76**
XYZ Limited — 76
A & E Page Industrial Holdings — 80

7. The factoring client — **84**
Who are they? — 84
How should the 'typical' client decide for factoring? — 86
Negotiations — 91
Prices — 93
Confidentiality — 93
Are clients getting what they want? — 95
The factoring/invoice discounting checklist — 96

8. Client relations — **98**
The key to successful factoring — 98
Structure and operation — 98
Security of funds — 99
The problem of fraud — 102
Client communications — 104

9. The factors — **108**
Bankers all? — 108
Growth and profitability — 110
Factoring people — 112

10. The marketing of factoring — **117**
Introductory sources — 118
The negotiation process — 119
Some Shibboleths — 124
Marketing, not just sales — 128
Advertising and public relations — 133
The factoring product — 137
The way forward — 145

11. The Association of British Factors and Discounters — **148**
Background — 148
Structure and activities — 149
The need for training — 150
Public relations — 151
A wider franchise? — 155

12. International factoring		**158**
Background		158
Export factoring		162
Direct export factoring		169
Invoice discounting		170
The benefits of export factoring		173
The international factoring scene		176
The export dilemma		187
13. Boom, bust and boom again?		**194**
The path to real growth		196
Appendix 1	Association of British Factors and Discounters: Members' annual combined sales 1986–1992	205
Appendix 2	Association of British Factors and Discounters: Factoring and invoice discounting clients—industry sectors 1990	206
Appendix 3	Association of British Factors and Discounters: Members and services	207
Appendix 4	Association of Invoice Factors: Members	213
Appendix 5	Sample sales ledger record	214
Appendix 6	Sample client accounting: Debts payable on maturity	215
Appendix 7	Case study—Cash flow forecasts	217
Appendix 8	Century Link—On-line reporting to clients	218
Appendix 9	Worldwide factoring: Members of Factors Chain International	222
Appendix 10	Factors Chain International: Worldwide factoring business	229
Appendix 11	International Factors Group: Members	234
Index		**243**

Foreword

Factoring occupies a unique position in the range of financing options available to business. Few financial mechanisms offer the convenience and the flexibility of factoring, or its cousin invoice discounting, yet none is regarded with as much suspicion by the business community.

Though factoring is now an industry largely owned by the big banks, many businesspeople, and not a few bank managers, still regard it askance. A reputation acquired in the 1960s for backing businesses on the verge of failure has clung to the factoring industry with remarkable persistency.

The factors have become more professional in their marketing efforts yet, as David Hawkins points out, still frequently present their industry in an unduly technical fashion to the confusion of many a would-be client.

Factoring made great strides during the late 1980s and annual growth rates of 25 per cent a year or more were not uncommon. But any illusion that it was a recession-proof industry were dashed at the turn of the 1990s when the factors' clients and the factors themselves suffered losses. Growth rates slowed sharply. Despite the downturn, however, factoring has succeeded in establishing itself as an important source of finance for a growing number of expansion-minded companies.

It has also proved its worth as a means of applying effective credit controls at a time when the problem of late payments has emerged as a serious threat to business. Some business organizations have called, unsuccessfully, for government intervention to ensure that invoices are paid on time. This may be necessary for the smallest of businesses but for those large enough to merit the involvement of a factor—with a minimum turnover of £100 000— factoring provides a market-based answer to the problem.

As and when the recession ends factoring should be poised for even further growth. The large loan losses run up by the banks on their small business portfolios have made many bank managers reluctant to lend. This has prompted widespread fears of a shortage of finance when the upturn comes. The mistakes made by the banks have persuaded many senior bankers to treat their factoring arms with greater respect.

More bankers are now prepared to accept that the factoring techniques of risk assessment and the close monitoring of factor's clients' sales ledgers gives the factor a greater insight into a client's affairs. Bank managers, reliant as they often are on incomplete or out-of-date financial statements, are much more vulnerable to unpleasant surprises.

At the same time the creation of the Single European Market and the stimulus that this is expected to give to trade within the European Community should increase demand for export finance. More countries have taken

FOREWORD

to factoring in recent years but the volume of export business is still very small compared with the level of domestic factoring. At the same time the risks of international trade have increased while traditional methods of financing are often perceived of as cumbersome and expensive.

Factoring remains something of a mystery in the eyes of many businesspeople. There has been no serious study of the subject for many years. *The Business of Factoring* provides a timely and practical guide.

Charles Batchelor
Growing Business Correspondent
Financial Times

1. *Factoring and invoice discounting*

Factoring and invoice discounting are among the fastest growing financially based services available to corporate customers in the United Kingdom. They are also among the least well known. It is beyond dispute that the services have made a substantial contribution to the individual growth of thousands of companies in this country and to the prosperity of the economy as a whole. Yet mention factoring to many commercial people and the reaction is negative, even hostile. The industry—for that is what is has become—includes as service suppliers all of the main clearing banks and other institutions and companies of impeccable pedigree. It remains widely misunderstood and is still regarded by many as a 'lender of last resort'.

Why is this? The reasons are many and varied. Perhaps the industry has been slow to promote itself. Perhaps the British commercial public is inherently conservative, even though anti-factoring sentiment is not confined to these shores.

Possibly the small to medium-sized company market, which traditionally has been the sector served by factors, is itself accorded insufficient esteem by the commercial chattering classes who mould opinion. Maybe when all is said and done, it is an expensive and cumbersome way to finance a business and some may say that the reputation is at least partly deserved.

This book will endeavour to explain the reasons for the attitudes that exist. It will try to set out clearly and fairly not only the pros and cons of the argument but also the basis on which the services are offered and operated. It is aimed mainly at the factoring client, actual or potential. It will seek to spread a little light about the industry and its services, how they can be used to maximum efficiency by whom and for what purposes. Of necessity it will dwell to some extent on technical detail but it will not seek to persuade the reader to become a factor. If it removes a little prejudice from a few minds and helps some entrepreneurs to make the right decisions for their business, it will have succeeded.

What is factoring?

Perhaps the root of much of the misunderstanding can be located in the fact that very often the terms 'factoring' and 'invoice discounting' are used on an almost interchangeable basis. This is quite incorrect. Despite the fact that factoring companies often provide both services they are separate and distinct and are designed to meet quite different needs.

Factoring is, in effect, a mix of services. The factor purchases the trade debts of a commercial concern—the client. These debts are evidenced by the invoices which the client raises on customers for goods and services provided on open credit. The factor in a full service situation will provide a computerized sales ledger service, will usually, though not always, provide credit protection against the risk that customers will not pay, and will collect the debts on an open and disclosed basis from customers.

Thus, clients are relieved entirely of the cares and responsibility of running a sales ledger. They deal with the customers from a sales and delivery point of view in the usual way, but hand over to the factor all the routine administration of customer accounts.

The client gains access to the factor's expertise in operating ledger systems which, even allowing for the advent of the microcomputer, are likely to be more comprehensive and sophisticated than his or her own. He or she gets the benefit of credit information systems available to the factor and a wealth of experience in the vital business of collecting cash.

For all of this, the factor will levy on the client a service fee, usually expressed as a percentage of the full face value of debts offered and which, as indicated below, reflects the cost to the factor of administering the account.

In addition, of course, the client will usually receive a financial facility. This is an advance geared in percentage terms to the debts offered for factoring at the time at which they are offered. Most factors say that they will provide facilities of up to 80 per cent of the full face value of debts, but in practice the level of advance will depend on a variety of elements, not least the financial strength of the client. The balance of the facility is paid by the factor either by reference to a fixed maturity date or, more usually, when customers make payment. The cost of the facility is usually calculated on a similar basis to that of a bank overdraft and is geared to bank base rates. The facility itself, as we shall see later, is usually more flexible than overdraft money.

This is basically the essence of factoring. It is a simple service made unnecessarily complex by some of its practitioners.

Invoice discounting

As already implied, confusion is compounded by the fact that most factors are also invoice discounters, and many clients and their advisers seem quite unable to distinguish between the two services.

Here again, the basis of the service is simple. Debts are purchased by the factor (i.e. the discounter) on a similar basis to that involved with factoring. However, clients continue to operate their own sales ledgers and to deal with the customers in collecting items outstanding. Usually, the arrangement between client and factor is not disclosed to customers. This has a number of implications which we shall examine later. Invariably, the client remains responsible for the customer credit risk, although just to complicate matters some factoring houses now offer credit protection to invoice discounting clients. The service is therefore fundamentally financial. By using it, the client derives an assured cash flow through the financial facility, calculated on a similar basis to the factoring arrangement. As it is geared to debtors, and generally the level of debtors is geared to sales turnover, the facility grows with the company's requirements. The client pays for the service through a similar mechanism to that already described in relation to factoring but, of course, the level of charges is lower reflecting the lower workload involved.

Invoice discounting is becoming increasingly popular despite sceptics within the industry who accord to it a degree of distaste displayed normally by, say, traditional jazz fans contemplating bebop.

We shall explore the arguments later.

Who are the factors?

A few years ago, this question would have been a simple one to answer. Now it is much more complex. All of the main UK clearing banks have factoring subsidiaries or divisions which operate on a more or less independent basis from their parents, although of course they derive considerable advantages from them. There are also one or two major independent factors owned by financial institutions, and a plethora of smaller independents who have entered the market in recent years.

So the potential factoring or invoice discounting client is almost spoiled for choice. Since most clients already have bankers they can, if they wish, endeavour to set up an arrangement with a subsidiary of their own clearing bank, or that of another. They can go to one of the many independents or, as sometimes happens, they can change banks and join factors at one and the same time.

Be that as it may, factors are not bankers. They are experts, or at least specialists, in debtor financing and the provision of the services sketched out above. The risk and rewards involved are quite different from those involved in banking and there is a strong body of opinion within the industry, probably valid, that bankers do not make good factors.

Factoring companies incur quite high overheads. The provision of full-scale credit and ledger services is an expensive and labour-intensive business, so with one or two exceptions, factors eschew expensive London premises and congregate in places such as the south coast and other parts of the Home Counties where labour and office space is marginally cheaper and more readily available. They compete vigorously for good management and staff, who are always in limited supply. They do not pay huge salaries, although increasingly many seek to offer their staff a good career structure, training and fringe benefits. Without doubt, experience in the industry brings substantial benefits in terms of variety of work and an excellent grounding in commercial practice, finance and, above all, the gaining and retention of clients. Factors gain considerable insight into the problems, joys and sorrows of small to medium-sized concerns in a very wide variety of industries. This can be rewarding in itself and people involved in factoring draw a quite genuine satisfaction from seeing their clients prosper and develop. They also take considerable pride in the standard of services offered to clients, although this can be tempered a little by the necessary and healthy cynicism which recognizes the fact that sometimes the debts offered by some clients leave a lot to be desired in terms of their validity. Perhaps for this reason factoring management rarely, if ever, take full-time employment with their clients.

Who are the clients?

These days, factoring clients come in all shapes and sizes and from a multitude of industries. Some of the largest companies in the land are using invoice discounting facilities to good effect. At the other end of the scale, several factoring companies are now offering facilities to companies with sales turnovers below £100 000 a year, although this, in general terms, has been the level at which most factors will start to become seriously interested in helping a business. All factors from time to time will consider helping 'new start' companies if they are favourably impressed by the calibre and commitment of the management and the likely quality of the debts to be offered.

The range is also wide relative to the industrial sectors involved. Some industries are inherently unsuitable for factoring because the nature of their business is such that a clear untrammelled trade debt is not created and therefore cannot be offered. But these days, almost any company with 'clean' open-account trade debts, reasonable management and a product or service sold to other companies as opposed to individuals, can offer itself for factoring. So as we shall see below, the potential scope is enormous.

Many of these client companies are owner-managed. Most are growing. Factors look for growth potential, for it is in relation to this that the true worth of a factoring or invoice discounting facility can be gauged.

Some general themes

We hear a great deal about small business and its contribution to the British economy. It is my contention that factoring and invoice discounting have not received their due share of credit for the encouragement and help that they have provided to this sector in recent years. Many years ago the Wilson

Committee, reporting on the performance of the City of London in funding business, drew attention to the so-called 'equity gap'. This referred to difficulties experienced by smaller businesses in raising development funds since, by definition, the security available to commercial lenders was modest and the more traditional sources of personal wealth have all but dried up.

Many things have changed since that time. Banks have improved their marketing. The British venture capital industry has developed. Government assistance is available to smaller businesses in both financial and other areas. Despite this, it remains difficult for many small to medium-sized concerns to raise expansion finance. Probably it will always be hard. Perhaps it is right that it should be. If you make it too easy for people to gain access to finance, results in terms of failed business can be dire.

Nevertheless, the Thatcher years are supposed to have ushered in an enterprise culture and a society in which high priority is accorded to the creation as well as the distribution of wealth, and smaller businesses are highly important in such an economy.

A rapidly increasing number of such businesses are using factoring and invoice discounting. Many of the proprietors of these companies will tell you that the factoring money has been the key element in the growth of their business and therefore in the generation of employment. Although factoring companies stress this aspect increasingly in their publicity activities it is unlikely that the industry as a whole is regarded as being especially important by industrial observers or, more significantly, by those who contribute to government policy-making in this area.

There is another dimension to this argument which relates to the service rather than to the financial element. It is well known that within industry as a whole, the credit control and collection functions are often poor relations within a company management set-up. The more glamorous areas such as sales and marketing frequently attract the better staff and the lion's share of resources.

Factors are specialists in this area and there is no doubt that they bring to a business a quality of credit and collection administration which improves dramatically upon the performance which the company could provide for itself. It is impossible to measure the impact which this must have upon business efficiency throughout the economy as a whole, but it is obvious that it is substantial and growing.

Even in the case of invoice discounting the industry makes a contribution to management efficiency. As we shall see, invoice discounters have a vested interest in ensuring that their clients' sales ledger administration and collection performance is as good as it can be. They insist upon the achievement and maintenance of certain accounting and collection standards in return for the provision of funds against debts. It follows then that the rapid growth of invoice discounting must have had some effect, again unquantified, on the administrative performance of British companies using the service. At a time when great emphasis is being placed upon commercial and administrative efficiency to allow British manufacturers and services to compete with foreign competition, this can have done nothing but good.

2. An industry in the making

Early days

An Order of the Common Council of the City of London stated in 1623:

> The clothier by himself and his household servant heretofore hath used to make his own sale to the merchant or draper to his profit and good content. But now diverse persons have cunningly interposed themselves to deal as factors and brokers between the merchant, draper and clothier.

These early factors were not universally popular. Like middlemen down the ages, they were open to criticism from all sides. Seventeenth-century contemporaries were loud in their condemnation. Factors were instrumental in raising prices. They controlled the market place, sometimes in a contrary way, depressing prices to suit their own ends. They held the wool manufacturers to ransom and preyed on their customers. Basically, they were early entrepreneurs who had spotted a market gap and sought to exploit it.

The seventeenth-century wool trade in England was well developed and widespread, with centres as far afield as Yorkshire and the West Country. It was subject to cyclic economic trends. London was growing apace and represented a major market, even though communications were primitive.

Cloth manufacturers were not always able or willing to undertake extended sales trips to distant markets. Similarly, they were unable to finance the lengthy period of credit generally required by the drapers. Unpopular they may have been, but the early factors appear to have fulfilled a need. From the beginning they provided the working capital industry needed to prosper and expand.

Contemporaries allege that they also achieved great wealth, often from humble beginnings: as one notes 'no more being required to set up as a factor than an ink-box and two quire of quills'. Things have changed somewhat since the seventeenth century!

Two points are relevant at this stage. First, factoring grew out of the textile trade. It was many years before the industry could bring itself to shake off this association and to diversify into other areas of business. Second, it is important to note that the first factors were commercial people, not bankers. They involved themselves in all aspects of the merchanting of cloth. They became acutely aware of customer needs and set out to fulfil them. This tradition persists.

THE FACTORS GO TO AMERICA

In 1620, the Pilgrim Fathers landed in what was to become the USA. Among their number were at least three London merchants who could be described as factors, purchasing merchandise and selling into the newly opened market.

During the following two centuries the US economy underwent extensive expansion, with progressive waves of immigrants first from the UK but eventually from the rest of Europe. There was considerable demand for imported products, and the skills the early factors had developed were ideally suited for these expansionist conditions. According to Peter Biscoe (*Credit Factoring*: Butterworths, 1975), by the second quarter of the nineteenth century the term 'factor' had become synonymous with that of commission agent. They appear to have concentrated primarily on the movement of textiles, representing European, frequently Lancastrian, manufacturers and performing a wide range of functions. Biscoe quotes the following commission rates, based on sales:

	Commissions on sales (%)
Sales foreign product	5%
Sales domestic product	2½%
Guarantee customer credit	2½%
Litigation	5%
Handling, collecting bills of exchange	1%
Drawing, endorsing, accepting bills	2½%

So by the end of the Civil War, there existed a factoring industry based primarily in New York and charging very good rates for its services. The tradition had existed for centuries whereby factors were prepared to provide finance to bridge the gap between manufacturer and customer payment. But it is difficult to establish precisely when factors began purchasing debts from their clients.

Certainly by the end of the nineteenth century, the US economy was becoming mature. The McKinley tariffs were designed to encourage domestic manufacture and this had the effect of forcing the US factors to turn their attention towards US domestic business and to concentrate their efforts on the activities they knew best. In 1890 the New York factors, Oelbermann, Dommerick & Co., dropped selling and storage from their product lines and concentrated on providing what was, in effect, a modern factoring service based on sales ledger administration, credit control and collection. As is the way with these matters, the competition followed, so that by the 1930s the US factoring industry was operating on a not dissimilar basis to that found today, whereby debts were assigned by the client to the factor, who dealt with customers on the basis of a notification of the assignment.

By the 1940s the industry was firmly established in the USA. On the other side of the Atlantic, however, there was little sign of any developments except for the fact that some of the London-based foreign banks were prepared to offer a form of invoice discounting service.

Back to Europe

This all changed very quickly. It is sometimes hard to recall the heady enthusiasm of the early 1960s. In the USA, the newly elected Kennedy administration proclaimed the 'New Era'. American business embarked on one of its more ambitious and optimistic periods. It also began to look towards a partially regenerated Europe as a market place. During this period, the USA was regarded in business terms as the home of free enterprise and as a centre of management excellence. New products emerged and new technologies developed, many of them based on the relatively new science of computing. The late 1950s saw the beginning of the growth of credit cards in Europe. Around that time the US 'exported' the concept of leasing to Europe. So the emergence of factoring in 1960 should have come as no surprise. The first UK factoring company was founded in that year and several competitors were quite quickly established.

There were inevitable problems. Quite naturally, US experience was used as a model. Unfortunately, the British market was not yet ready for a full factoring service under which the client received credit protection as well as the full sales ledger accounting and collection services. Some of the early participants in the market were therefore driven to offer the services as finance pure and simple and as a straight alternative to a bank overdraft or a loan. This may have had the effect of planting in the minds of the commercial public the idea that factors were merely the 'lenders of last resort'. Certainly during that period the crucial issue of selectivity of clients was not always handled effectively, so that some of the early participants, both factors and clients, did not come out well from the experience.

During the early 1970s, however, the UK clearing banks began to participate in factoring and so there began the long process through which the concept of service factoring gained ground and the benefits began to be perceived. Within a few years, all of the 'Big Four' clearing banks had become involved, although Barclays were subsequently to withdraw from active participation for a long period.

So the basic shape of the industry was laid down by the mid-1970s. At that point it made little impact on the UK commercial public, however. By 1976, total factored sales turnover was less than £1 billion, despite several years of quite hard publicity and sales efforts by the main players in the market place. Substantial growth was still some way off, and much of the marketing of the era has a prim, almost evangelical flavour to it. Those of us who were active in the industry at the time recall that the entry of the clearing banks was expected to bring about huge and rapid growth. It did not do so, and the reasons for this are perhaps obscure. The rationale for the banks' involvement was simple. This was the beginning of the age of integrated service marketing. The banks were in the business of providing their customers with all the services they could possibly require. Factoring was a financial service, so it had to be provided, if only to demonstrate the breadth and power of the banks' services. This was fine so far as it went. Unfortunately, the policy underestimated the degree of conservatism present not only in the public at large, but also among bank managers.

The reality was that it would take a number of years and much blood, sweat and marketing expenditure for the industry to gain any measure of acceptance comparable to that enjoyed by other financial services. Not only were the clients and their accountants sceptical, but people within the banks themselves were hardly within the vanguard of financial change in the 1970s. Bank managers in those days took a great deal of convincing that factoring was appropriate for their customers.

For all this, the entry of the clearing banks did bring substantial advantages. Their very involvement made it possible to present the industry as soundly based and respectable. It had arrived and it was not going to go away. The fact that most main factoring companies were owned by banks did give management the self-confidence to go out and sell their services.

It gradually became possible for the factors to attract, as management and staff, capable people who were committed to the development of the industry and who were able to acquire the somewhat odd mixture of skills and knack that are required to administer and sell factoring. The banking shareholders have shown considerable wisdom in allowing these people, most of whom were not bankers by background, a fair degree of operational independence and scope. So after all this effort and change the industry has gone a good way towards persuading at least a proportion of the British commercial public that the views expressed by the City burghers in 1623 are now not relevant.

The industry today

This process of persuasion has some way to go. There are some 10 000 companies using factoring and invoice discounting services in the UK today, according to the figures produced by the industry association or trade body, the Association of British Factors and Discounters (ABFD).

This figure illustrates at once the progress that industry has made towards acceptance and maturity, yet provides a tantalizing reminder that in many ways its development has hardly commenced. Estimates vary widely as to the

AN INDUSTRY IN THE MAKING

total potential market for factoring and invoice discounting. I have seen a figure as large as 250 000 quoted by industry sources as being the size of the 'universe' that the industry could address. A more conservative approach would be to take the total number of businesses that fall within the appropriate turnover bands and the Standard Industrial Classification Codes that factors address and make the assumption that, given the right conditions, a high proportion of such companies would use the service. My own estimate based on this is that there are between 60 000 and 100 000 companies in the UK who could factor their debts or use an invoice discounting facility if they wanted to and could find a factor or discounter who was willing to offer an arrangement. On this basis, even ignoring the more bullish statistics put about by some people in the industry, and of course the potential for further growth in the small to medium-sized corporate sector, market penetration still has some way to go.

Every six months for many years now, the ABFD collects from its member companies statistics for the turnover they have achieved in their various services. This is, of course, the sum total of the sales turnover of the clients who have offered their debts for factoring or invoice discounting. The figures provide indications of the factors' market shares, and the growth of the industry generally. Not all factors are members of the Association, so the statistics are not a complete indicator. Nevertheless, the combined turnover of the unaffiliated factors is comparatively low, and the ABFD statistics provide the best yardstick as to the progress of the industry, aside from the profits of the major factors. The turnover figures are shown in block diagram format in Appendix 1.

Until the quite extraordinary conditions brought about by the recession which commenced at the end of the 1980s, the industry had expanded, year by year, in a way that compares favourably with most other financial sectors. The ABFD tends to judge performance not by return on capital employed but in relation to overall sales growth, and on this basis most people in the industry, and associated with it, are probably reasonably content with the progress that has been made. Total turnover has expanded from £5.6 to £15.9 billion in the period from 1986 to 1992. Thus, sales grew by a factor of 2½ during the five-year period, continuing a growth curve that had started five years previously, in 1982, when total turnover was just over £2 billion. Until the recession, the Thatcher years seemed to be good ones for the factoring business. But the overall figures are misleading. While invoice discounting has certainly grown, factoring—the original core product of most of the ABFD companies—has not shown anything like the same propensity to growth. As Appendix 1 shows, during 1988–89 the invoice discounting product overtook factoring, and the gap between the two products has grown wider ever since.

The reasons for this are not hard to pin down. In an era when cheap and efficient microcomputing facilities are within the reach of every business person, it cannot become easier to sell a service which has at its core the provision of efficient sales ledger administration. In the early days of the factoring industry, sales staff used to make a point of showing potential clients the gleaming, high-tech computing facilities that the factoring companies possessed and everyone else, certainly in the small company sector, envied. Those days are past. If the service element is to be sold, its benefits rather than its features are the key issue. There are signs, disturbing to some people, that the factoring industry has given up the effort of selling the virtues of its services, relying very much more on the attractions of an expanding finance line to entice clients into serviced facilities. A theme of this book is that, while some growth and respectability have been achieved, the potential for the service remains largely unexploited, and this has unfortunate effects not just upon the industry, comprising as it does the factors and their shareholders, but also on their clients and, perhaps more important, their potential clients.

THE CHALLENGES TO TODAY'S FACTORS

Of course, factoring growth has to be judged in relation to the circumstances within the market place. Most factoring clients tend to see the arrangement as a relatively short-term one. They use factoring or invoice discounting facilities at a certain stage of their commercial development and replace them with the appropriate mix of funding and bought-in skills when they feel it necessary or realistic to do so. In practice, this tends to be when they become 'bankable', that is to say, when the business reaches the stage where sufficient growth has occurred to be able to provide a bank with the spread of assets required as a base for the consideration of a lending proposition. So the average 'factoring life' of a client is perhaps three to four years, depending upon a number of elements. First, the skills and service of the factor: if the factor is efficient, and can demonstrate to the client the continuing relevance of the service, the client may well be retained. Most of the leading factors can point to clients who have continued to benefit from the service for very long periods. Second, of course, it has to be recognized that factors, for better or worse, have become established in the higher risk, smaller businesses sectors, where inevitably, and particularly during recession, the loss of clients through failure or fraud is greater than in other areas of the economy.

Consequently, factors are in the position of having to replenish their stocks of clients on a continuous basis in order to stand still, let alone grow. One of the main challenges facing the factoring industry is to develop the product it offers, and perhaps to cultivate other products or services which have the effect of sustaining greater client loyalty. It remains to be seen whether this will be achieved.

But the bald figures conceal other trends. As we shall see in Chapter 12, export factoring is not just a non-growth business, but is in virtual decline. In an era when barriers between nations have broken down to a greater extent than at any time since the nineteenth century, this fact may be received with surprise in some quarters, especially by anyone who has had any experience of how a well set-up factoring arrangement can assist an export-based business to perform. We will be exploring this oddity later.

Similarly, the proportion of factoring business wherein the factors provide their clients with credit protection against non-payment by customers is in relative decline, either because people do not want to pay for it or the factors, or some of them, are reluctant to provide it. Here again, the casual observer would perhaps be forgiven for believing that, in recessionary conditions, the market would be hungry for a form of credit protection which, if utilized correctly, would ensure that effective cash flow was accompanied by the peace of mind that comes from knowing that bad debts will not be suffered. It apparently is not: the real growth is occurring at the invoice discounting end of the business and some of the factors, even those who are members of the ABFD, are not providing factoring services in the full traditional sense.

Does this matter? In one sense, no. In the long run, and perhaps even in the short term, the market place will determine which service people buy and use. The quality of a service, even its very content, will be moulded and shaped by what people are prepared to pay for. From the point of view of the management of an individual factoring business, operating in a tough market sector and trying to produce an acceptable return on shareholders' investment, it does not matter too much where that return comes from. If people want invoice discounting or recourse factoring, why not give it to them at a reasonable price which allows the factor to make a profit?

Broader and more objective considerations also exist. There are good reasons for the belief that the industry is not playing entirely to its strengths. Although the impact of recession has hit the industry hard, wider and more long-term economic trends and conditions are favourable to the kind of rapid and substantial growth that many people believed would take place after the industry was introduced to the country in the 1960s. Appendix 2 shows, in pie-chart form, the industrial and commercial sectors from which factoring and invoice discounting clients are drawn. At first sight, there is nothing especially remarkable about them. The reasons for the smallness of the construction industry sector will be explained later. What is important to note is the widespread nature of the factors' businesses. The richness and diversity are impressive, especially when one considers that by contrast, in 1987, some 80 per cent of the clients of the US factoring business were still in the textile industry. UK factors, in comparison with their US cousins, have a major achievement to their credit. They have developed an industry capable of servicing wide swathes of British industry.

The exposure to such a broad gamut is critically important. Factors, and to a lesser extent invoice discounters, obtain, through the daily operation of their service, an intimate view of the requirements, quirks and special features of the client's business. A great deal can be learned about a company, its customers, the industrial sector within which it works and the commercial practices which prevail, by the fairly mundane process of running a sales ledger. As a consequence, the British factoring industry has within it a wealth of knowledge about a wide range of industries and trades. Bankers could argue that they, too, possess such broad experience. Certainly good practical banking is partly based upon a broad knowledge of commercial practice in different business sectors, coupled with an astute appreciation of human nature. But most bankers will admit that the nature of their dealings with customers does not allow them to gain the detailed understanding of the operations of small and medium-sized companies that it is open to the factors to acquire.

In my view, and I think it is shared by others, these advantages have not been exploited to the full by an industry which, if anything, is over-modest about the contribution it has made and could make. For there are other major features of modern commercial life which could work increasingly in its favour and which could ensure that the growing imbalance between factoring and invoice discounting is kept within bounds.

It is commonplace to talk about the decline of British manufacturing. In recent years, a combination of government policy, the discovery and revenues derived from North Sea oil, and the basic fact that large areas of British industry were archaic, have meant that the manufacturing part of the economy has declined. Pessimists believe that this may be permanent and will continue to lead to irreversible decline in economic performance and in the share of world markets. Others hold to the view that the shrinking of the manufacturing sector was a necessary prelude to the slimming-down process which was required to enable Britain to compete effectively in the new European context. Whatever one's view of the matter, there can be no doubt of the continuing importance of a strong manufacturing sector to the UK economy. It may be a different manufacturing sector, but it will be one just the same.

Moreover, the factors have an important role to play in developing it. Appendix 2 shows that over 70 per cent of factoring or invoice discounting business occurs when someone sells something they have made or distributes something that someone else has produced. If we go back to 1984, the corresponding figure was virtually the same. So despite the comparative decline in the volume of British manufacturing, the factors have continued to support the making of products. They are prepared to get involved with service industries, but overwhelmingly, their growth has been based on manufacturing.

That is not all. In recent years, the contribution to economic success of the small to medium-sized business has been increasingly recognized. People have realized, in an era when full employment can no longer be taken for granted, that the flexibility and drive which can be provided by the small company is an indispensable element in the modern economy. Coupled with the major shift towards European markets that has been brought about by Britain's gradually increased involvement with the EC, it becomes increasingly clear that the role which could be performed by factors in the life of the nation has, if anything, been underplayed.

For if nothing else has been proved, it has been made clear beyond doubt, during the past 25 years or so, that an effective factoring service can bring considerable benefits to exactly the kind of business that can profit from these trends in the context of both domestic and international business. The potential exists but there remains a substantial gap to be bridged if it is to be realized. Some observers appear more bewildered than anything else that it has not been bridged, and that the reputation and image of the industry is still so mixed.

After all, the industry is established and here to stay. It is well supported and capitalized. Of the 12 members of the ABFD listed in Appendix 3, no fewer than eight are either subsidiaries or part of the corporate groups of clearing banks, and the parent companies of the other four are well established organizations. So the fears expressed in the early days of the UK factoring industry that the business of factoring would come to be associated with relatively small-scale, rather marginal, financial organizations, has proved ill-founded. The factoring industry is respectable almost to the point of dullness so far as its leading members are concerned.

Thus far, despite the predictions of some who would prefer to see the industry in more independent hands, there has been no great move away from clearing bank ownership. The 'independent' factors, themselves part of well-established groups, have not as yet been able to persuade large numbers of the commercial public of the benefits of a second line of finance, provided by an organization not owned by the clearing banker who provides the overdraft. There are considerable benefits to a small business from such an arrangement, both from the point of view of the security of the funding line advanced and the ability to negotiate costs.

But there has been an influx of new players into the market place. Besides the members of the ABFD there are at least 30 companies offering factoring or invoice discounting services, and until the impact of the recent recession hit home, the number was growing. Some of these are very small. Others specialize regionally or by industry. The shareholders tend to be smaller organizations than the major banks, and there are a sprinkling of non-financial sector companies who have formed operations, attracted no doubt by the returns that, in good times at least, are available from factoring and, in particular, from well managed invoice discounting.

Some of these factors have formed a professional body which, on paper at least, is a rival to the ABFD, although in terms of annual factored turnover there is no comparison between the members of the two organizations. The Association of Invoice Factors makes no bones about its role in life. It is, purely and simply, a trade association for factoring companies who are not aligned to the clearing banks. As such, it naturally represents itself and its membership as having a degree of independence from the clearers which, in these days when the major banks are not always the most popular of organizations, does provide some people with an element of choice which is important to them. The list of the Association's members is shown in Appendix 4.

So the future factoring client is not starved of choice when contemplating use of the service. Whatever else it may or may not be, the factoring and invoice discounting market is highly competitive. The consolidation among the bigger players in recent years through the re-entry of Barclays Bank and the arrival of important contributors such as Roy Scot Factors, the Royal Bank of Scotland subsidiary, coupled with the entry of many smaller players, has given the market an appearance of maturity. Mature markets tend to slow down in growth terms, and the immediate reaction to this is to say that factoring has a long way to go before it can be considered to be deeply into its produce life cycle.

At the same time, there is no doubt that the development of invoice discounting is confronting the factors with some quite severe difficulties, in terms of presentation and marketing, product development and service. In the six-year period to 1990, the four major factors consolidated their hold upon the non-recourse factoring market place to the extent that their joint market share grew to around 90 per cent. Simultaneously, the smaller companies gained more of the non-credit insured (recourse) market, and we have now reached the point where nearly 40 per cent of invoice discounting is offered by companies outside the ranks of the Big Four. Given the respective costs of entry and operation to the markets this is not surprising, neither is it especially undesirable, but there is no doubt that trends of this kind do have an effect upon the idea that the factoring industry is one that is based upon service, the enhancement of the administrative standards as well as the financial health of the client's business. Much of this book is about this kind of issue.

Factors have moved towards improving and extending their services. Several, for example, as we have already seen, offer facilities to very small concerns turning over less than £100 000. There are several other interesting experiments in progress which we will examine in more detail later. Investment in people and computer systems has been considerable. Most major factors are very conscious of the need to provide high quality service at all times, and some have developed electronic methods of communicating with clients so as to streamline and speed up their services.

Above all, the pressure of competition has meant that the price of factoring and invoice discounting facilities has been reduced, so much so that some people feel that, in responding to market forces, some of the factors are cutting prices to the point where it becomes uneconomic to provide good service and to make sufficient provision for loss.

Is the industry doing enough? Will we ever reach the point where it is totally accepted, so that it becomes perfectly normal for all companies within the appropriate industries to have a factor? We are still some distance from this ideal, desirable as it may be from the point of view of the factoring industry, and indeed it may never be reached. In the same way that bankers may, for the foreseeable future at least, have to live with the fact that some individuals in the community will never open a bank account, there may be a level beyond which the factoring industry will find rapid expansion almost impossible.

3. *The services*

Trade credit and factoring

It is difficult to imagine a world without trade credit. The facility to receive the benefit of goods or services and to pay for them at an agreed future date is something taken for granted by most people in business, and yet without it much of the commercial world would grind to a halt. Yet it is perhaps surprising, given the importance attached to money in most western societies, that suppliers are prepared to entrust customers with goods without payment on delivery.

All too frequently, customers breach this trust. Often they do so because they themselves have been kept waiting by their own customers or because existing banking or other financial lines are inadequate to sustain a sufficiency of working capital. It has been estimated that the total volume of pure trade credit exceeds by a factor of two or three times the total volume of funds provided by bankers and other financiers to businesses, even though the variety of institutions, banks, confirmers, discount houses, leasing companies and forfeiters represent a highly complex and vast financial superstructure without whom, once again, commercial life would not exist.

Factors are among this group. As we have seen, they have been around for a long time in one form or another but it is only comparatively recently that they have represented an important force in assisting the provision of trade credit. To date, at least, they have avoided involvement in consumer credit and they will not provide facilities to companies supplying customers who are individuals rather than other companies. Neither will they become involved in purchasing trade debts which are subject to long open-account sales terms. Their services are geared primarily to companies selling on short-term open account and there is very little point in trying to persuade a factor to provide the kind of long-term credit facilities sometimes offered in the capital goods or construction industries.

Similarly, it is a waste of time asking a factor to handle individual customer deals through a factoring or invoice discounting arrangement. Many companies, especially in the export field, experience credit or collection difficulties with one or perhaps two major customers, and it is tempting to try to lay off these problems to any third party willing to provide financial and collection facilities. Factors, like credit insurers, require a spread of risk.

So what will factors do? They will consider helping almost any company which can demonstrate the following:

THE SERVICES

- a reasonable 'spread' of debtors, either UK domestic or international
- open-account payment terms up to 60 days from the date of invoice
- record of consistent customer payment and relative absence of dispute
- some history of corporate profitability or at least its potential.

On this basis, the contribution made by the factor or the invoice discounter to the process of trade credit is most marked. The factor's services, comprising as they do a financial facility backed up by sales ledger control, credit advice and perhaps credit insurance, are purpose-built to enable the company to trade on open-account terms and indeed to allow the effective use of credit as a feature of a company's marketing policy.

The rest of this chapter will examine in detail the mechanics of factoring and invoice discounting before going on to consider the way in which the services can be utilized to the best possible effect.

The full factoring service

At various times, factoring has been described as 'old line' or 'main line' to distinguish it from discounting and as already indicated, it comprises several elements. First, the factor purchases from the client open-account trade debts and perhaps finances them at the date of purchase. Second, the factor maintains the whole of the client's sales ledger both from a book-keeping and a general administration viewpoint. Then he or she collects the cash due from customers in accordance with the sales terms. Finally, he or she may, although this is not universal, provide credit protection, that is, take responsibility for losses brought about by the customer's inability to pay. Many factoring companies offer non-recourse, i.e. credit-protected, facilities to at least some clients.

In essence, the service is simple. Once agreement has been reached between factor and client on terms, customers have to be advised that a factoring arrangement has commenced, that the debts created through existing and future sales belong to the factor and that in future payment should be made to him or her. At the commencement of the relationship it is important to write individually to existing customers drawing attention to the new arrangement and pointing out the advantages it can bring. Most factors have specially prepared letters for this purpose which are generally prepared on the client's letterhead. Slightly more imaginative clients may wish to devise their own means of telling customers that they are setting up a factoring arrangement. In particular it may be desirable to send specific letters to slightly sensitive or important customers making it clear to them that the factoring facility will enable the supplier to perform more efficiently, rather than less, and that in fact the provision of the financial support will ensure continuity of supply. In practical terms, problems seldom arise at commencement since factors have very well oiled procedures for taking on clients. The whole process can be very quick and painless even though it will usually involve the assignment of existing debts, and a certain amount of sales ledger reconciliation may be required so as to ensure that information passed from client to factor is accurate and comprehensive.

Invoices are, of course, the evidence that debts have been generated. The copy sent to the customer will bear a printed capital notice of assignment or factoring legend stating that the debt has been assigned to the factor and payment is due to him or her in accordance with the sales terms. Aside from this aspect, the client company will raise its invoices in the usual way. The second copy of the invoice will be sent to the factor and it will be this copy which will be used for processing and for accounting. Invariably, the factor will require a schedule upon which copy invoices should be listed, totalled and submitted for acceptance and processing. Similar procedures apply to credit notes. Some factors go to great lengths to ensure that clients are properly 'educated' in their procedures so as to minimize any problems in relation to this routine paperwork. They may have a number of requirements in this area, none of which are onerous in themselves and which will tend to have the effect of improving clients' daily administration and, hopefully, their relationships with their customers. Such items include:

1. A quoted customer number (allocated by the factor) which will appear on a regular listing sent from the factor to the client. The intention of this is to minimize the risk of invoices being allocated to the wrong customer account. If the number is quoted correctly such errors are, in theory, impossible.
2. Factors may expect clients to quote more diligently than in the past the correct trading style or even registered name of the customer with whom they are dealing. Usually they will insist, so far as they are able, on accurate postal addresses and details of 'statement addresses', where these are different from the normal place of business of the customer.
3. The factor will insist on clear trading terms being notified to him or her for inclusion in factoring records and for terms to be shown quite clearly on the face of invoices.

This may sound a little tiresome and pedantic, and it can cause difficulty for a client whose administrative procedures hitherto have not been particularly efficient. There are good reasons for all of these requirements which simply reflect sensible commercial practice. Clarity in these matters can do no harm to the factor, the client or in the long run, the customer.

On receipt of the schedules of invoices the factor will process them. The debts will be formally acknowledged and credited to the client account. The process of crediting is in some factoring agreements taken as the actual point at which the debts are accepted legally for factoring. The individual invoices will be allocated to the customer accounts, usually on the day of acceptance which, again, is generally the day of receipt.

Any invoices that are not acceptable for any reason will be rejected at this stage, perhaps because they are not clear or are arithmetically incorrect or duplicated. As can be imagined, clients do manage to perform all of these feats at various times and the factor's staff have to be fairly vigilant in dealing with the paperwork. Again, similar procedures apply in principle to credit notes which are also listed and which, of course, must be exact copies of the credit notes sent to customers.

The crediting of the schedules to the client account will invariably give rise to payment availability to the client who can then draw off the funds up to the agreed level. Some factors ask their clients to wait 24 hours to enable invoices to be processed for this purpose; others will make payments against the physical schedules received in the morning's postbag. Telegraphic transfer payments can be made if required, although this facility may be available only for payments above a certain figure and will be charged for. Factors or discounters will pay direct to the client's bank or to the company itself. On occasions they will pay directly to third parties, for example important suppliers, although this will only be done in accordance with the client's instructions. The facilities are totally flexible, quick and reliable. Above all, the finance available grows with the size of the debtor book and does not have to be continually negotiated against fixed security in a way that a bank overdraft all too often does.

Most clients develop close working relationships with their client relations executive within the factoring company, who controls payments and is usually prepared to do everything possible to ensure smooth payment procedures and occasionally to meet exceptional requirements. Generally speaking, so long as the terms of the offer of factoring are clear and the client follows the relatively simple rules set out in the client's operating procedures, client payment should cause very little difficulty. Where it does, poor communication is frequently to blame.

Through the client accounting system, the balance due after prepayment will become available for payment to the client at the end of the credit period, as described in Chapter 5.

Once the sales ledger has been set up, customers notified of the commencement of factoring and the existing debts assigned to the factor, the day-to-day running of the sales ledger can begin. The factor will take full responsibility for liaising with the customers and, when the debt is due, for collection. Directly invoices are received they will be posted to the appropriate customer account on a daily basis. Customers will be sent, each month, open-item statements showing the up-to-date position and containing a copy of the notice of assignment indicating that the debt has been assigned to the factor and that it should be paid to him or her.

Sales ledger administration, ostensibly simple, causes much difficulty to many business people. However, factors are geared up to process paperwork on a regular, indeed daily basis, and procedures are designed to ensure that queries are dealt with promptly, cash allocated properly and that statements and all written material is clear. As a consequence, it is normal for factoring companies to achieve dispatch of accurate, open-item statements to customers very shortly after the turn of the month or at whichever date the client wishes. It has to be said that small or medium-sized businesses in the UK are not generally as punctilious and as well organized as this, and simple and fundamental as it is, sales ledger administration does represent an important service for many of them. If well performed, it also has the effect of reducing to a minimum adverse customer reaction since most customers, and in particular large companies with complex payment arrangements, do appreciate clarity, timeliness and accuracy.

This is not to say that mistakes do not occur. Factoring companies are no more perfect than other organizations and it is by no means unknown for errors to be made. Generally, however, these are small in number when compared with the vast number of transactions that the industry is handling on a daily basis.

Credit control and advice

Many full factoring arrangements are non-recourse: in other words, the factor assumes the customer credit risk on the debt purchased. Debts taken over at commencement usually remain at client risk since it is not practicable to have a credit check on large numbers of debts outstanding on a retrospective basis. After the initial assignment it is necessary for the factor to assess the creditworthiness of customers before invoices are offered and accepted. Businesses differ greatly and so does the credit quality of their customers. Where the sales turnover of a company is mainly repeat business, it is not difficult for a factor to establish, before the factoring arrangement begins, credit limits which reflect the sales pattern seen within the client's business. Where sales distribution is more random, difficulties can occur, but usually these should have been foreseen prior to the commencement of the arrangement, so that limits can be established. In assessing credits, the factor will take into consideration the kind of criteria normally adopted by trade creditors, i.e. financial strength, payment track record and net worth.

Over the years, however, factors have developed a number of advantages as compared with other trade creditors. The sheer breadth of their business means that they have in-house records of many thousands of customers in many industries. They are able, therefore, to monitor payment patterns in a sophisticated and detailed way. This information, coupled with the published data, should form the basis of more liberal credit judgements, although obviously in the wrong circumstances more information can have the effect of leading a factor to restrict credit. Moreover, the non-recourse factor has a vested interest in providing, within reason, as much credit cover as is prudent and possible. The factor's income comes from service fees levied on turnover and money charges. Both are determined to some extent by sales growth, and sales growth is not assisted by restricted credit.

Much of the credit assessment work is carried out before the factoring arrangements are in place. If, when the business is under consideration, it is likely that the factor's credit department will be unable to cover a significant proportion of the client's debtors then it may well be that the business is not suitable for non-recourse factoring and such an arrangement will not be entered into. Some potential clients would do well to regard such an outcome as something of a warning light! Assuming reasonable cover can be given, however, credit limits will be established. These should be large enough to meet anticipated trading requirements and to minimize detailed communication between factor and client. The factor will regularly produce information on the credit limits that have been allocated to customers and the client can ship against these limits in the full and certain knowledge that the factor is accepting the risk. Nowadays, many factors use electronic communication systems to update their clients in this respect. Where an exceptionally large order or an account is negotiated the factor will consider special requirements as a matter of routine. This will usually involve the client completing some sort of order approval form giving details of the customer and the size of the order and, importantly, the anticipated delivery date. The factor can then consider approving the order for credit purposes and if there is to be a regular trading pattern with the customer, establishing a routine credit limit within which the client can work.

Of course, credit can be withdrawn if the factor comes across information which calls in doubt the creditworthiness of the customer. He or she will stay on risk in respect of invoices raised up to the date upon which a formal notification of the withdrawal of credit approval was sent to the client. This may be done in relation to a specific account on a daily basis or may perhaps be included on a stop list sent to the client on a regular basis. Once again, the electronic systems being brought into effect by factors play an important role here in speeding up communications between the two parties (see Chapter 7).

In cases where specific credit approval is not given nor a credit limit established the factor will still usually insist upon handling the debt. The client will offer the invoice in the usual way and it will be accepted, but designated as 'unapproved' or 'client risk' debt. The item will receive exactly the same service as do approved debts, and of course the customer will not be aware of any difference in treatment. Most factors will sue for collection of unapproved debt if their client wishes them to do so, although the costs of so doing will usually be for the client's account.

The main difference in treatment will be that many factors will not finance unapproved debts or offer the full percentage advance provided for approved debt. Very often, the question of credit cover is less of a problem to the client than is the level of finance required. So any disagreement can spill over from a simple matter of the factor's view of the creditworthiness of a given customer to the question of funding of the client's business. In an ideal world, clients should try to follow factors' credit advice. They are paying for the service and for the factor's credit experience. Credit is an art not a science, however, and sometimes clients think that they know best. Sometimes they are right, possibly because they have been dealing with the customer in question for many years and that customer has always paid the bills even if possibly on a somewhat delayed basis. In disagreements of this type the result is usually some kind of compromise in which the factor's client relations executive should, of course, play an important rôle.

Collection

Cash collection is in some respects the most important part of the factoring service. It is the area in which the performance of a factor can be best judged and from which really effective savings can be derived. It is also the area which can cause most trouble if not handled well.

In the early days of the industry in the UK a number of factoring companies won no prizes in this area. The reasons are not difficult to imagine. If a factor has advanced too much money against an indifferent quality debt, it is tempting to collect cash from whatever customer is prepared to pay and forget about servicing the full sales ledger. Good collection requires clear administration, good communication and trained, motivated staff. Some of the early factors had few of these attributes.

Their present-day successors do possess them, and their performance can be gauged by the reductions they achieve in the average time customers take to pay, without complaint. There is nothing particularly clever about efficient collection. What is required, besides the motivated staff, is good and clear information. To that end, many of the factors have invested heavily in computer accounting systems, which should ensure that the quality of the information provided in-house and to customers is timely, accurate and clear. Clients have a vital part to play in this, of course, because they provide the raw information material about their customers and the goods or services provided, and if this is inaccurate or incomplete the factor and the customer, and indeed both of them in due course, will have problems. Hence, most factors go to some lengths to try to train their clients and, more particularly, the client's staff, in attention to detail in this respect.

The monthly customer statement has already been mentioned. It will, of course, identify to customers items which are not due for payment but will also point out amounts that are due or overdue. The importance of open-item statements, as opposed to those showing brought-forward balances, cannot be over-emphasized. Although on the surface they are an administrative detail, they do make a considerable difference to the quality of a company's credit administration and collection. Many British companies do not allocate cash regularly and rely on balances brought forward. Consequently, it is difficult, sometimes impossible, to resolve problems with customers relating to short payments or discounts taken out of time. If you cannot identify each invoice on an account and relate specific payments to it, you cannot keep on top of the inevitable queries that can arise, particularly on large accounts, and considerable staff time can be wasted in both the supplier's and customer's offices. You cannot easily record such entries as store order numbers or locations against specific items. Small matters in themselves, but they can make a real contribution to effective accounting and cash collection.

The factor, at the commencement of the arrangement, will suggest to the client an appropriate collection cycle. This can be varied depending on the client's view of the need for a gentle or tough attitude towards recalcitrant customers, although as the factor has bought the debt and is financing it he or she will be unlikely to allow special treatment to all customers. This would be a total contradiction of the objective behind factoring in the first place. Frequently, compromise is necessary in this area.

Routine procedures are that the statement will be followed by at least two, possibly three, reminder letters of increasing severity prior to considering instruction of solicitors. These letters will be accompanied by frequent telephone contact with customers by the credit department staff who soon get to know the prime customers well and to use the client's contacts. For larger sums it may be necessary to visit customers and employ telex or facsimile communications to deal with particularly urgent or large outstanding debts.

Legal action is taken as a last resort. Normal practice is for the factor to send a copy to the client of the final reminder letter, which is normally the last before instructing solicitors. If the client opposes legal action, most factors will withdraw credit approval at that point and may re-assign the debt to the client. They will, of necessity, withdraw funding by ceasing to provide the on-account payment in relation to that particular debt.

This can be an area of difficulty in terms of client relations, for obvious reasons. The client may not want the customer sued while recognizing the factor's need to collect. The existence of the factoring arrangement can be an advantage here because it does bring about a subtle change in the relationship between supplier and customer. At this stage of the proceedings, the complaining customers can be told 'this is now out of my hands as the factor has bought the debt, and if payment is not made, then any further action is entirely up to the factor.' This can take the sting out of an otherwise somewhat tense commercial relationship.

Factors will send clients regular details of the state of play on the sales ledger, either by way of an aged analysis or a summary of the debts purchased and outstanding. As already indicated, some factors are doing this electronically. Others stick to paper. Either way, it is obviously important for clients to stay in touch. It is their business and their customers that are being handled and the client needs to know just what is going on. Equally, wise clients will leave the day-to-day administration to the factor. After all, the client is paying a fee for the service and it is pointless becoming involved in routine matters unless asked to.

Clients will certainly be asked to become involved in situations where customers dispute invoices that have been sent to them. The resolution of disputes is perhaps the most important element in the successful operation of credit control and collection. Customer disputes can occur for all sorts of reasons: late deliveries, deliveries of the wrong type, size, quality, colour of product, no deliveries at all! Customers may, of course, raise disputes on a frivolous basis simply to cover up for the fact that they are unable to pay for perfectly legitimate supplies. Different industries vary considerably in this respect. Factors become quite expert in identifying genuine from frivolous disputes. They are usually prepared to give the client the benefit of the doubt in any dispute. In other words, when a customer refuses to pay either a whole or part debt because of a dispute they will normally permit the client a period of time in which to resolve the matter by sending to him or her the details of the dispute so that the client can resolve the matter with the customer with minimum delay. Usually a period of 30 days is given, which effectively puts the client on notice that some urgent action has to take place. If the client has not resolved the matter within the stipulated period the factor will retain the right to reassign the item to the client, leaving him or her to collect directly from the customer. If, on the other hand, the client indicates clearly that the dispute has been resolved or did not exist at all in the first place the factor will proceed to endeavour to collect from the customer, although of course the client may be required to supply more information as to the technical nature of the dispute.

Generally speaking, these procedures seem to work in most cases. Critics of factoring argue that the existence of disputes is one of the reasons why the service can never work efficiently because of communication difficulties on a three-way basis between the factor, the client and the customer. In practice, so long as the level of dispute within a given business remains within reasonable bounds, no serious difficulty arises. Indeed, the procedure can work as a discipline on a client ensuring that disputes are attended to quickly and efficiently.

Full factoring—who needs it?

With the development of cheap and universally available microcomputing, sales ledger accounting packages are readily available. Anyone prepared to spend a little money and some time and trouble is perfectly able to run competently a sales ledger which would generate accurate and timely information both for internal use and for customers.

Credit insurance is available for companies concerned to minimize or eliminate bad debt risk, and overdraft finance can be obtained from the banks. Why, therefore, are companies still using factoring services and why does the use of the service continue to grow?

There are a number of reasons. Factoring provides a package of services which can relieve the entrepreneur of a great deal of routine work. Most small companies are operated by people whose expertise is technical or sales-based. Few can afford expensive high-quality financial support. Most do not have a full-time finance director or even a full-time accountant. The classic argument used by factors, therefore, is that by allocating the credit and sales ledger administration functions to them, time and resources are released which should enable the entrepreneur to get on with the vital business of producing and selling products. The point has been made *ad nauseam* in hundreds of articles and factoring advertisements, but is nonetheless valid. People operating in bigger company environments are apt to be innocent of the day-to-day pressures under which smaller businesses work. Lack of time is often the main enemy, and poor organization the cause of much difficulty and even business failure. The ability to 'subcontract' such an important part of the operation, hopefully in the certain knowledge that the function will be performed effectively, is a real blessing in the right circumstances.

Second, the credit protection aspect, although much less emphasized, can be important. The main non-recourse factoring houses, having been in business for many years, have developed credit assessment skills of a high order. They have dealt regularly with many thousands of customers in their time, and have in-house knowledge of customer payments and track records in a very wide variety of industries. They are, or ought to be, in a position to provide as rapid responses to requests for credit approval as can most credit insurers who are dependent upon outside information sources (used also by the factors) to assess realistic credit levels. Credit insurers can no doubt point to a number of features of their service that stand up well alongside those of factors, but that is not the point. The fact is that the factoring client, if he or she so wishes, can get 100 per cent protection against bad debts as part of an overall package, and this can be invaluable for a growing company. Few factoring clients start to use the service for credit protection but some of them come to appreciate its finer points as the relationship develops.

Then there is collection. Many critics of factoring will argue that the imposition of the third party between supplier and customer must have a deleterious effect. No doubt in some cases it does, but as we shall see later, these days such cases tend to be few and far between. On the other hand, most factors can point to a string of success stories where they have been able to reduce significantly the number of days customers take to pay without upsetting them. How is this? It is quite simple. Customers respond to effective credit control, which as we have already seen involves regular, clear reminders that a debt is due. Clearly produced open-item statements sent regularly at the end of the month, augmented by well-written, to-the-point follow-up letters, do tend to work particularly when accompanied by the regular attentions of well trained collection staff. Very often, factoring clients are unable or unwilling to learn the techniques of credit collection themselves. Thus, there are examples where the total cost of a factoring facility has been paid for simply by the interest savings on debtors outstanding once the factor has been successful in reducing the average time taken by customers to pay.

Then there is the finance. The critics will tell you that people use factoring services purely for the money. Of course, there is some truth in this. Undoubtedly, most full factoring clients initially approach a factor because they feel they need additional finance. Indeed, research commissioned by the Association of British Factors, as it then was in 1989, confirmed that of a sample taken by the researchers, Burson Marsteller, 69 per cent gave their reasons for use of the service—to release capital and improve cash flow. Many will have talked to their bank managers and will have been refused the additional facilities required. Factoring finance is not cheap, but then few of these clients could command 'blue chip' funding rates and many years' experience of factoring clients indicates that although many, perhaps most, have money in mind when they sign a factoring agreement they later come to appreciate other aspects of the service.

Fundamental to the argument is the fact that factoring finance promotes corporate growth. Because factors know about debtors and are in a position to control the operation of the sales ledger they can release more funds against the debtor asset than can bankers. These funds, used wisely, will promote growth, and if they are coupled with effective credit control and collection there is an element of stability underpinning the companies' growth.

So this mixture of motives is why people continue to use full factoring services. Whether they continue to do so in sufficient numbers to enable the factoring industry to grow in the manner to which it has recently become accustomed remains to be seen and this perhaps depends upon the factors as much as upon the clients. This is a topic for a later chapter.

Recourse factoring

Some factors and some clients prefer to operate without any credit insurance within the factoring package. A recourse arrangement is just that. In other words, the client is responsible for bad debts arising from the failure of customers to pay, but aside from that the service is almost identical to a full factoring or non-recourse arrangement. The factor takes responsibility for the administration of the sales ledger, for collection from customers and for the provision of a financial facility where required. With recourse arrangements, of course, factors must retain the right to require their clients to re-purchase debts at a given point in time, since by definition recourse factors carry no responsibility for the final insolvency of the customer. In practice, recourse factors tend to pursue outstanding items through collection to legal stage even if they may hold an additional reserve on payments on account in respect of items which have reached, say, 60 days past the due date shown on invoices.

ADVANTAGES OF A RECOURSE ARRANGEMENT

Why, therefore, should a client enter into a recourse arrangement as opposed to a non-recourse one? It depends very much on the requirements of the company. If finance, plus capable sales ledger administration, is the prime need and if the client is quite confident about the creditworthiness and quality of his or her customers there is no reason why the client should plump for a credit-insured facility, especially perhaps as competitive quotes may be obtainable from recourse factors, who logically should be able to provide a cheaper service by virtue of the fact that there is no credit insurance element contained within it. There are more subtle reasons, however. With non-recourse factoring, the level of funding available is very often, almost always, geared to the level of credit protection that the factor can offer, in the light of the credit quality of the client's customers. This is quite logical. A factor's prime security for the funds advanced lies in the quality of the debts accepted. If, as part of the service, the factor is providing credit protection and advice, it would be foolish almost to the point of perversity to finance unapproved debt entirely on the same basis as approved.

Non-recourse factors are not necessarily too rigid about this. So long as the majority of a client's customers are reasonably creditworthy and the debt is well spread between a reasonable number of accounts, the factor will probably provide a facility against all of the outstanding accounts. But cases will always arise where the non-recourse factor's view of customer quality and spread will not coincide with that of the client, and in such instances it is not uncommon for additional reserves to be held against the availability of payment on account to the client.

Generally, recourse factors take a more liberal view of customer debt since they are not on risk from a bad debt point of view and can afford to consider the 'spread' of customer accounts in gauging the quality of their security. They claim, therefore, to be able to release more cash, pound for pound, than is usually feasible under a non-recourse arrangement. This is, of course, an important issue for the client requiring the maximum level of facility to finance growth, especially if the client is not over-concerned about bad debts. These claims have not been verified by any independent research, and there are, without doubt, plenty of cases which tend to support the opposite point of view. The variety of circumstances arising during the course of a factoring relationship, between factor, client and customer, are myriad, and it is possible to prove all kinds of points by reference to specific cases, where experience is not at all typical.

Another key advantage claimed in favour of recourse factoring is its simplicity. If you are expecting someone to take the risk that your customers will not pay, it is axiomatic that you have to provide detailed information about these customers to the factor and sometimes wait a little while for an indication that the factor will assume the risk. In a recourse arrangement this does not arise. Recourse factors usually provide advice to clients about the advisability or otherwise of accepting a given customer order but they are not assuming the risk, and this is invariably a fast process and, indeed, one that the client is not obliged to follow. So the whole relationship is simpler and, possibly, quicker.

Adherents to non-recourse factoring would no doubt dispute a good deal of this, and argue that their service is equally effective, just as quick and not at all restrictive in terms of the funds made available. In many cases, they are no doubt quite correct. When full service factoring works well it works very well, and many clients have had cause to bless the fact that the factor was on risk when they have heard the unpleasant news that a customer has been lost, not because of any failing on their part as a supplier but because the financial pressure became too great.

Just the same, the trend in the market is towards recourse arrangements, indicating that overall, the credit protection facility is less important to many businesses. The ABFD statistics clearly highlight the trend. In 1985, a surprising amount of factoring was transacted on a recourse basis—ignoring invoice discounting, no less than 33 per cent in fact. By the end of 1991, this figure had grown to 48 per cent. Even more significant has been the gradual take-up of this variant of the service by the factoring fraternity. In 1985, only Alex Lawrie Factors, whose business has always been based on recourse facilities, were providing them in a big way. Of the total recourse business turned over, Lawrie had some 76 per cent of the market. Most of the other major factors provided recourse facilities, but overwhelmingly, they were providing credit protection.

By 1991, the picture had changed. Of the 12 members of the ABFD, six provide more recourse factoring than non-recourse. The main bastions of the full service factoring discipline are these days the major bank-owned factoring companies, such as International Factors and Lombard Commercial Services, whose recourse portfolios still represent a relatively small minority of their total business, while S. P. Business (Europe), the Security Pacific factoring company acquired during the year by Century Limited, remained the only factor who had not followed the lead of Alex Lawrie, and moved over, at least partially, to recourse factoring.

And the trend in the UK is muted as compared with that in the world generally. Indeed, the above description of a factoring service could be considered as being over-biased towards UK experience if one considers the market from a global viewpoint.

Later, we shall be dealing in detail with the statistics provided by the Factors Chain International in Appendix 9. These show quite clearly that, in the world at large, recourse factoring is of considerable importance and is almost on a par with the full factoring service. Both services have to be considered in the light of the surge of growth provided by invoice discounting, but there is no doubt that for many factors and clients world-wide, recourse factoring is even more important than in the United Kingdom.

Does this mean that the credit protection element of the factors' services is no longer valid in the sense that it is a service that people are prepared to pay for? Not really. It probably reflects developments on the supply side of things rather than any major shift in demand. In the early days of the UK factoring industry, those responsible for establishing factoring services looked towards the USA as a model for their work. In the USA most factoring is non-recourse, indeed, the whole service is based upon the principle that the factor takes the credit risk. It has just happened that way, historically.

Accordingly, US factors have built up very large resources in terms of credit information, market knowledge and the capacity to disseminate it. Now this is all very well once the data has been accumulated, especially if it is captured in an appropriate electronically based format, so that it can be stored and distributed cheaply. But as anyone who has started to develop a database from scratch will tell you, the costs can escalate in a quite alarming way. So it is no accident that the clearing banks have been the standard bearers of UK non-recourse factoring. They have been the only ones able to afford the expense of the data gathering and retrieval, the staffing and not least, the costs of dealing with clients who have been promised a fast turn-around of their requests for credit approval.

New entrants to the factoring market place have learned this lesson assiduously. They have tended to start on a recourse basis, build up a customer credit track record through practical experience, and utilize this information at the appropriate time when clients come to them for non-recourse facilities and they feel competent to provide them on a cost-effective basis. To an extent this has occurred in the UK but it has also happened, so I am reliably informed, in important factoring markets such as Italy, and is re-occurring in places such as Hungary, where the factoring gospel is a relatively new one but may proffer great potential.

Invoice discounting

All of the factors without exception, however, are providing invoice discounting. The service is thus closely related to factoring and the two services are certainly confused in the minds of many members of the commercial public.

Invoice discounting is, however, a quite distinct service, aimed at a different sector of the market place and at companies with totally different needs and attributes. It is, of course, purely financial in scope. The client sells his or her debts to the factor, who in this context, of course, is a discounter, who provides an agreed payment facility expressed as a percentage of the debts in exactly the same way as a factoring facility. The arrangement is confidential, that is to say, there is no notification to customers that the debt evidenced by the invoice has been assigned and financed. By definition, therefore, it remains for the client to take responsibility for the collection of the debt and to account to the discounter for this collection process. This is assisted by the establishment of a trust account in a bank nominated by the discounter and which he or she controls, and into which receipts from customers are paid by the client.

From the discounter's viewpoint, invoice discounting is inherently more risky than is factoring. The discounter does not control the sales ledger and normally has no direct contact with customers. He or she is entirely dependent upon the efficiency and honesty of the client in offering debt for discounting that is valid and collectable. The discounter relies upon the client for collection and has to assume that the client's staff are competent in this respect and capable of handling the administration of the sales ledger. Discounters depend upon their clients to warn them of impending disputes or other problems with customers which could have an adverse effect on the payment pattern and thus the quality of the receivable and the discounter's security.

With all of this in mind, the discounters, and for the most part, the factors, for they are one and the same, have evolved quite separate procedures and principles to permit them to contain their risks. In the first place, criteria for new business is far tougher than for factoring. Any discounter will expect a serious invoice discounting proposition to relate to a company that has some track record of profitability, strong management and a stronger balance sheet than many factoring clients can proffer. Discounters have to be convinced that the likelihood of their clients failing is reasonably remote, for no other reason than if a corporate failure does occur then the discounter will be faced immediately with the task of recovering the advances made for customers who, immediately prior to the crash, have no inkling of the involvement of the discounter, and that the sums due for goods or services provided are due to him or her, not the administrator.

Discounters differ in their precise balance sheet and operational criteria, but because of this risk, it is unlikely that a company without a net worth of £50 000, sales turnover of at least £1 million and probably more, and a history of profits, will find it easy to obtain discounting facilities. They will also be expected to offer other qualities. At the initial survey of the business, the discounter's staff will put under the microscope the details and capacity of the client's staff and management in terms of sales ledger operation, customer relations, accounting and, above all, cash collection. The quality of management within the business will almost certainly also receive close scrutiny as will the prospects for the enterprise, its market place and quality and spread of customers.

Once the agreement has been signed, the discounter will require the client to provide regular, probably monthly, information about the continuing relationship with customers. An aged analysis of debt will be asked for early in the month, almost certainly accompanied by a sales ledger reconciliation and copies of the customer statements that the client has sent out. As with a factoring arrangement, the level of prepayments will be governed by the discounting agreement, but that document will undoubtedly permit the level of the facility to be altered if the client is unable to cooperate in any of these areas.

Despite all this, and the attendant risks involved, there is no doubt that invoice discounting has strong attractions for both providers and recipients of the service. As we shall see later, there has been no shortage of organizations prepared to become involved in the business, and all of the factors, in recent years, have utilized the skills developed in the choosing and monitoring of factoring business to develop invoice discounting capacity. The discounting element of their business has developed to the point where it is, in many ways, becoming more important than the original factoring service from which it was derived.

So far as new providers are concerned, it is not altogether surprising that they choose to cut their teeth on the provision of discounting rather than factoring. Costs of entry are comparatively low. There is no requirement for expensive credit control staff or information resources other than those required to monitor accounts. The principal requirement with regard to staff is expertise rather than numbers, and if the risks are high the return on capital employed can be excellent so long as the operation is properly run.

From the client's viewpoint the service is highly beneficial, as is amply demonstrated by its growth rate. The client receives funding against debtors well in excess of that which a bank would normally provide through overdraft or other lending facilities secured on debtors. The facility grows with the increase in sales. It is confidential and is comparatively inexpensive, these days often comparing well with overdraft facilities in cost terms. A number of high growth household business names have used invoice discounting in the course of reaching their current pre-eminence, and many more continue to do so.

Operationally, the service is simplicity itself. Clients forward to the discounter schedules of invoices in very much the same way as has already been described for a factoring facility. Prepayments are made by the discounter, usually through CHAPS facilities up to the level of the facility stipulated in the agreement, less any extraordinary reserves. Subject to the control mechanisms mentioned above, there are very few disadvantages from the client's viewpoint, and because discounting facilities are normally offered to better organized, staffed and financed businesses, these, in practice, cause very few problems. Most of the clients usually operate computerized sales ledger facilities [most discounters will insist on them] and the administrative chore presented to them by the discounter's monthly work requirements is no real problem. The service is here to stay.

Management buy-outs

In recent years the development of management buy-outs (MBOs) has been an important feature of the UK commercial scene. The emphasis placed on the more productive use of assets in the 1980s, the development of the venture capital industry, and the willingness of the City to go along with ambitious managers willing to take risks with whatever personal wealth they have acquired, has resulted in a veritable boom which has received a further boost as a result of the recession, as receivers are appointed to basically solid but cash-starved businesses a proportion of whose managements become convinced that they can turn the business round.

The buy-out will always involve the purchase of either the share capital of the target company or specifically identified assets which have been hived off, usually by a receiver, and which it is believed can be put to good use by the management team. Rarely, of course, can the management team finance the purchase of the shares or assets from its own resources.

So the banks and the venture capitalists have developed some quite novel techniques for providing the necessary finance. Most people are familiar with the sometimes highly leveraged deals seen in the USA during the 1980s associated with 'junk bonds'—sometimes huge corporations were purchased via consideration based at least partly on paper stock the value of which was questionable—but the UK seems to have missed the worst excesses of this, and although some MBOs have failed, others have gone on to provide career and business opportunities that might otherwise have gone begging.

The fact remains that MBOs are by their nature fairly risky. The acquiring management does not have the wealth to buy the shares or assets, and so inevitably the financiers have to provide equity loans and sometimes 'mezzanine' funding to enable the deal to be concluded. This needs to be carefully structured if the business is not to be too highly 'geared' so that it becomes unable to handle the burden of interest which it will carry into its new life.

Here factoring, or more particularly invoice discounting, can play a vital role. As we have already seen, invoice discounting can provide substantially more funds against the debtor asset than can a bank overdraft facility. So it is ideally suited to complement the funding 'mix' of venture capital, management equity or loan, bank finance or overdraft, which has to be put together, sometimes in a very short time, if a rival bid for the company is on the table.

The assembling of this package, and the legal and commercial implications of MBOs, can be complex. Some of the factors have therefore begun to establish specialist units, whose role is to work in tandem with the other professionals involved with the buy-out providing the specialist input in relation to the funding of debtors. They will also make sure that the various agreements between the parties contain nothing which would inhibit the factors' ability to fund. Rarely, in fact, will factoring or discounting money be used to purchase shares or assets, but it is available as an ongoing working capital facility, growing with sales, to the new management team as the business gets under way.

In assessing an MBO proposition, the factor or discounter will apply very much the same standards to the quality of the customers and sales ledger as for any routine new business. Inevitably, however, more emphasis will be placed upon the strength and track record of the management team, its ability to cover all of the main business functions, and its clarity of vision in terms of developing the business it hopes to acquire. The latter aspect will, of course, be expressed through a detailed and well structured business plan, and it is through this document that the team will be judged initially. The submission of a poorly thought out or unrealistic business plan will probably do more to scupper the ambitions of management than anything else. It is also vital that members of the team demonstrate their capability of producing realistic forecasts and plans. Simply asking the auditor to knock out a set of figures will not suffice—the team must understand collectively and individually the full implications of the plan and be capable of implementing it.

Agency or bulk factoring

Agency factoring was originally a system whereby a confidential invoice discounting facility was provided by a factor on the basis that the debts were assigned to a company with a name similar to that of the client, perhaps, for example, with the word 'sales' added after the main corporate title, but which was in reality an agent for the factor, even sometimes operating from his or her office. The purpose of this, of course, was to obscure the existence of the arrangement from customers, giving the impression that they were dealing with the sales company of the supplier.

This practice has all but died out. These days, factors offer agency arrangements to clients on the basis that the client is responsible for sales ledger administration and collection along the same lines as for invoice discounting but on a disclosed basis. Protection against bad debts may also be included in the service.

The inelegantly named bulk factoring is yet another variation, against leaving the client responsible for collection, but on the basis that payments are made to the factor's account in accordance with instructions contained on the invoice. On the face of it, these arrangements are neither fish nor fowl nor good red meat, since they do not provide that element of service which is the charm of a full factoring facility and lack the confidentiality of an invoice discounting line. These services can be useful to some clients, however. Some relatively new companies do not meet the somewhat stricter criteria laid down by invoice discounters in terms of the level of turnover and history of profitability. At the same time, they may be businesses which the factor would be prepared to support on a disclosed basis, even though possibly the characteristics of their sales ledger are unsuitable for the full factoring service. This is usually because of a very widespread number of customers and low average invoice value, both of which have a direct impact on the factor's cost and accordingly on the charge that has to be made. So there is a place for agency and bulk factoring and quite frequently, successful clients 'graduate' from these services to achieving the status of full invoice discounting clients.

Maturity factoring

Some companies use factoring for service without any financial facility. Thus, they receive the full package of services with the factor running the sales ledger, providing credit control and protection and collection from debtors. They also receive an assured cash flow because most factors will offer arrangements under which a fixed maturity period is calculated reflecting the average time taken by customers to pay, at which point the factor is committed to paying the full amount to the client less service charge and other routine deductions. An alternative is 'pay as paid' arrangements through which the factor will pay the client as and when customer payments are received.

Only a few factoring clients use maturity services. But most factors can boast some element of maturity business, frequently among the larger companies, some of whom are household names who value the combination of bad debt protection and assured cash flow that the facility provides. Sometimes there is an international element, since quite obviously credit protection in foreign markets can have added attraction.

Export factoring

Export factoring provides all of the facilities offered in the domestic arena, plus more. From the client's viewpoint the system works in a very similar way although it is likely that the exporting client will get more for his or her money than the company using full factoring for domestic debts. For example, the client will receive the benefit of 'local' credit approval and collection in the country concerned. The export factor's correspondent factor will have facilities which will be at the disposal of the UK exporter. So a credit line can be established in the light of information gleaned in the country and assessed by credit professionals there. It is possible that the exporter's agent will be able to work closely on the ground with the local factor, thus both speeding up the process of credit assessment and doing everything possible to ensure that the majority of sales are covered by credit approval. Collection is also eased. Statements will be in the language of the country concerned and local practice will be followed in the way dunning letters are sent or telephone contacts made. Local advice on appropriate sales terms can be made available. Most export factors, as part of their service, offer currency protection to the exporters.

Factors, like other credit insurers and financiers, have to take into consideration the notion of 'political' as well as commercial risk. So clients wishing to export to a number of Third World countries are still often best advised to proceed only on letter of credit terms, and if possible arranging for the letter of credit to be confirmed by a bank of good standing. But we live in changing times. The list of Factors Chain International members spans the globe (Appendix 9): there are factors established in some exotic places, and the list is growing all the time. While the majority of cross-border factoring takes place between companies in established markets, the opportunities for growth are very great, and as experienced factors develop their business in an increasing number of markets the potential contribution factoring can make to world trade will also expand.

The costs

Throughout the gamut of factoring services—full factoring, invoice discounting, international, bulk and agency—the charging structure adopted by factors is virtually the same, as follows:

1. A *service charge*, also known variously as a factoring commission, administration charge or fee, levied on the full face value of debts offered at the date they are offered for factoring.
2. A *finance charge*, also described as a discount charge or money charge, levied on the payments on account taken by the client for the period that the funds are made available to him or her.

This structure applies to factoring and invoice discounting overseas as well as in the UK. In more than 25 years of operations here, factors have rarely departed from what has become the conventional means of charging for their services and for the use of their money. This may confirm that, seen as a group, they are conservative, even unoriginal in their dealings. It may, on the other hand, simply reflect the fact that this is the most effective method of charging, and that, so far at least, no one has come up with a better one. The system at least is proven and well accepted, if not always fully understood by clients. It is relatively open and straightforward. Any client armed with a calculator and minimal common sense can work out costs. It is instructive to take each charge in turn and consider how it is applied to each service. Then we will be better equipped to consider the crucial issue of value for money.

Service charges are applied to the gross value of invoices as they are accepted for factoring. The level of the percentage charged is agreed prior to the commencement of the factoring relationship and is enshrined within the factoring agreement which is drawn up between client and factor. Thus, although factors may vary the charge from time to time, alterations are not casually made. The charge, which attracts VAT, is applied as a debit to the client account against every invoice offered for factoring. It provides factors with their basic income, compensation and profit in return for which they provide the services described above. As might be expected, factors are expert in assessing the costs and risks of operating sales ledgers and providing credit protection. So it is not usually difficult for the potential client to get them to give cost indications. Generally, service charges will fall within a range of 0.4 per cent to 2.5 per cent of sales turnover. The precise figure applied to a particular client's account will be determined by the characteristics of the business as well as its inherent desirability. The factor will take into consideration the client's current level of turnover, forecasts of sales and the extent to which these can be taken seriously, allied to the potential of the business in the longer term. The number of customers involved will be considered; both those with balances outstanding at any one time, and potential and the number of pieces of paper likely to be handled will also be considered carefully; that is to say, invoices and credit notes which will be dealt with on a routine basis.

Most factors have formulae which they apply to the costing of full factoring business and which reflect the juxtaposition between sales turnover, average invoice value, customer numbers and the bad debt provision that influence their costs. The precise level of service fee quoted to a particular client will depend as much on these elements as the inherent desirability of the account in terms of the factor's experience of the industry or the strength of his or her desire to help the particular company concerned.

Service charges are applied in exactly the same way to other services described above, namely invoice discounting, bulk and agency factoring. In these cases though, considering the relatively low workload incurred by the factor the level of charge is lower. For invoice discounting one would expect a service of between 0.2 per cent and, say, 0.6 per cent of sales turnover, depending upon the general desirability of the business. In this context, desirability will be assessed by the discounter more in terms of the inherent risk involved, or perceived to be involved, with the particular business proposition that is under consideration rather than the workload or handling characteristics that it presents, although these will also be considered.

For agency or bulk facilities, the service charge rates will be more than for discounting—between 0.5 per cent and 0.75 per cent is normal—and they can be even higher, depending again on the characteristics of the business, the factor's view of the risks involved, and the likely workload to the factor's staff in monitoring the account.

In all cases, whether for full factoring, domestic or export, agency or bulk and even for most invoice discounting arrangements, factors will invariably expect a minimum service charge arrangement under which, should the service charge levied not meet an agreed level during a specific period of, say, a quarter year after the date of commencement of the factoring arrangement, then the difference between the charge actually levied and the minimum will be debited to the client account.

The rationale for these arrangements is, of course, to protect the factor in a situation where a client's projected turnover has failed to materialize, thus generating less income for the factor than anticipated, perhaps to the point where he or she failed to cover the costs incurred.

Moreover, in the vast majority of cases, the provision is never implemented. Minimum service charges are very often pitched so low that nothing short of catastrophe could cause turnover to drop to such a level. But they can be of significance when relatively new businesses are being offered for factoring or in volatile markets. Before signing agreements with large minimums, clients should be absolutely certain that they expect to achieve targets, or that, alternatively, the arrangement cannot be negotiated on another basis.

Finance charges are levied on the finance used by the client under whichever type of factoring or invoice discounting agreement. It is debited to the client account as the funds are drawn down. As cash is credited to the account on a daily basis (see Chapter 5) the net effect is to ensure that the client pays only for the money drawn down, so the charges are fair and open.

Rates charged depend very much on the financial strength of the client and the consequent attractions to the factor of the particular business. In most cases, factors attempt to match the rates charged by banks on overdraft facilities to the small to medium-sized corporate market, so most finance charges are probably in the range of 2½ to 3 per cent above the base rate of whichever clearing bank the factor uses for the purpose. Competitive pressures in recent years have meant that factors rarely get away with rates much in excess of this, although very small factoring cases may find themselves paying perhaps one or even two points above the average.

On the other hand, especially in the invoice discounting market place, the larger, better capitalized and more efficiently run businesses have sometimes been able to obtain rates from discounters which provide little in the way of margin to compensate for the risks involved.

Generally, the cost of money appears to excite little controversy among factors, discounters and their clients. Service charges can be another matter entirely.

Is factoring expensive?

Many of the problems faced by the factoring industry have the costs of the service at the core. Often, the criticisms are based on sublime ignorance as to the basis on which factors charge. Many people confuse the two basic charges outlined above, assuming, for example, that the finance charge is levied irrespective of the funds employed, or, to use an extreme case, but one that most people in the factoring business have heard, that the reserve held on payments on account by the factor is, in fact, the service fee. If factors were, in reality, retaining as charges up to 25 to 30 per cent of the face value of their clients' invoices, they would not have many clients, but I have heard this fiction put about by people who ought to know better.

Better informed critics put forward the point that, if a company is reviewing the possibilities for obtaining working capital, factoring is generally ruled out because, if you take the total charges involved and apply them as a cost to the level of funding that can be raised, even if it is accepted that factors can release more cash against debtors than can bankers, the result of the exercise produces very expensive money indeed. This is unquestionably true, if you regard the exercise as being a totally financial one.

Indeed, if a company is capable of obtaining bank overdraft or other borrowing facilities sufficient to enable it to expand at exactly the pace desired by the shareholders, and the management is totally competent in all areas of credit control and sales administration, then that company has no need of a factoring or invoice discounting facility. Such companies do exist, but I would venture to suggest that, in the real world, there are many more who are in no position, particularly in the economic conditions experienced recently, to negotiate with their bankers on every facility they are likely to require.

Moreover, the 'self-sufficient' argument assumes not only that the factoring service is of little worth, but that it is, of necessity, expensive. To an extent, this point of view has entered the conventional wisdom of the commercial world over the past 25 years aided by some strong vested self-interest on the part of several groups in the business community and, as argued in subsequent chapters, the factors and their supporters now face a particularly difficult task in removing it from the minds of many people. This is unfortunate, not least because many factoring clients have found that genuine benefits can flow, not just in terms of increased funding but in business efficiency and reduced costs from a factoring arrangement.

So let's take a practical example—a 'typical' factoring case. A company turning over, say, £750 000 per annum, selling a product to the retail sector so that it has, say, an average invoice value of perhaps £400 going through around, say, 100 'active' customers. As we have already seen, factors, in quoting a service fee, will take into consideration the workload involved in handling such an account. They will also look carefully at the trends within the business and the risks. In crude terms, it might be that a factor would quote such a company a 1.5 per cent service charge which would result in a total cost of the factoring service, as opposed to finance, of £11 250 per annum. It might be more or less depending on the elements mentioned above, but this is a reasonable guide.

Then you must add the cost of finance. Let us assume that the debt turn is around 75 days—in other words, customers are taking 2½ months to pay. This gives, on average, a sales ledger balance of approximately £150 000 and a particular client requires, say, 65 per cent payments on account against debtors, around £100 000. At today's interest rates this will cost him around £10 000 per annum. So if you add the funding costs to the service fee you have £21 000 plus as a cost of the factoring facility. This is a lot of money for a small business to absorb, so are not the critics quite right in their judgement?

It depends on how you look at it. Let's deal with the finance costs first. We have to assume that the client is not drawing on the facility frivolously. So the £100 000 is being used as working capital within the business and if it were not made available by the factor it would have come from another source. This source, invariably a bank, would charge for it. The charge might be slightly less than that of the factor but it could also be higher. Unlike the factoring finance, the facility would not grow with the expansion of sales and debtors in the way that a factoring financial facility does. It will almost certainly be the subject of some kind of upper limit or would require constant renegotiation as the company expanded plus, of course, the provision of additional security.

Now let's look at the service charge element. Before the company began factoring it would have incurred costs in administering the sales ledger. Just as there is no such thing in business, or in life, as a free lunch a sales ledger costs something to operate. Labour is the key element in the cost equation. Very often, the debtor control function in small companies is carried out at a surprisingly senior level—quite frequently by the managing director. Managing directors are often the last people to estimate carefully the costs of their time, but for the sake of argument let's assume, in our hypothetical company, one half day per week of senior management time is committed to debtor control (it's often very much more than that!) and that salaries plus direct overheads amount to, say, £40 000 per annum. That is approximately £4000 per annum assuming that the manager devoted 10 per cent of his or her time to the function. Then there is the cost of the credit clerk who will also do some of the company's book-keeping and will be responsible for administering those customers with whom the MD does not necessarily get involved. It is reasonable to assume that, say, between a quarter and a half of this person's time will be allocated to credit collection and sales ledger accounting work. At current salary levels this gives us between £3000 and £5000 a year.

Then there is the cost of the accounting system itself. Even a cheap microcomputer will incur depreciation. There is stationery, both for the computer and for correspondence, postage, telephone calls, perhaps occasional customer visits, all of which should properly be allocated to the sales ledger and collection operation. I am no accountant but I think most people would accept that at least £3000 a year could be consumed in this way. Already we have identified costs in our hypothetical business nudging £12 000 a year. That is £750 more than the factoring charge at 1.5 per cent. This ignores the costs of any credit insurance arrangements which the company may think it prudent to make. It ignores the cost of the management going back and forth to the company's banker's negotiating fresh overdraft levels, and preparing the inevitable cash flow forecasts and business plans that accompany such visits. It ignores any potential savings made in the annual audit bill because the auditors' task in preparing the balance sheet is made easier by the existence of a clear monthly client statement and one debtor—the factor. Most of all, it ignores both the possible benefit of quicker cash flow brought about by better sales ledger administration and a reduction in debt terms, together with time saved through the early identification and resolution of disputes and the possibility of obtaining a substantial reduction in time and material costs by using the factor's funds to negotiate cash discounts for prompt payment to suppliers. I have known cases where, by the shrewd purchasing of factoring, clients have been able to cover the cost of the entire facility by this means.

Of course, I can be accused of using figures selectively. Certainly there are many businesses where the opportunity costs argument is less obvious. If, for example, our hypothetical company had been turning over £750 000 through, say, only 25 'active' accounts with an average invoice value of £10 000 it is still possible that the factor might seek to charge, say, £8000 per annum service fee, or just under 1 per cent. In these circumstances it is obvious that the credit control and sales ledger workload is lower and the alternative cost, depending on senior management involvement, would be less onerous.

It is equally obvious that each company's vital statistics and organization and management practices vary considerably. Some managing directors, I have no doubt, are paragons of correct management practice, leaving all routine administrative detail to conscientious, well trained and relatively lowly paid staff. In such cases the comparisons I have quoted are irrelevant.

Moreover, none of these arguments apply to invoice discounting, agency or bulk where, with the possible exception of credit insurance through an agency arrangement, clients receive no services beyond the prompt provision of cash. Yet factors still charge service charges to invoice discounting clients even though the level of charge is lower than that for factoring. How, in practice, can this be justified?

The answer, of course, is that the market justifies it. We have already noted the growth of invoice discounting, and this is the largest single argument in favour of the existing practice. When clients pay a service fee or perhaps a fixed charge, they are in effect paying a premium for the funds made available through the invoice discounting facilities. They know that this facility will expand with growth and that it is not available elsewhere, notably from the banks. They appreciate that if it is put to good use within the business it can generate really spectacular growth, increasing the wealth of all participants. In this sense, irrespective of the extent of their financial sophistication, their instincts are probably sounder than those of the critics.

So where does all this leave us? Are factoring and invoice discounting grossly overpriced services or are they the finest thing ever to be developed for the British commercial classes? The answer undoubtedly lies in the middle. In the right circumstances they can deliver considerable benefits, both in a financial and administrative sense. Where a company has genuine growth prospects, a lively well directed management and yet needs support in the service areas I have described there is no doubt at all that factoring can provide the key to growth. Invoice discounting can produce corporate 'lift-off' in a dramatic way. Undoubtedly, factors are guilty sometimes of persuading companies to use their services where these circumstances do not exist. No doubt some tightly controlled small businesses end up offering

THE BUSINESS OF FACTORING

their sales ledgers to factors, possibly because their bank manager or other adviser said they should, only to find that either the chemistry or, more particularly, the factor's procedures and staff do not suit the business or its customers. Such cases exist, although they do seem to be relatively few and far between. Moreover, the fact of the matter is that problems of this kind can usually be resolved quite quickly. No factor will wish to retain a client who is totally unhappy with his or her service. It's too risky and it's simply not cost-effective.

4. *Risks, security and law*

Some critics say that factoring is risk free. 'You have the invoices', they say, 'what's the problem? All you have to do is to collect the advances from customers.'

A moment's reflection confirms this to be nonsense. Quite clearly, the non-recourse factor is at risk, simply by virtue of providing bad debt protection, but in many ways this is the least of the risks involved. The main losses suffered by factors are incurred overwhelmingly in financing clients. A little more reflection will make it clear that in a wicked world such as ours, organizations handing over cash in exchange for pieces of paper called invoices are taking risks. As we shall see later, it strains credulity to believe that every debt offered to factors is valid and collectable.

No provider of funds can escape risk, nor should they expect to. In some ways, however, compared with others in the financial community factors are particularly vulnerable; after all, they are dealing with a sector of the market place where risks are endemic. Smaller, fast growing companies fail more often than do larger ones, and when they do the amounts involved are greater than are normally lost in the consumer credit market place. Yet the factoring and invoice discounting worlds are competitive and fast moving. In order to attract and keep business, factors have to undertake obligations to finance debts. When a batch of invoices arrives on the factor's doorstep, the client expects payment that day, or at least within 24 hours, and not in two or three weeks' time when the factor has had time to consider the matter. In most factoring companies every day of the working year, decisions about the level of funding on specific clients have to be made, and quickly. The consequences when a decision is wrong can be painful.

On the other hand, factors have developed defences against risk. This chapter explores some of them, having first identified the nature of the risk, and looks at some of the quirks associated with this sometimes strange business. The discussion will lead into the quasi-technical areas of security and law. It is not the intention to offer a legal treatise. In order to understand the attitudes of factors towards their clients and their businesses, it is necessary to touch on certain technical points. These aspects will be kept as brief as possible.

Customer risk

When factoring is without recourse and where a bad debt has been properly credit approved, a factor will pick up the bill when the customer becomes insolvent. In this situation, the factor will be in the position of having to deal with the administrative receiver or liquidator as an unsecured creditor. Any loss incurred will obviously be for his or her account so the client receives the full credit protection provided for in the factoring agreement.

In recourse factoring arrangements, or cases where a non-recourse factor has not approved either part or the whole of the debt for credit purposes, any loss will be for the client's account. The factoring agreement will contain provisions obliging the client to re-purchase from the factor an unapproved debt either in whole or in part at a specified time, usually a given number of days from the due date for payment or at customer insolvency. Sometimes the factoring agreement will provide guarantees from client to factor relative to the payment by customers of unapproved debts, and this guarantee can be invoked by the factor in circumstances of insolvency. In practice, most factors will usually continue to provide clients with collection services in respect of unapproved debts up to and even beyond legal stage, even though the debt is the responsibility of the client and not the factor.

So what is the scale of losses suffered by factors with regard to bad debts? Like most financial institutions they are a little reluctant to say too much about their losses in public, although a good deal of complaining takes place in gatherings of professionals within the industry. Certainly from time to time one hears stories of quite substantial customer bad debts incurred by the non-recourse factors who, naturally enough, will do all they can to minimize losses, although many within the industry would argue that a certain level of customer loss is a necessary concomitant to the provision of an effective credit insurance service.

The scale of losses throughout the industry as a whole is known through the statistics provided by the ABFD. For example, we know that in 1987 members of the association suffered customer bad debts in the order of £2.6 million. This is a substantial sum, but perhaps when considered in the context of overall industry turnover of £7 billion for that year it seems less significant. The situation is not improving, however. The figure had grown to £5 million by the end of 1989 and, reflecting the onset of recession, had increased to £13 million by the close of 1992. So just over four years' trading had seen a very substantial increase, and the continuation of what is perhaps the worst UK recession for many years will not improve the position. An increase of this kind, which is not necessarily spread evenly throughout the 12 member firms, some of whom do not even provide credit protection, is beginning to look distinctly unhealthy.

Should the industry as a whole be unduly concerned? As already mentioned, it could be argued that as one of the prime purposes is to provide clients with bad debt protection, then occasional losses are inevitable, and that factors must take the rough with the smooth, the good years with the bad and will build up reserves to cover such contingencies. Moreover, the factoring companies have developed sophisticated credit systems and large departments specializing in the granting of credit. They have substantial information sources at their disposal including, of course, track record information of payments from a wide range of customers in many industries. So the scope for technical improvement is limited.

Moreover, competition between factoring companies is intensifying, and although it may be that few clients enter into a factoring relationship for credit insurance purposes only, once they have received the benefit of the service and have seen the factor assume the odd bad debt, they want to retain it and to ensure that the factor shoulders most of the risk. So are the non-recourse factors on a credit treadmill which will get steadily more difficult to handle? Some people within the industry believe so and cast doubts on their capacity to continuously service endlessly increasing exposures and overall volumes of customer risk.

On the other hand, the industry itself has been adjusting. Further examination of ABFD figures shows quite clearly that the traditional, non-recourse factoring is in relative decline. In 1985, 36.8 per cent of the members' total turnover was in respect of non-recourse sales; by 1990, this had shrunk to 22.9 per cent, reflecting the substantial increase in undisclosed invoice discounting, most of which is with recourse to the client. True, there was an increase in non-recourse turnover during the five years from £1.7 billion to £3.1 billion—an increase of 82 per cent. But the increases respectively for recourse factoring and confidential invoice discounting were 150 per cent and 320 per cent.

These statistics, of course, mask a still greater risk. The fact that invoice discounting is increasing apace means that the risk of losing money by advancing to invoice discounting clients becomes still greater, so whether the trend towards invoice discounting which has accompanied that away from non-recourse business represents a less risky option is open to question.

Client risk

Certainly if you ask any factor what it is that keeps him or her awake at night, the risk of losing money on customers or on advances to clients, the reply will undoubtedly be—on advances to clients. Customer risk can be managed, even taking into consideration service pressures from clients; the factor can ensure to some extent that his or her credit-protected portfolio is spread and, if necessary, can even lay off some of the customer risk to other credit insurers.

Risks of client losses are an entirely different matter. Factors these days take great care to try to write good client business. They may avoid certain industries entirely. They may raise the criteria applied to taking on new business; as we shall see later, they have various methods of controlling their risks and ensuring that clients stick to the guidelines that are laid down. But

THE BUSINESS OF FACTORING

in a competitive market place they cannot stand still; they have to continue to write business, and inevitably an increasing number of clients means more risk of serious loss.

The risk becomes clear in three main ways, through fraud, client insolvency and the dilution of debt. All of these adversely affect the security of the factor by reducing the quality of the debt assigned. Sometimes all three occur at once, and very often one element leads to another. When difficulties occur, the problem can escalate with frightening speed, leaving the factor holding virtually worthless debt as security against cash advanced.

FRAUD

Few clients actually enter into a factoring or invoice discounting arrangement with the specific intention of committing fraud. Some have done, both in the UK and in other market places, but such events are happily rare and it serves little purpose to linger over them. Fraud in factoring is not uncommon, however. The financial pressures of running a small business can be considerable, and bad luck or reduced circumstances can drive people to do things which in normal times they would not contemplate, especially as sometimes the action itself seems mild or even innocuous. Probably some factoring clients commit fraud without knowing they are doing it. On the other hand, business pressures, the need to pay wages or to placate a demanding creditor can often bring out the worst in people.

Ignoring payment due

The most common example of client fraud is simply hanging on to the factor's money. Customers quite frequently ignore assignment notices on invoices and statements indicating that payment is due to the factor and proceed to pay the client either out of habit, or because the client has asked for the money. In these circumstances, of course, the money belongs to the factor, who has bought the debts and has almost certainly made a payment on account. The right course of action, therefore, is for the client to pass the cheque immediately to the factor. Sometimes they bank it, sometimes it is a genuine clerical error. All too often, it is a response to cash flow pressure.

Pre-invoicing

This is also a fairly regular sin. Here again, it can be apparently innocent. The client raises an invoice before the goods are dispatched or the services are performed; this can arise through some kind of administrative error or it can simply mean that the client needs an urgent injection of cash and is, in effect, anticipating receipt of an order or trying to finance the manufacture of goods against customer demand. So long as the order does materialize, perhaps the worst that can happen is that the factor will collect his or her money a little later than the theoretical due date calculated by reference to the invoice date. So long as the client is continuing to trade, no great difficulty may ensue. If, on the other hand, the client ceases to trade before the goods are actually delivered then quite clearly there is no chance at all that the factor will collect from the customer. Clients also suffer from severe bouts of absent-mindedness in relation to the prompt raising of credit notes and sending copies of them to their factor. Quite clearly, in these cases the factor is going to be hard pressed to collect from the customer, who is expecting to receive a credit note and will not pay until he or she does so.

These kinds of occurrences are surprisingly commonplace in the factoring world and one would go so far as to say that all factors have at one time or another come across such situations. Inevitably, such actions by clients, whether brought about by administrative error or by intent, are clear breaches of the factoring agreement and as such entitle the factor to terminate the arrangement immediately and demand back from the client the funds advanced. In practice, of course, the circumstances which gave rise to the problem in the first place indicate that the chances of the client paying the factor quite substantial sums involved are negligible, and so the factoring company has to decide in these cases whether it will continue to provide a service and on what basis.

Quite clearly, once this state of affairs has arisen the relationship between client and factor can seldom be the same again and it is frequently best to endeavour to resolve the situation by managing the client's cash flow and giving him or her the opportunity of finding alternative funding. This is, of course, easier said than done. The factor usually has to make a judgement as to whether the indiscretion was committed deliberately or by a combination of inefficiency and administrative failure.

'Fresh air' invoices
No such defence can be put forward when, as sometimes happens, a client assigns the factor debts which are known in the business as 'fresh air invoices', which relate to a debt that simply does not exist and has little possibility of coming into existence. In this situation, the factor will normally immediately terminate the factoring arrangement and proceed to try to collect from customers such debts as appear to be valid. Very often, of course, such circumstances result in loss which, particularly in recent years, has been very substantial indeed.

Why do clients do it? They must know that sooner or later the factor or invoice discounter will uncover the fraud. People are perennially optimistic and when severe cash flow difficulties occur it is easy enough to rationalize actions which purport to keep the company going, to keep the staff and workforce employed, especially as many can persuade themselves that a large order or major distribution deal is just around the corner. What is really tragic about such situations is that in many instances, if the client were sensible enough to alert the factor to the problems that he or she is suffering from, it is quite often perfectly feasible to work out an arrangement under which payments on account can either be made on a more regular basis or even increased, provided, of course, the potential problem can be perceived as a short-term one. Factors, like bank managers, will always appreciate candour from their clients and will usually do all they can to help the company in difficult circumstances, particularly of course as it is in their own interest to avoid precipitating a receivership if at all possible. It is also very noticeable that in circumstances where the factor and client are able to cooperate to weather a storm of this kind, then very frequently the relationship becomes stronger. The client appreciates the help that has been given, and a new level of trust and understanding can develop between the two parties which can be used as a basis for genuine business development.

Insolvency/receivership

Fraud is always accompanied by financial difficulties. Sometimes, however, the client can be impeccably honest and still run into insoluble financial problems so that the company has to go into administration or possibly liquidation. Here again, the factor will have the right under the terms of the factoring agreement to terminate the arrangement, to cease making payments on account and to demand back the balance of the funds in use already advanced. The latter right can be a little theoretical. The fact that the client company has called in or had a receiver imposed upon it will invariably mean that it is unable to meet any demand for the repayment of factoring or invoice discounting advances. So the factor's practical response to any such situation is to look to the customer to pay sufficient of the debts assigned to him or her so as to recoup investment in the business. When news of a client ceasing to trade is received in the factor's office all hands will go to the cash collection pump. Invariably, customers will be sent statements and will be telephoned with requests to pay promptly the amounts that are due, and here lies the rub and the risk. When companies fail, the risk of dispute and non-payment becomes far greater. The cessation of the business nearly always implies some failure of control or direction. Failure to control finance, the inability to plan effectively, poor reporting systems, bad product quality, indifferent delivery, all of these things tend to happen and indeed are the cause of the financial crises in the first place. Similarly, they all affect the customers of the business and, in turn, the factor. In the pre-insolvency shambles, what can go wrong will do so. Money and time are short as desperate management try to run the business and generate cash to pay persistent and worried creditors. Sales may be made at all costs, perhaps giving rise to bad or doubtful debts. Goods will be pushed out of the factory before they are properly manufactured against the customer's order. Records will be poorly maintained, proof of delivery documentation may simply not exist. All of these situations may result in non-payment.

In these circumstances it is easy to see how factors lose money. Nowhere is this more apparent than in undisclosed invoice discounting. Here, the first intimation a customer has of the discounter's involvement will come when the supplier has had the receiver appointed and the factor has written to indicate that the balance on the bought ledger in favour of the client has in fact been assigned and is due to him or her. The need for clear and speedy communication with customers is paramount if the customer is not to ignore the discounter's request for payment and simply forget about the debt, raise a late dispute or send the goods back.

Where a factoring service has been provided on a disclosed basis the factor's risk is easier to contain. Here, the customer will at least be aware of the factor's existence and will be accustomed to paying him or her. Difficulties can still occur and a certain amount of pressure may still need to be applied. It may be difficult if not impossible, for example, to get disputes resolved even though it is quite common for the management and staff of a company in administration to continue to cooperate in order to sort out customer disputes. But at least the element of surprise is absent and factors, as opposed to invoice discounters, have a better chance of getting their money back. In either case, they are quite expert in so doing. Most invoice discounting sections or divisions of a factoring company will have a collection unit, whose job it is to liaise promptly with customers in circumstances of this kind so as to minimize risks. Quite clearly, they will endeavour to identify the larger amounts owing on the sales ledger so that these can be recouped first and applied against the funds in use.

In some instances, it may also be important to liaise closely with a receiver. Legally, factors or invoice discounters own the debts that have been assigned to them, and this ownership remains intact despite the appointment of the receiver. In practice, however, there is always the risk that customer payments may go to the receiver, and it is important to ensure that these are passed over quickly. It is in the interests of both sides to work together, and very often the receiver may request the factor to collect all of the debts outstanding over and above his funds in use so that any surplus cash can be applied for the benefit of the creditors. This also has the advantage, of course, of ensuring that the customers have only one point of contact for payment purposes, and saves the receiver the cost of setting up his or her own collection arrangements. It is very much in the interests of the factor to provide the receiver with as much help as possible. At the same time, a wise receiver will provide the factor with as much information as possible from the client's records and staff about the details of disputes, possibly copies of proof of delivery and other documentation, all of which will make the task of collection much easier and therefore of benefit to both parties.

DILUTION OF DEBT

So factors are at risk especially when businesses break down and when fraud is committed. It is not unnatural, therefore, for them to pay considerable attention to anything which dilutes or reduces the value of the debts that they have purchased. The most obvious source of concern is, of course, the humble credit note.

Consider a business for which the factor has provided a 75 per cent on-account payment facility. Only on rare occasions will the factor's funds in use actually represent the full 75 per cent, leaving a 25 per cent plus reserve which is held in case of just the kind of problems outlined above. Let's assume that the client has some misfortune. Perhaps a new product line is badly received by the market, manufacturing or delivery problems occur, one or two important customers are not happy with the supplies received. Suddenly the level of credit notes issued, expressed as a percentage of debtors, substantially leaps to, say, 10 per cent or even 15 per cent. It is almost certain that a situation like this, with a sudden surge in the level of credit notes actually issued, will be accompanied by increased disputes, and others will be impending.

At this point the factor's security becomes strained. In offering the company facilities at the outset he or she would have surveyed the business (see Chapter 10) and taken a view about the level of facility which the company required and with which he or she was comfortable. The sudden change for the worse will inevitably bring about some reassessment, perhaps a necessary reduction in facility levels.

Similar problems can occur with customer disputes and even cash discounts offered for prompt payment, especially where, as in some companies, some kind of bulk purchase discount is offered at the end of a season or particular period as a reward for placing orders up to a specified level. Unless factors are acquainted of these details by their clients, they may be taking unnecessary risks by continuing to advance at a higher level than the business justifies. A little later we will be considering in detail the client relations function, which is important in the management of factoring risks. For the moment, it is enough to note that the well organized factor will use modern computing techniques to record information on all these aspects, endeavouring to reflect trends and changes in the client's business as indicated by the movements in turnover, number of accounts, number and level of credit notes and disputes, and, above all, the speed with which customers pay. Taken over a period, properly structured statistics such as these can provide a valuable insight into the workings of a business and provide the factor with the opportunity to meet difficulties before a rising adverse trend becomes deeply established. At this point, of course, discussion would take place with the client, who in some instances may be less aware than the factor of the trends within the business which are causing concern.

Financial weakness

With all of these problems in mind it's small wonder that these days factors and invoice discounters are sometimes cagey about the type and quality of the business they take on. There are some companies where the risks, from a factor's viewpoint, are far outweighed by the positive benefits. We shall see later something of the detailed procedures factors used in taking on business and we have already touched on the broad criteria used by them in securing business. These criteria will vary from company to company and are rarely applied in a totally rigid way, but quite clearly factors are not interested in companies that are about to cease trading. Even where the current trading position appears to be quite healthy, factors have to assess carefully the quality of a client's trade debtors. If the company's fortunes do deteriorate, it is frequently the case that the only source from which the factor can realistically expect to recover his or her funds is from customers. If the quality of debt is flawed, so is the factor's security. Nor are factors at all keen to provide evidence to those who accuse the industry of being 'the lender of last resort'. On the other hand, most of the companies who approach factors are small businesses with higher risk profiles than bigger companies. It is essential, therefore, that factoring companies and, to an even greater extent, invoice discounters, apply quite rigorous standards to new business and to the monitoring of existing accounts.

A GOOD RISK?
To some extent this is done through experience rather than by detailed financial analysis. To be sure, the quality of debt is thoroughly analysed: that is inevitable, but at the smaller end of the business the quality of the client's balance sheet is perhaps less important to a factor than to a lending banker. Factors will invariably want to see evidence of profitability. They will wish to be sure that the shareholders have shown financial commitment, either by way of issued share capital or loan stock. If the company is financed mainly by directors' loans the factor will usually wish to see them subordinated before being prepared to provide additional finance against debts.

Examination of past growth and future prospects is important. This leads to consideration of product, production and distribution. Factors will scrutinize in great detail the way in which people receive and fulfil orders, raise invoices, operate their sales ledger systems, credit check and control their customers and collect cash. They will do this from two points of view. First, they will wish to ensure that the characteristics of a given sales ledger are such that it can be handled effectively, and at reasonable cost. Second, they will wish to see evidence that customers have paid reasonably promptly in the past, although they will accept that by providing more efficient sales ledger services they can often justify taking on business to effect improvements in this area.

Like the banker, the factor is very concerned about the quality and characteristics of the people involved in the business. A certain amount of prudent due diligence on the past activities of the directors will take place and will be reinforced by discussion about the company, its history and its plans for development. In view of the risk of fraud, factors are not unnaturally concerned about the honesty of individuals, and any strong doubts in this area will lead to the business being rejected very quickly. Similarly, the factor will be encouraged at evidence that profitability has been ploughed back into the business and has led to some growth. A well-prepared business plan will also engender confidence, as will the production of regular cash flow forecasts and management accounts. Evidence of financial control is important, especially when large facilities are under consideration and particularly in invoice discounting cases.

Unlike bankers, factors are concerned mainly about the one aspect of tangible security which affects them—the debt. A good factoring debt will make up for many other deficiencies or weaknesses. If company management can convince the factor that he or she will be able to collect funds advanced if difficulties occur they are well on the way to getting the facility offer. In other words, while a company's financial past is important it is considered against the background of the general suitability of the business for factoring services. This flexible approach has perhaps been the main reason for the growth of factoring in an increasing range of industries.

Sometimes factors will consider taking on 'new start' businesses. Like other lenders, however, they will be sceptical unless the proprietors can provide some evidence of likely success. Factors are as aware as anybody else of the high failure rate existing in the new start area. The existence of firm orders from a good spread of customers will provide encouragement, as will evidence of solid financial commitment by the proprietors. It must be remembered, however, that by definition, many new start businesses will have no choice during their early trading months, or even years, but to sell to a narrow customer base and this provides a factor with a concentration of debt that is not attractive. Most factors say that they will give new starts a fair hearing; however, most new start businesses probably do not get past the initial discussion.

RISK AND THE INVOICE DISCOUNTER

All of this applies, with increased force, to invoice discounters. Discounters are even more vulnerable than their factoring colleagues, to fraud, corporate failure and dilution of debt. At least through the day-to-day operation of running the sales ledger, factors are in close contact with customers who are aware of their existence, and the fact that the debt represented by the invoices payable on their bought ledger is payable to them.

The confidential discounting arrangement provides none of this protection and discounters, in achieving reasonable security, have to fall back on their capacity to select clients who are likely to stay in business or who at the very least, if they do face difficulties, are unlikely to attempt fraud. Consequently, discounters will be more demanding than factors, both in the criteria that they set for new business, and in insisting upon regular audit of clients once they have been offered facilities. Discounters will also expect a regular flow of monthly information from their clients with regard to the detailed operation of the sales ledger, and the clients' success in collecting effectively from customers.

Who *cannot* factor?

In the preceding paragraphs we have considered the threats to the factor's security brought about in various ways. While these threats occur in only a minority of cases, the possibility of loss when such events do transpire is not inconsiderable. So when assessing new business, factors and invoice discounters inevitably have to take into consideration the possibility that such circumstances may occur and that they may find themselves dealing with the need to collect from customers in order to recoup the funds in use which have been advanced to a client who has failed to continue to trade. This is at the core of their security. So long as a client continues to operate, few difficulties may occur and it could be argued that almost any debt, for whatever period, could be factored so long as a supplier continues in business. Unfortunately, when the going gets tough the real risks start to emerge and inevitably the losses can be painful.

THE IDEAL BUSINESS FOR FACTORING—OR NOT

It is for this reason that factors and invoice discounters prefer businesses in which the obligations of the seller are performed and completed at around the time the invoice is raised and the debt comes into existence. Any residual liabilities, responsibilities or tasks are unwelcome, since by definition, should the client cease trading and the customer insist upon his or her rights in terms of follow-up service or supply, the factor, who has purchased the debt, is unable to provide it. So businesses selling equipment with a strong element of after-sales service, for example, are less than attractive to factors. Suppliers of capital equipment are unlikely to receive a rapturous reception from a factor. Usually, capital goods sales contracts provide for 'stage payments' reflecting such events as the placement of order, manufacturing time, installation and commissioning and so on. In theory, these could be factored (factors have been known to try!), but in practice they do not provide ideal business.

Seen from the viewpoint of the company requiring the finance, it is prudent to endeavour to match the finance period with the likely life of the asset in question. Factoring finance is essentially short-term working capital appropriate for funding an expanding business and focusing on companies with good products and effective management teams. To use it as a substitute for medium-term bank funding or for leasing, which is designed specifically to finance capital equipment, is quite wrong in itself, irrespective of the attitude of the factoring company.

Contra-trading

Other areas of business activity pose difficulties. Obviously, whatever the industry, factors or discounters will be loth to become involved in any business where contra-trading is a regular feature. This practice, where both parties involved in a transaction are selling to and buying from each other, and where, from time to time, one or the other will settle the balance outstanding by matching the respective debts and making payments reflecting the difference, is, naturally enough, an anathema to factors. It is also surprisingly common, so its existence within a business does not of necessity mean that a factor will not become involved. If the factor likes the look of the business in the round, he or she may offer a facility but on condition that the contra-trading is stopped by mutual agreement between the two sides. Alternatively, in cases where this is difficult to achieve, it may be possible to hold an additional funding reserve against the contra'd element of the business and yet still provide sufficient funding to the business as compared with overdraft facilities.

Seasonal business

Paradoxically, factors will sometimes look askance at businesses which are of a predominantly seasonal nature, especially if this feature is accompanied by an element of suspected financial weakness. The seasonality of the textile trade provided factoring with its historic roots, but things have moved on, and where the sales pattern of a business is closely linked with a particular time of year, its very irregularity can mean that the exposure of a financier can be heightened, particularly if a given line or product is badly received. For this reason, few factors will get involved in businesses closely associated with agriculture, for example.

Other businesses which may prove unattractive

Other businesses which will be unpopular with factors include those, for example, where it is practice to take in free issue stock which belongs to the customer and upon which some kind of added-value process is being carried out, so that in a situation where the supplier ceases to trade, there will be almost inevitable dispute concerning payment. Indeed, factors will be unlikely to become involved in any business where there exists the likelihood of high levels of dispute. Their security rests solely upon the quality of the debts sold to them, and if there is any aspect of the client's business that looks as though it could give rise to a weakening of that security, they will, at the very least, ask a large number of questions before becoming involved.

Of course, their attitudes differ. Each factor has different approaches to differing sectors of industry. For example, I know factors who will, for reasons which to them are valid and based upon hard practical experience, regard the furniture industry as being comparatively high-risk. Others see little problem in taking more exposure within it. Some do not particularly like 'high tech' businesses, and although this attitude has always seemed to me to be a little outdated, they are perfectly entitled to take that point of view, which again may well be based upon hard practical experience.

Sale or return goods
Similar circumstances occur in relation to arrangements for 'sale or return'. Here, the supplier is providing goods to the customer on the basis that payment will be made as and when they have been sold on to a subsequent customer. The client is unable to provide any kind of warranty to the factor that the invoice is raised in respect of a valid debt which is payable on a clear, due date since, by definition, the customer has the option to return the goods and thus avoid payment.

Building and construction industry
Further difficulties arise in relation to the building and construction industry. Invariably, the practice in the industry is such that payments are made against certification by architects or engineers, and until such certification is received the debt cannot truly be said to exist. Contracts in the industry are frequently subject to retention agreements, so that payment is released only when it is clear that the supply of services or materials have been undertaken fully and completely to the satisfaction of the client and the client's professional advisers. In cases where a supplier may have become insolvent or, for some other reason, is unable to undertake the necessary remedial work, payment may never be released. Indeed, in general the relationships between contractors and subcontractors within the industry are such that it is entirely impracticable for a factor to be sure that the debt he or she is handling will be paid by means of one simple invoice and one payment.

For these reasons, factors and invoice discounters avoid capital goods and construction industries notwithstanding the fact that this, of course, means that a very large area of business activity effectively falls beyond their reach.

Reservation of title

Another difficult area that has caused concern in factoring circles in recent years is reservation of title (ROT), whereby a supplier places within the contract of sale a condition that reserves to the seller the ownership of goods until the supplier has been paid. This gives the supplier the right to either reclaim the goods by direct action or to insist that any proceeds are due to him or her.

Quite clearly, this can cause a potential difficulty in a situation where the goods in question have been resold by the customer, who may then assign the debt that thus arises to a factor. In this situation, where the buyer (the factor's client) gets into financial difficulty, a factor can come into conflict with the supplier as to just who is entitled to payment.

ROT has been around for a long time, especially in Europe, but its importance and apparent use have grown in recent years, especially in the light of the well-known *Romalpa* case (*Aluminium Industry Vaassen BV v Romalpa Aluminium Ltd*) where, in 1976, the Court of Appeal upheld the rights of the supplier to retain his right to the proceeds of sub-sales of the goods, that is, onward sales by the supplier's customer even where the original goods may have been incorporated into another product. This became known as 'prolonged reservation of title'.

The consequences for factors are obvious. Many potential clients will be purchasing goods from a variety of sources. If a supplier's contract of sale contains a clear term reserving title in straightforward language, legal ownership can be said to reside with the supplier. These facts can be checked during the initial survey of the business, and the prepayment facility geared to the level of likely ROT, but there is nothing to stop a client from subsequently contracting with a supplier who has clear ROT in his or her sales terms.

The position has perhaps been complicated by a degree of ambiguity, particularly in relation to what is realistic in respect of sub-sales of products. If you take *Romalpa* to its theoretical limit, an unpaid component manufacturer, who had taken the trouble to render his product identifiable, through a part number or coding system, could remove it from a machine sold and paid for by the ultimate customer. Indeed, the outcome of recent legal cases appears to support that point of view. In *Borden (UK) Ltd v Scottish Timber Products Ltd* (1981), the court ruled that as the resin supplied had been converted into glue, mixed with wood chippings and pressed to form chipboard, the seller's goods had been consumed in manufacture and thus there was nothing to which the reservation clause could attach.

On the other hand, in *Hardy Lennox Ltd v Grahame Puttick* the court took the view that as the transformer supplied was still in its original form, albeit now part of an engine, the clause was still effective to reserve ownership to the seller. Informed legal opinion appears to hold to the view that the removal of goods fixed to other products is probably effective when they are identifiable and can be removed in one piece without damage to the surrounding article.

From the factor's point of view, of course, the key question remains: just how can it be ensured that the assignment of the debt to him or her will receive priority as against any claim made by the client's supplier under an ROT clause? Where goods are not easily identifiable, the inclusion in the factoring agreement of a warranty provided by the client that the debts offered for factoring do not arise through the operation of ROT will probably provide most factors with sufficient comfort for them to offer facilities.

In dealing with easily identified products, the factor may have to fall back on the ruling in the classic case of *Dearle v Hall* (1823), through which the commonsense rule has been adopted that, where there is dispute between two assignees of debt, the first to notify the debtor has the prior right. This applies in a situation where the assignee giving notice was unaware of the existence of an earlier assignment at the time he took assignment of the debt. In practice, factors will provide customers with notice through the assignment clause on the invoice, and confidential invoice discounters, if their security procedures are effective, should be able to beat most commercial suppliers to the punch by declaring the existence of the assignment of the debt, once it becomes clear to them that their client may be facing some financial strain.

The classic rule laid down in *Dearle v Hall* has been reinforced somewhat quite recently by the outcome of the case of *Pfeiffer Weinkellerei-Weineinkauf v Arbuthnot Factors* in 1987. Here, in addition to illustrating the fact that even in such delightful industries as the wine trade, disputes and difficulties can still occur, the court's ruling was to the effect that priority will be accorded to the party which was first to give notice of entitlement to the sub-purchaser. Here, the factor was first to give notice of his rights to the sub-purchaser and had priority over the plaintiff supplier.

The factor's security

So far it has been a gloomy story from the factor's point of view. Of course, difficulties of the kind described above do not occur all the time. The purpose of this chapter is primarily to point out that there is genuine risk associated with the provision of factoring and invoice discounting services and to provide some explanation for the procedures and attitudes within the factoring industry which are discussed later. It also helps to explain why factors do not provide finance against 100 per cent of their clients' debts or indeed anywhere near this figure.

In addition, it is important to recognize the various defences factors have in the face of these risks. They can be broadly summarized as follows:

1. First and foremost, a clear assignment of debt will afford factors some protection since at least by this means they will have the security of the debtors for recovery.
2. There will always be a factoring agreement, which will place obligations on both parties but will spell out very clearly the factor's rights in the relationship.
3. Other forms of security may be available.
4. Factors have developed various means of reducing or minimizing risks by virtue of their client relations procedures and audits.

It is now time to examine some of these aspects in more detail.

The assignment of debt

The early days of the factoring industry in the USA were bedevilled with a bewildering variety of methods through which the factor could obtain satisfactory security. In some states, simple written assignments were taken; in others filing in the local public office was required; in yet others, it was necessary to notify debtors of the existence of the assignment in order to perfect it.

As interstate trade developed during the nineteenth century, it became clear that some degree of uniformity was required, not just with regard to the assignment of debt, but with the governing of all commercial relationships. At the turn of the century a movement for a Uniform Commercial Code was under way, and by the middle of this century, such is the pace of change in these matters that American factors were able to register a security interest under Article 9 of the Uniform Commercial Code. This effectively gave them the security they required to carry on their business.

At the time factoring was 'exported' to the UK, however, this happy state of affairs had not entirely come to pass, since Article 9 had not been universally adopted in the USA and American factors were getting the security they needed by the outright purchase of debts. Other considerations which existed at the time, for example, the restrictive provisions of the then Money Lenders Acts, the fact that the factors did not possess banking status, and above all, the difficulty of taking a fixed charge on a book debt, inclined the early UK factors to follow their US counterparts and to seek to purchase debts rather than lend against the security of the asset.

Quite obviously, if the debt is taken as security, it is necessary to register a fixed charge over the debts at Companies House, since without this registered charge the factor would have no claim as against other creditors, including a liquidator, should the client cease to trade. In principle, there is no reason why factors should not operate on this basis nowadays, and indeed some do, especially in situations where they are concerned about ensuring maximum security and perhaps countering any prohibition on assignment that a customer might raise.

Nevertheless, old habits die hard, and it is still probably the case that most factoring and a fair proportion of invoice discounting still take place on the basis of the purchase of debt by the factor from the client.

The transfer of ownership of debts is accomplished through their assignment. Debts are 'choses in action', intangibles which cannot be picked up and taken away. The Law of Property Act 1925 governs the assignment of debt, and in order to meet the provisions of section 136 and to create a statutory or legal assignment it is necessary to meet three formal requirements:

1. There must be an absolute assignment of the whole debt, not by way of charge.
2. The assignment must be in writing and signed on behalf of the assignor (client).
3. Written notice must be given to the debtor.

If the statutory formalities are not met in any way, then any assignment is deemed to be an equitable assignment. This does not need to be in writing and does not require notice to the debtors involved to render the assignment valid (although of course failure to give notice, for example, in confidential arrangements does raise the risk that customers will claim contra-rights or set-offs).

In practice, the effect of equitable assignment is little different from the legal one. There is a practical difference which emerges when the factor is suing to recover debt. In this situation, under an equitable assignment, the factor should join with the supplier as a co-plaintiff. But anyway, most solicitors sue in the name of the factor, relying on the rules of the Supreme Court.

Another overwhelming advantage of taking an equitable as opposed to a legal assignment is that the former does not attract Stamp Duty. The principle behind stamp duty is that it is levied on instruments, not transactions, and if, as with an equitable assignment, there is no instrument, then there is no duty. Since the level of duty is 1 per cent of the face value of the debt assigned, it is clear that the imposition of the duty upon all debts would have a grievous effect on the factoring industry. Thus, except in circumstances where they wish to perfect their rights by taking a legal assignment—perhaps, for example, before taking legal action for recovery—most factors rely on equitable assignments for handling the greater part of their business.

More problems with assignment
The problems concerning assignment do not end here, however. Factors are not the only people in the commercial world who require security for advances made. Banks and other lenders invariably impose a fixed and floating charge over the assets of a company so as to protect their lending

position in case of need. Quite clearly, where either a fixed or floating charge exists it will be highly imprudent for any factor to attempt to purchase the debt. The practice has therefore grown whereby factors request banks or other financiers for a waiver, the effect of which is to release the debts from the fixed and floating charge so as to enable the factor to complete an assignment of the debt. The waiver, which is normally in letter form, confirms that the bank or lender is aware of the intention to enter into a factoring arrangement, and agrees with the release of the debts usually subject to the understandable proviso that the bank's rights under the charge will be unaffected, in as much as they refer to sums payable by the factor to the client, i.e. amounts over and above collected funds in use.

Banks have been giving waivers to factors for a number of years now, and they show no sign of ceasing to do so even when the factor is a subsidiary of a clearing bank competitor. There are signs, however, that bank managers, on receipt of requests for a waiver, may well refer the account briskly to their own factoring subsidiary so that a competitive quotation may be provided. In addition, of course, they may well insist upon a reduction of overdraft facilities as a condition of granting the waiver. This by itself is reasonable. After all, they are giving away security and are therefore entitled to reduce their overall financial exposure, especially as the factoring arrangements should provide the client with a higher level of funding.

Another threat to the clean assignment of debt is the practice of some customers to insert, into their standard purchase contracts, clauses prohibiting the assignment of the debts generated by sales under the contract. Their reasons for doing this can only be speculated upon. On the surface, a customer would seem to gain no advantage by such action and it can only be assumed that this practice is followed to ward off factors or other collectors who may be suspected of being rather more efficient in obtaining funds for their clients than are the suppliers themselves. More charitably, it may be that such customers, who are frequently major companies, local authorities and government departments, fear the consequences of loss if they should, by error, make a payment incorrectly to a supplier who then ceases to trade, causing the factor to return to them for a second payment.

Whatever the reasons, the problems have become more serious since the ruling in the *Helstan* case of 1978. Here, a local authority exercised its rights under a contract prohibiting assignment and was upheld by the court. If the practice became very widespread it could, of course, have a serious and unfortunate effect on the factoring industry.

Some factors attempt to cover this risk by providing a general requirement in the factoring agreement that any debt not validly assigned and paid to the client is held in trust by him or her for the factor. An alternative is to take a fixed charge over such debts so that in the event of the client ceasing to trade, recovery could be achieved from the customer. In the absence of this, the only option available to the factor is to gear the level of advance payments to the amount of debt on the sales ledger which is unaffected by the prohibition. If this intention is made clear during the initial negotiations it may be possible for the client to persuade the customer to drop the provisions.

THE FACTORING AGREEMENT

The factoring contract or agreement between the client and the factor is basic to the factor's security since it provides the framework within which the arrangement works and sets out the rights and obligations of the factor and the client.

A potential client studying a factoring or invoice discounting agreement will be struck immediately by its imbalance. It will invariably appear to be heavily weighted in favour of the factor. The reasons for this are obvious. Factors are the party to the agreement who are at risk, whose money is on the line; the objective of much of the agreement is to minimize that exposure. It is vital for factors to have proper documentation which spells out clearly just how they have obtained absolute and unfettered ownership of the debts that have been purchased. It is also essential at the outset that clients understand that the warranties given are to be taken seriously. Such an approach will do much to underpin the relationship between factor and client. Indeed, if the relationship develops into a good one the factoring agreement should rarely be referred to, since almost by definition its objective is to deal with difficulties that occur, and in a good relationship these are minimized.

There are two main types of factoring agreement, 'facultative' and 'whole turnover'. A facultative agreement gives the factor the option of accepting debts at his or her discretion. In other words, the property within the debt does not pass to the factor until such time as the debts have been formally offered by the client and accepted by the factor, so in a facultative agreement factor has the absolute right to control the flow of debts from the client. The factor can accept or turn them down at will and, in theory at least, the client has the alternative of offering them to another party for discounting, factoring or finance. However, once the debts are accepted by the factor they become the property of that person and he or she has priority against any other lender or claimant.

In a 'full turnover' agreement the debts are deemed to be offered to the factor as and when they have been credited to the account which the factor maintains for the client. The agreement will provide for all of the company's turnover (or, as defined, a division thereof) to be sold and purchased by the factor. On this basis, they become the factor's property without further ado by means of an equitable assignment of all future debts to which the agreement relates. Therefore, through full turnover agreements debts become the factor's property irrespective of notification to customers, which obviously provides increased security, and this assignment would take precedence over any claims by a subsequent debenture holder. Moreover, the existence of a full turnover agreement effectively prevents the debts from being offered to any other party.

This form of agreement also has advantages for the client since the factor cannot arbitrarily refuse to accept a debt, although very often non-recourse factors will insert into their agreements the provision that finance will be available only on debts which are approved for credit protection purposes.

Either form of agreement will clearly indicate the identities of the parties involved, the commencement date of the arrangement and usually provide a series of definitions of the inevitable legal terms that arise. It will also deal with the warranties and undertakings provided by the client. From the factor's point of view this is the most important part of the agreement, since it is crucial to his or her security interests. The warranties and undertakings will sometimes be couched in quite complex legal language and may appear onerous. In essence, however, they are simply confirmation by the client that the goods or services which underlie the debt offered have been delivered or performed and that they meet in every respect the provisions of the contract of sale between the client and the customer. Therefore, the debts offered are also free from any dispute or counterclaim by the customer and have not been charged or put at the disposal of any third party. The client also warrants that the debts offered are sold to the customer on an 'arm's length' basis; in other words, that the debts are due on open account from third parties and not from an associate or subsidiary of the client's own company. Usually, the client undertakes to perform a series of actions which assist the factor to collect legally valid and binding debts from customers. The client pledges to cooperate fully with the factor if required in the collection of a debt, to deal promptly with disputes and not to offer customers terms of sale which differ in any way from those indicated on the invoice which has been factored.

The warranties are not really onerous. All that they do is to place upon the client the responsibility for ensuring that the debts are valid and collectable. The agreement will also deal with provisions for appropriation of receipts, and the manner in which credit balances should be handled. It will give the factor the right to inspect the client's records from time to time and will, of course, provide for termination of the arrangement.,

On the latter aspect, the factor would normally retain the right to terminate the agreement where the client is in breach of it, goes into liquidation or receivership or becomes otherwise insolvent. Normally, however, the agreement will be terminated by the giving of at least three months' notice on either side, although in some instances factoring agreements can be terminated only on an annual basis by the client, usually on a date linked to the anniversary of the commencement of the arrangement.

In general terms, clients will find factors reluctant to amend the basic provisions of their factoring agreements. They are an important element in the factor's security and he or she will regard the main principles within it as being non-negotiable, unlike such issues as price and other conditions which can be negotiated in a competitive situation. It may also be possible to negotiate on any conditions which are attached to the offer of factoring, although their inclusion in the offer in the first place will normally mean there may be some reluctance to bend on certain critical points.

Nevertheless, directors of companies asked to provide indemnities or guarantees of the debts should not necessarily do so. Some factors require them and others do not. Salespeople for those that do will tell the potential signatories of these documents that they are not guarantees such as those given on a bank overdraft. In legal theory this may be the case, since all that they are doing is to warrant, on a personal basis, that the debts offered for factoring are valid and collectable. They can also take comfort from the fact that, in the unfortunate event of their company ceasing to trade and the factor needing to recover his or her moeny, the factor will undoubtedly look initially to the debtors for the funds required. However, directors should be under no illusions. Indemnities and guarantees sometimes called for by factors do make it clear that in the event of a factor facing loss, usually because he or she is unable to persuade customers to pay, he or she is empowered to turn to the individual directors of the client company for reimbursement.

Of course, any director controlling the business properly should have few qualms about the validity of the debt. If so, that person has no business offering it to the factor. What cannot always be ascertained is the possible effect upon the business, and the debts owing to it, should the company cease to function.

OTHER FORMS OF *SECURITY*
Sometimes, when considering a facility of some size, or a case of complexity where the quality of the debt is marginal, factors will take into consideration elements of security which are not based on debtors. For example, it may be possible to refinance a potential client's business by advancing a full facility of up to 80 per cent (or sometimes even more) enabling the company to repay its overdraft and gain access to increased working capital from factoring. In such circumstances, it is likely that the factor will wish to take a fixed and floating charge over all the assets of the business in the manner similar to that of a bank, the main benefit from this arrangement being, of course, that the factoring facility will grow with the expansion of the business itself.

Occasionally, factors may put together financial packages involving such elements as stock finance and, possibly, the making of advances against commercial or other properties. In such cases, of course, the factor becomes no different in practical terms from a banker offering a loan on security. For various legal reasons, factors have historically avoided being seen as offering a loan on security and have gone to great lengths to ensure that words such as 'loan' or 'interest' are not used in factoring documentation. With the passage of time, many of these reasons have disappeared and it would seem likely that in due course some of the factors have become almost indistinguishable from banks so far as their commercial activities are concerned.

5. *Accounts and accounting*

One of the main objectives of this book is to assist business people to understand the mechanics of factoring and invoice discounting and to help clients get the maximum benefit from the services that they are paying for. Accounting is at the core of the services, and I make no apology for devoting a chapter to it. For both factoring and discounting clients, the operation of the sales ledger is critical—a separate book could be written on the topic—but here we concentrate upon the client accounting system which forms an essential bridge between the two parties, and a medium of information without which the relationship cannot work well. It provides clients with part of the mechanism through which they can measure the performance of the factors, identify and control the costs of the facility and regulate the supply of cash to their business.

All too often, clients do not understand the accounting procedures of their factor, and delegate the supervision of accounting arrangements to auditors. Quite obviously, the auditor has a key role relative to the production of management and audited accounts for the company. But it is equally important for any managing director, let alone the finance director, of a business to be aware at any one time of the amounts owed to the company and by it. This can only be accomplished, in the context of factoring, through an understanding of the accounting information that the factor sends each month, either by post or via the electronic communication system set up for the purpose.

Sales ledger accounting

The sales ledger is the fulcrum of the factoring or invoice discounting relationship. If, in the case of factoring, the factor cannot effectively run a client's sales ledger, or with invoice discounting, the client fails to perform, the relationship will not endure.

In Chapter 3 we touched upon the procedures of factoring and upon the sales ledger function. We discussed briefly the virtues of 'open-item' accounting systems as opposed to those based on brought-forward balances. Such a system requires, above all, a regular account reconciliation together with the frequent application of cash received from customers to specific invoices. Factors can spend considerable time ensuring that their customer accounts are well reconciled, especially where customers insist on making payments on account, usually in round figures that are not always easily applied to specific invoices.

Reconciliation problems can also occur when customers, for whatever reason, make deductions from payment, possibly because of incomplete delivery, or take cash discounts out of time. There may be the raising of debit notes and round sum payments. The factor's accounting system has to be able to cope with all of these, usually for thousands of customer accounts. The secret of doing so rests on effective routines, performed swiftly. When anything other than a perfectly straightforward payment is received, an effective factor will raise a query with the customer (or perhaps with the client, if a dispute appears to have arisen) that day. It is usually in the customer's interest to respond quickly, and to indicate the basis upon which a given payment has been made so that the account can be reconciled and the next customer statement show an accurate position.

In cases of difficulty, and especially where customers do not respond, the factor may have problems in 'cleaning' the account. Most factors have in-house specialists in this area who are skilled in the detailed and sometimes tedious business of reconciliation. Well-designed monthly statements with tear-off payment slips showing the invoices outstanding can also reduce the incidence of difficult payments.

Here, factors have advantages in comparison with even the best organized of small to medium-sized businesses. Aside from the fact that their staff are specialized in sales accounting and ledger administration, the simple fact of the application of a daily routine assists in ensuring that the account is maintained on an up-to-date basis.

Most factors organize the sales ledger operation on an alphabetical basis by client. In other words, each client's customers will be listed alphabetically on the computerized record dealt with by a specific sales ledger clerk. An alternative is to operate a single alphabetical customer 'run', encompassing customers of all clients. Each system has its advantages, but in general terms the former appears to be more prevalent these days, since it enables the operator to develop customer knowledge and contacts in the light of specific knowledge of the client's business.

Whatever procedure is adopted, it is essential for the sales ledger record itself (a sample of which is shown in Appendix 5) to contain the vital basic information required for efficient customer liaison. This comprises the document or batch number of invoices, possibly the customer order number, the amount due with VAT, the document date and the due date. Equally essential are the details of the customer, the name and address particulars, details of any special payment arrangements or locations, named contacts and telephone numbers. Most factors' records will carry much more than this, including details of the highest and last customer payments, the existence of the customer's account on other client ledgers and the dates and amounts involved in any legal action, court judgment or dispute. All of this will be recorded and will enable the credit or sales ledger personnel to keep at least one step ahead in their dealings with customers.

Finally, there has to be an efficient back-up service if the ledger is to

ACCOUNTS AND ACCOUNTING

operate effectively. Factors are dealing with many thousands of customer accounts. They therefore take some pains to ensure accurate descriptions of customers' trading styles, addresses and track records. Here, good client liaison is essential since much of the information is provided originally by the client and it has to be checked by the factor's staff and updated as fresh information becomes available through the operation of the ledger.

Client accounting and payment availability

Factoring clients receive each month a client account from their factor which sets out the detailed accounting relationship between the two participants. Generally, these take a similar format, although different factors use different names to describe the accounting process which, in essence, is the client account. In the vast majority of cases, factors account to their clients on the basis that the purchase price of the debts purchased from the client is payable on the date that the factor collects from the customer as and when the credit period has expired. Just to complicate things, however, some factors operate on the basis of 'maturity periods' calculated by reference to the average time taken by customers to pay, and this system, although impeccably fair and open, does require a little more explanation.

For the purpose of illustrating the first principle, the following 'dummy' (figure 5.1) has been constructed:

	Sales ledger a/c					Current a/c			
Date	Item	Dr.	Cr.	Bal. £	Date	Item	Dr.	Cr.	Bal. £
1/3	Bal b/f			50 000	1/3	Bal b/f			28 000
2/3	Factored invoices	10 000		60 000	2/3	Cash		2000	26 000
2/3	Cash		2000	58 000	3/3	Payment to client	5000		31 000
5/3	Cash		4000	54 000	5/3	Cash		4000	27 000

Figure 5.1 Client account

For illustrative purposes, it has been assumed that the client account is in two parts: a sales ledger control account and a client current account. The sales ledger control account is credited or debited with any items which move the balance on that account, for example, invoices or credit notes factored, cash received from customers, items reassigned or other adjustments. The current account is mainly a vehicle for the debiting of payments from the factor to the client, but it is also credited with cash receipts from customers. For purposes of illustration, there are brought-forward balances of £50 000 and £28 000

69

respectively, and on the second day of the month a schedule of invoices amounting to £10 000 are offered and accepted for factoring and debited to the sales ledger control account. For the sake of simplicity, factoring charges and other relatively minor adjustments have been ignored. In practice, of course, these would be debited to the current account. As at 2 March, the accounting position between factor and client would be as follows:

Gross debtors	£58 000
Less current a/c	£26 000
Net client balance	£32 000

This closing balance represents the amount standing to the credit of the client in respect of debts purchased by the factor and not yet paid by customers. If the factoring arrangement were to cease at this point the client would have the option of repurchasing the debts from the factor for the sum of £26 000 or leaving the factor to collect the outstanding amounts and pay the funds over upon receipt, once his or her funds in use were extinguished. Assuming a continuing relationship, however, that the client elected to take a payment on account on 3 March, and that this is followed by further cash receipts from customers amounting to £4000, the payment availability to the client, as opposed to the amount due, is as follows in figure 5.2:

Date	1 March £	3 March £	5 March £
Sales ledger a/c	50 000	58 000	54 000
70% as for factoring agreement	35 000	40 600	37 800
Less current a/c	28 000	31 000	27 000
Cash available	7 000	9 600	10 600

Figure 5.2 Payment availability

From this it will be seen that this simple accounting system takes into consideration both payments on account up to the availability plus the 30 per cent 'reserve' payments due to the client when customers make their payments to the factor.

The accounting and payment system is easy to operate and understand. In practice, life is rarely so straightforward, and the main area of potential difficulty which can arise in relation to payment availability relates to the holding by the factor or discounter of additional reserves on payment. Most factoring or discounting agreements will make provision for the factor to hold back payments in situations where, for example, the debts purchased have reached a given number of days past the due date, or where there exist heavy concentrations of debt on a few customer accounts. From the viewpoint of the factor, there are usually good reasons for implementing such systems. They do not wish to do so. Quite obviously, their own profitability is affected if they are unable to advance funds up to the maximum level possible provided for in the factoring agreement. But equally, no factor or discounter will wish to advance in say, high-risk concentration situations, where it is felt that the client by continuing to trade almost exclusively with a handful of possibly dispute-prone customers, is exposing both the factor's security, and his or her own business, to unacceptable risk.

Problems of this kind are best resolved, if at all possible, before the factoring arrangement commences. If a client knows that it is likely, for instance, that a heavy concentration situation will probably occur in certain seasons of the year, or following receipt of a particularly large order, it is best to review the position with the factor before commencement, so that a policy can be arrived at which will secure the client's cash flow to the greatest possible extent, and safeguard the factor's security. Sometimes these problems prove to be intractable, but very often they can be resolved by sensible discussion.

In accounting and payment terms, any additional reserve will be spelled out in something like the manner shown in the example in the daily balance summary in Appendix 8, where there is deducted, from the sales ledger current balance, an amount for disapproved debt comprising, in this case, disputes and customer accounts not approved from the viewpoint of credit worth. The availability percentage is applied to the resultant 'approved' sales ledger balance, from which is deducted the current account balance to give the cash availability. So the client will be notified of the details of any deductions over and above the formal reserve required under the terms of the factoring agreement.

Where the factor is accounting on a 'maturity' basis, the accounting is somewhat different. As indicated in Appendix 6, the client account is again divided into two parts, this time the debts purchased account and the client account. During the negotiations for the factoring facility the factor will have established that, on average, the client's customers pay after a certain period of time. This period, the 'maturity period' for the purposes of the factoring agreement, is used as the basis of the client accounting system, which also takes into consideration the existence of the sales ledger control account:

1. *Sales ledger control account.* As already indicated, the client's factored sales ledger will be debited with invoices offered for factoring and credited with credit notes, cash and discounts taken by customers in accordance with the client's standard credit terms. Quite clearly, therefore, the balance shown on the sales ledger control account will reflect the

actual payment pattern by customers or, to put it another way, the factor's skill in collecting efficiently from them.
2. *Debts purchased account.* This account is part of the client accounting system proper. The credits to the account consist entirely of the totals of the schedules of offer accepted by the factor. The debits to it are simply the same amounts being transferred to the client account at the expiry of the agreed maturity period, which as we have already seen reflects the average time taken by customers to pay on a daily basis. There are no other entries into the debts purchased account. The balance on the account therefore represents the sum of the debts that have not matured at the date it is produced.
3. *Client account.* This account receives the credits from the debts purchased account at maturity. It will also be debited with prepayments to the client, service and discount charges, any cash discounts taken by customers and credit notes issued by the client. Where non-recourse factoring is in operation, the account will receive debits for any bad debts incurred at client risk.

Under this system it will be seen that where customers are paying, on average exactly in line with the specified maturity period, the credit balance on the debt purchased account should, in theory and at all times, equal the debit balance on the sales ledger control account. On the assumption that the initial calculation is correct, the schedules of offer will be transferred from the debts purchased to the client account at exactly the same time as the customers pay.

In practice, life is not like that, of course, and there will always be a discrepancy between what is forecast and what actually happens. Therefore, it is apparent that if the balance on the sales ledger control account consistently exceeds that on the debts purchased account, then customers are, on average, taking more time to pay than was forecast at the time factoring commenced. Quite obviously, the reverse situation is true where the average figures are reversed.

The main benefit to clients of this system is that they enjoy an entirely predictable cash flow since the factor pays in full at the end of the maturity period irrespective of whether or not the customer has paid. For this reason it is probable these days that the factors who operate the system reserve it for clients with whom they feel comfortable in cash flow terms. It also provides the client with a very clear view of just how the factor is performing in relation to the originally stipulated maturity period. It is essential for the factor's client executive to keep under review the actual movements on the account as against those that have been forecast at commencement or subsequently, and to make adjustments accordingly. If those adjustments are consistently upwards, factors may have some explaining to do in terms of their cash collection performance although a lengthening of the debt-turn may occur due to circumstances beyond their control. If the movement is consistently down, then it is likely that at least part of the benefit is due to effective credit control.

In client payment terms, the client account will automatically gain credit for transfers from the debts purchased account. Thus, irrespective of amounts drawn down as prepayments, the client will receive benefit in accordance with the stipulated maturity period. That being so, it is necessary to consider interest considerations since it is not feasible for the factor to change maturity periods on a daily basis. Therefore, most systems of this kind incorporate items such as an interest credit adjustment which, over and above the standard interest charge based on the debit balance of the client account, will be recalculated in the light of the average time taken by customers to pay by virtue of daily comparison between the average balance on the sales ledger control account and that on the debts purchased account. Because of the mechanics described above, this calculation will provide either a credit or debit to the client depending on whether the actual collection period is in advance or in arrears of that stipulated under the maturity arrangement.

Client's audited accounts

For many years factors have been able to claim that the effect of factoring on a client's balance sheet can provide advantages as compared with other forms of financing. As we have already seen under a factoring or invoice discounting arrangement, the client is not indebted to the factor to whom the debts have been sold. Consequently in the USA, and to some extent in Europe, auditors have felt free to regard factoring finance as being 'off balance sheet'. This can lead to not inconsiderable advantages for some clients.

Take, for instance, a client company with a simplified balance sheet with the following characteristics. I have assumed for the sake of illustration that all of the assets and liabilities are current:

	Current assets £		Current liabilities £
Cash	10 000		
Debtors	200 000	Creditors	250 000
Stock	150 000	Net worth	110 000
	360 000		360 000

On this basis, the client company has a current asset/current liability ratio of 1.44:1. This is reasonably healthy but is capable of improvement. Such improvement can be achieved by the introduction of a factoring facility. Let us assume that one is put in place, that the client draws down 75 per cent of debts offered and sensibly uses the money to pay creditors. The impact of this can be illustrated as follows:

	Current assets £		Current liabilities £
Cash	10 000		–
Debtors	50 000	Creditors	100 000
Stock	150 000	Net worth	110 000
	210 000		210 000

The current asset/current liability ratio now shows more than two to one. At a stroke, the apparent creditworthiness of the business has been improved, even though, of course, net worth has remained the same. The debtor figure is, of course, the factor's reserve, or balance due.

Of course, any reasonably shrewd observer, in reviewing the accounts of the company, will note the sudden drop in debtors, and will probably reach the correct conclusion concerning the worth of the business. Similarly of course, the profit and loss account will have to take account of the factoring service and discount charges.

In any event, it is unlikely that the current state of affairs will be allowed to persist. In May 1990, the Accounting Standards Committee, the body entrusted by the various professional accountancy bodies with the delicate task of addressing problems in financial reporting, and subsequently replaced by the Accounting Standards Board, published ED (Exposure Draft) 49 as a proposed Statement of Standard Accounting Practice, which under the title 'Reflecting the substance of transactions in assets and liabilities' addressed the issue of off-balance sheet finance.

As drafted, it contained little good news for the factoring industry. While recognizing the contribution that factoring is now making to the financing of business it saw the existence of a factoring facility as being essentially a lending arrangement between factor and client based on the security of debts. Accordingly, if adopted in its original form, it could have had implications well beyond the simple issue of whether factoring arrangements should be treated as being off-balance sheets. The Exposure Draft went to the heart of the relationship between factor and client.

The ABFD took up the matter with the Accounting Standards Board— thereby illustrating the importance of having an industry-wide body capable of putting forward a broad industry view—and persuaded them as to the merits of a number of revisions in the draft standard. The effect of these is to remove any threat to the legal assignment of debts, but to maintain the position under the original document where factoring advances appear on balance sheet. This is based upon the view that although the debts are assigned legally from client to factor, the arrangement is essentially a financing one. There remains the possibility of further changes in stance, however. The Board's task in reviewing the position encompasses a field far wider than factoring alone, and it remains possible that changes brought about by the effect of reviewing practice in other areas could still impact upon the factoring industry.

6. *Some cases in point*

Factors are rightly fond of using case studies to illustrate the benefits their services can bring to businesses. They are right to do so because it is a fact that no amount of description or elaboration of the benefits of the services can bring home the advantages in the same way as the impact upon a business achieved over a period of years and expressed in terms of growth, increased profitability and return on capital employed.

It is no exaggeration to say that probably hundreds of cases could be put forward to justify the advantages of the services—far more than for many other financial and service industries. A moment's reflection will make it clear why this is so. Factoring, and to an extent, invoice discounting, impacts upon a business at a crucial stage of its development. By the time a factor is prepared to offer a facility, the business has invariably been around for at least a couple of years. It is 'established' in the sense that it has achieved at least some market penetration, evidenced by the customer list, which hopefully confirms the fact that a measure of repeat business has been transacted with some reasonable quality accounts. There is at least some management structure in place, and hopefully, developed products. But there will also be huge constraints on growth, brought about by the inevitable shortage of funds and management expertise. Factoring will address the former difficulty, and it may have considerable impact upon the latter.

Therefore, in choosing case studies it is necessary to try to illustrate the totality of what the factors have to offer. For this reason, the first case study retreats into fiction. I have constructed a scenario for an imaginary company operating within a manufacturing industry, selling on credit terms to a reasonable spread of business customers. It could be involved in a wide range of sectors—the advantage of the fictitious approach lends flexibility—and the important point to appreciate is that, like so many businesses, initial capital introduced by the working directors is quickly utilized and the business is soon highly dependent on bank finance.

XYZ Limited

THE BACKGROUND

The company has good prospects. Its order book is full and it will be seen from Appendix 7 that it is expanding quickly. Indeed, the problems associated with expansion provide the main worries for the directors. The bank has been supportive and helpful and has granted overdraft facilities of £80 000 secured by a fixed and floating charge. Until recently, the business was able to operate within this, but due to the development of a successfully modified product line, orders have picked up and the overdraft has been under pressure. The bank agrees to increase the overdraft facility to £100 000 on a temporary basis against the background of firm orders. Nevertheless, the directors are increasingly aware that it is unlikely to approve the further extension of the overdraft unless security is forthcoming. There is none available.

Keeping the status quo—without factoring
Forecast A shows the effect on the business if the directors make no alternative financial arrangements. Fast growth has brought with it a quite dramatic increase in debtors, despite the efforts made by management to insist on prompt payment. In case it is felt that these are overstated for purposes of proving the point, it should be said that such situations are by no means unusual in small to medium-sized businesses. Most factoring companies could point to examples such as this, where increases of more than 50 per cent of debtors have occurred during periods of rapid growth. Inevitably, the growth results also in substantially increased purchases of raw materials and semi-finished goods, together with some increases in costs, as more labour is taken on to fulfil the manufacturing requirements.

As a consequence, there is an inevitable strain on the overdraft. By month 7 the revised temporary limit is under pressure and the following month it is breached. The directors request the bank for a further extension and the bank manager, who knows them well, turns a blind eye to the fact that the series of temporary excesses occur. As one of the directors remarks during this worrying period, 'we are paying the penalty of success'. Indeed, in many ways the company is riding high. There are record sales figures, and in due course it should make excellent profits. Cash flow is a constant concern, however, and the directors make a determined effort to collect outstandings and reduce the somewhat lengthy debtor period. This pays off by virtue of a distinct improvement in cash generated by the turn of the year which enables the bank to be pacified. Nevertheless, the bank's area office asks for the company to produce a revised business plan, which exercise the directors feel is a profound waste of time since the bank has made it clear that it will not be prepared to grant a further overdraft without adequate security.

Moreover, the company faces the problem of how to finance what appears to be continual expansion. A number of options are considered. The company was introduced to a director of a venture capital company who shows some interest in arranging for a substantial injection of equity. This would carry with it a number of advantages. The equity introduced would, of course, strengthen the company's balance sheet. The funds would permit the directors to take on badly needed additional staff and management and to commence a marketing and publicity campaign which would, they are sure, improve still further their expansion prospects. The venture capital company would adopt a 'hands on' approach by having one of its own directors sit on the investees board, and it is probable that through this arrangement the company would receive valuable advice, management skills and business contacts.

In addition, the venture capitalist would assist in providing the framework through which the business could be planned and developed effectively. Quite clearly, the venture capital company would expect to be in a position to sell its shares after a reasonable period, say five years, so that both it and the directors would benefit considerably if the business grew consistently to the point where the shares became tradable.

The directors considered the advantage of this. There are also disadvantages, of course. They are aware that the raising of venture capital can be a lengthy and time-consuming process. They are busy people and while producing a reasonable business plan holds no fears, they are concerned that the negotiations could consume considerable time and effort. More fundamentally, they are, at this stage at least, by no means sure that they wish to sell a proportion of the share capital of a business which, after all, is now only just beginning to take off after some very hard years of effort and worry.

For the same reason, they are reluctant to contemplate introducing a further private shareholder, particularly as such a person would probably require some say in the day-to-day running of the business, and the directors do not wish to overcomplicate the operational side. Moreover, they are aware of the difficulty of finding people with the required level of funds and the correct attitude. Private investors have invariably accumulated their own wealth after a period of considerable effort and some risk, and when investing in private companies tend to expect a major share of the equity as a reward for putting their money on the line.

The directors contemplate changing their bank with a view to obtaining an increased overdraft and perhaps loan facilities. The auditor believes that this could be the best option for the business, but at this stage is unable to suggest a bank who is likely to make available substantial additional funding without increased security. Furthermore, the directors have a feeling that the existing bank, despite what they consider to be a somewhat restrictive attitude towards lending, is by no means worse in its attitude and approach than its competitors. They feel some loyalty to it, since it was, after all, the bank which gave the company its first overdraft facility when in fact, as one of them puts it, 'the risks were far greater than they are now'. They consider the possibility of providing additional security. Both have a reasonable amount of equity within their private homes which could be remortgaged in order to introduce fresh funding, possibly on a loan basis so that the money could be repaid once the company's cash flow position has improved, hopefully after a couple of years' increased trading. One of the spouses is firmly against this option, however, and they drop the idea.

SOME CASES IN POINT

THE FACTORING IDEA
Finally, the directors consider factoring their debts. They have heard of factoring, of course. A number of their suppliers use factoring companies and they have, from time to time, in a desultory way, discussed using it themselves. Until now, however, the requirement has not been seen to be too pressing. Furthermore, they have received the impression—they are not sure where from—that it is, as one of them puts it, 'something of a last-ditch type thing'. Nevertheless, they telephone one of the suppliers who uses a factor asking for his views—which are more or less favourable. They discuss the matter again with their accountant who, after a certain amount of hesitation, says that she would support the discussion with a factoring company, and then they review the relationships they have had with the various factoring companies who have sent to them monthly statements on behalf of clients and conclude that few problems have in fact been caused by the factor's involvement. Indeed, it occurs to them that their view of the standing of the supplier has not suffered in any way. Thus reassured, they make enquiries with several factors. Things move quickly thereafter and within a few weeks the company receives an offer of a full factoring arrangement with a service charge of 1 per cent, a finance charge of 2½ per cent above base rate for funds utilized, with a financial facility of 75 per cent of the full face value of debtors. They have to admit that they found the negotiations with the three factors they talked to refreshingly different. The people concerned seemed to want to do business and explained quite clearly the requirements the factor would have in terms of the presentation of paperwork, the provision of information and, indeed, the overall contractual relationship. The directors were also impressed by the apparent willingness to work with the existing bank on the basis that an attempt should be made to negotiate arrangements whereby at least some of the overdraft facility was retained, even though the factoring facility would effectively provide funds which would replace the full £100 000. They were also agreeably impressed with the openness of the negotiations; they were invited to visit two of the three factoring companies to see how the service worked in practice, and their requests to be allowed to talk to one or two of their existing clients was met without hesitation. In addition, the directors felt that the contractual arrangements were not particularly onerous. All they had to do was to effectively provide a clean valid debt and to attend quickly to any customer disputes that arose. As this was their existing practice they saw very little difficulty in dealing with this aspect.

The potential with factoring
Forecast B shows the impact of the arrangement if it was introduced at month 3 of the identical cash flow. Sales have been assumed to have been running at the same level as costs. The difference, of course, is that the

company will receive a substantial boost to funds at month 3, the on-account payment on the debts existing at the time the factoring arrangement commenced. This gives the directors the option of repaying the overdraft in full, although as I have said, we have assumed that the bank is content to permit the continuance of a small working overdraft secured against the assets within the business remaining once the debts have been assigned to the factor.

An assumption has been made that post-factoring the collection performance improves marginally, but no allowance has been made within the purchases figures for the company to take advantage, by virtue of its improved cash flow, of savings via prompt payment discounts. Assuming that it did so, something of the order of £15 000 could be saved over the whole year if a 2½ per cent discount for prompt payment was obtained. This could, of course, provide a saving in excess of £13 000 factoring service fee. It has also been assumed that the cost of factoring equates to that of bank money although, quite obviously, the total costs of the finance are higher than under the previous arrangement if the increased funds available are being put to good use within the business.

The revised cash flow, of course, shows a dramatic position: at the end of the year the company has more than £30 000 (possibly an unrealistic figure since it would not need to draw the factoring funds and pay interest on them in order to obtain a lower rate of interest through bank deposits), but this is shown for purposes of illustration. The costs of the facility are reduced by savings on supply credit and bank overdraft. As is usually the case, the full 75 per cent facility is not used all of the time so there is a small reserve always available for drawing contingencies or particularly effective use within the business. Above all, the directors have relative peace of mind and can concentrate on developing their business in the way they have planned.

I could be accused, of course, of presenting a somewhat rosy picture. Not all factoring cases are like this. In many cases, the funds are not effectively used. Not all companies can attain growth on this scale, nor are the issues so clear-cut. Nevertheless, most factoring companies could point to actual clients where performance is not very different from this hypothetical one.

A & E Page Industrial Holdings

The background

In 1981 Tony Page, now Managing Director of the family paper and packaging business, moved from his native London to the very different environs of Merthyr Tydfil in Glamorgan, to lend a hand with the reorganization and direction of the business. At that time—and here we are in the real world, not the imaginary one—the business exhibited many of the characteristics that I have described above. Dependable Packs Limited had

SOME CASES IN POINT

been established by Tony Page's elder brother Arthur in 1962. In the years before Tony left a comfortable job in the computer industry, the business had become established as a prime supplier of specialist packaging to the motor industry.

The late Arthur Page had started life as a window cleaner in Grays in Essex. A natural entrepreneur, he spotted a clear niche in the motor industry and developed a business capable of meeting its requirements. No fool but not perhaps a natural manager, he shrewdly moved the business from his native London to Wales to take advantage of the generous grant aid available to expanding businesses, and by the time the younger brother was recruited, turnover was running at some £700 000 per year through a solid customer base, but one which was still heavily concentrated on the motor industry.

But there were problems other than concentration. Profitability was low—around £2000 per annum pre-tax. Cash flow, despite the existence of a factoring facility, was tight and there was constant pressure on the overdraft limit. Indeed, technically the company was insolvent, and a great deal of management time was spent in keeping creditors, including the statutory ones, at bay. Reporting and accounting procedures were primitive, even nonexistent, and as a consequence, management was unaware of the profitability of various product lines, and was unable to concentrate upon marketing them.

There was no strategic planning and the company was going nowhere. As is all too often the case, the fact of the matter was that the man with the determination to get things started apparently lacked the managerial skills which are required to develop a growing concern. But at least Page senior had the vision to bring in someone who could do this.

Tony Page was brought in to look after the administration of the business, leaving his brother to concentrate on sales.

A change for the better—with factoring
One of the first things Tony turned to was the factoring arrangement with the then Barclays Factoring Services. The company had been pushed hard towards this recourse arrangement by the local bank director who, it was believed, was anxious to reduce the bank's exposure on overdraft. The facility was providing few favours. The service fee payable was of the order of 3 per cent, with finance at 4 per cent plus base rate. Service standards were indifferent, although things improved after the Barclays business was taken over by Anglo Factoring, with whom Tony was able to negotiate vastly improved terms (1.6 per cent service fee, 3 per cent plus base for an 85 per cent advance). The facility was non-recourse, so the recurring nightmare of bad debts was eliminated. Anglo were apparently perfectly capable of providing more than adequate levels of credit protection which, with the enhanced level of funding, gave the business the support it needed.

THE BUSINESS OF FACTORING

Over the years, the packaging and paper business has almost run the gamut of the factoring industry. In 1987, the Anglo Factoring business was sold to Security Pacific who in turn sold out in 1991 to Century Factors, the Close Bros Plc subsidiary. Generally, the changes have had no adverse effect although there appears to be little doubt that the initial relationship developed with the Anglo Factoring management and staff contributed greatly to the development of the business.

Substantial changes have been brought about. The corporate structure has been reorganized with the original trading company, Dependable Packs Limited, being joined by a sister company, Castle Corrugated, with the shares of both being held by a family-owned holding company. These changes merely reflect the improvements that have been effected in the trading arrangements. Castle, located at Monmouth since its formation in 1984, produces corrugated board, and allows Dependable to concentrate upon the flexible packaging products in which it has developed considerable skills over the years. The dependence on the car industry is long gone. There is now a spread of accounts in a wide variety of industries.

Moreover, the management structure has been improved dramatically. In 1986, the group recruited Tony Withnall, an experienced production manager with the Dunlop Group, enabling Ken Humphries, the long-time production manager, to take over sales. The sales side was strengthened on the Castle side of the business also.

The outcome of all this has been evident in the results. In the year to June 1992, the group turned over some £6.75 million, with a profit before tax exceeding £300 000. In the midst of the worst recession in living memory, they expect to at least repeat that performance in the current year, and may better it.

There is a balanced and skilled management team. There is a better product range addressing a wider market sector. The business is soundly based and set for further expansion once the recession ends, and the directors have no doubt about the part that factoring has played in helping to achieve this situation. The availability of substantial—up to 85 per cent—finance against credit approved debtors has meant that they have been able to concentrate upon the important aspects of purchasing, manufacturing and selling products without having to worry constantly about the company's cash flow, or spend time dealing with creditors, bank managers and others who habitually take up much of the time of busy directors of cash-hungry companies. This comment, which sounds like a direct 'lift' from a factoring company publicity sheet, in fact came quite spontaneously from one of the directors. They also appreciate the credit protection. Currently, the vast majority of the debts offered to Security Pacific (now re-named SP Business Finance (Europe) Ltd) are approved for credit purposes. They set a target of 5 per cent unapproved debt, and monitor the factor's performance on a daily basis. Admittedly, the industry is one which is virtually ideal from a factoring viewpoint, the spread of debt and the credit quality of the customers providing a firm basis for a good factoring relationship.

Not that the factors escape criticism completely. Over the years, Tony Page has noted differences in quality at various times between the factoring companies that have handled his company's debts. As a computer specialist, he feels that in some respects the quality of the data processing sometimes leaves something to be desired. He believes that the introduction of electronic processing of invoices is long overdue and that the industry generally has been cautious and conservative in relation to the introduction of advanced technology. He believes that there is scope for improvement in the speed with which cash is processed, and he has noted distinct variations in the quality of the staff training provided by the factors and in the consequent attitude of staff to his business as a client.

For all that, Tony Page would not wish to face the commercial future without the factoring service that has developed his business. For their part, factors should listen carefully to what clients of this calibre have to say. It could determine their own future.

7. The factoring client

Who are they?

We have already noted that, compared with experience in the USA, companies in the UK using factoring and invoice discounting services are drawn from a very wide range of industrial sectors and industries. As long ago as 1981, a report produced for the National Commercial Finance Conference analysed the US factoring market and concluded that it was important to spread the industry into 'new' factoring markets. Over 150 in-depth interviews were conducted with companies to ascertain why it was that the factoring trade was not more widely spread. All the usual reasons for lack of growth were trotted out: cost; the notion that the existence of factoring was a sign of financial weakness; the danger of upsetting customers; and so on. The intention of the report's authors was to ease the way for the expansion of the industry into a wider market place. They failed. A recent check of the US scene revealed that factoring is still overwhelmingly based in the textile and carpet industries and shows no sign of becoming more widely spread.

As we have seen, this is not the case in the UK, nor in areas of Western Europe, where the breadth of industrial involvement is quite impressive. The overwhelming majority of factoring clients are manufacturers or distributors. The 1990 statistics produced by the ABFD indicate that some 46 per cent of factoring clients actually produce something, while a further 30 per cent distribute products. The service sector, while growing, still only represents some 17 per cent. This breakdown is not altogether surprising, of course, given the characteristics of the service and the factoring industry's requirements in terms of quickly realizable and collectable debt. It is the manufacturing and distribution sectors which provide the best security for factors. This is, perhaps, another point which should be taken into consideration by the shareholder banks.

If one considers the statistics provided by the British Bankers Association for clearing banks' sterling lending to UK residents for the period 1983–90, it becomes abundantly clear that the manufacturing industry sector has declined substantially as a percentage of the whole. In 1983, 16.3 per cent sterling lending was directed at manufacturing industry. By 1990, this had declined to 10.6 per cent. Financial services, as a sector, have shown a substantial increase, from 8.8 per cent to 15.2 per cent, and it is possible that some of this money was on-lent into the manufacturing sector. Nevertheless, the figures tend to confirm, in a very dramatic way, that the British manufacturing sector has received less attention from the City in the past 10 years than perhaps it should have done. To some extent, the factoring industry is exempt from this criticism, and this point should be borne in mind by its shareholders.

The ABFD statistics contain no surprises when it comes to the size of clients. Around 30 per cent of clients produce a turnover of less than £250 000 per annum, and this sector is growing as factors reduce their minimum turnover requirements and actively seek to help still smaller businesses. Only 5 per cent of clients have a turnover of more than £5 million. The factoring industry has failed to penetrate the upper echelons of British manufacturing industry, even though, of course, some large companies do make use of confidential invoice discounting services. Here again, there would appear to be a market for increased invoice discounting participation if clearing banks were prepared to persuade major industrial groups to use the service. Generally speaking, they are not prepared to do so.

For all that, the members of the ABFD were able to report at the end of 1992 that nearly 10 000 companies use their services. In addition to this must be added the clients of the smaller factoring companies, of whom there are some 30 in total. So on the basis that these each have an average portfolio of 25 to 30 clients, it is not unlikely that there are some 11 000 companies in the UK using factoring or invoice discounting in one way or another.

The paradox is that in general terms we know very little about who these people are. The only research that has been carried out into the make-up of the factoring client base was commissioned by the ABFD in 1988. Other than this, there has been very little attention directed by academics or industrial researchers into the make-up of the companies that use the factoring industry.

Those of us who have been involved in the industry know beyond all doubt that the overwhelming majority are managers of small businesses. However, it is usually the owners of the businesses concerned, or at least the people who run the business day by day, who have a substantial equity stake within it. Moreover, they are normally male (although fortunately in recent years more women factoring clients have begun to emerge), white, Anglo-Saxon, middle class. They are the sort of people that run businesses on the edge of most major towns in the UK, within sections of industrial estates or converted industrial premises.

Most of these small businesses are run by enterprising people who have frequently given up well-paid and more secure careers in the larger end of British industry for the pleasures and insecurity of running their own businesses. Often they are very interesting people and are highly competent in their chosen craft or business. It is very common to find engineers, computer people, technicians of all kinds, who exude enthusiasm for their product, their company, their market place and their customers. Such people work very long hours, often for a level of remuneration which is comparatively low, until such time as their company has achieved expansion and success. This kind of drive and enthusiasm is essential at this level of industry if businesses are to be developed.

On the other hand, the overwhelming enthusiasm and concentration on the business that some factoring clients possess can be almost destructive. It can lead to an attitude which dismisses as irrelevant, for example, activities of competitors, the possibility of a drop in orders or other calamity. Potential and actual factoring clients suffer from other drawbacks. Few small companies of this kind have a formal management structure which recognizes the difference between the basic business functions—general management, marketing and sales, finance and operations. In very many cases, managing directors will effectively perform at least one, possibly two, of these functions in addition to their own. Sometimes, in reality, they will cover the lot. All too often, lines of responsibility are blurred, business plans are sketchy, administrative and financial systems weak, job descriptions non-existent. Most fundamental of all, and this is a sad comment on the educational and training systems in the UK, most of these people have had very little formal business training. Experience, yes; training, no.

This is quite extraordinary when one considers that the difficulties and problems involved in running a small to medium-sized business are very substantial indeed. Entrepreneurs need to be aware of all aspects of business life and all the services available to them and the support which can be garnered from various organizations and sources. They need skills in man-management, finance, marketing, sales, as well as, probably, technical capacity in such areas as engineering, production and design. In recent years, the government has been trying to plug some of these gaps through the Enterprise Initiative Scheme, which appears to have had some success. All the research appears to indicate that the better planned the business, the better trained the workforce, the more likely it is that a small business will survive.

This obviously has implications for the factoring industry, which has a continuing interest in the development and survival of its clients. The fact that most of the people within the market place have relatively little industrial and commercial training tends to make them act in certain ways in relation to the factoring industry.

How should the 'typical' client decide for factoring?

It is worth considering just how the 'typical' company goes about the process of entering into a factoring arrangement. Very often, the business will have been in existence for two or three years. Initial finance will have been provided by the directors, coupled with some secured overdraft. As time goes by, cash flow pressures increase, hopefully for the good reason that the business is expanding rather than for any other. Inevitably, there is discussion with the bank, and the manager may well recommend factoring at this stage. Possibly the auditor will also do so, often qualifying his or her recommendation with the usual reservations about cost, over-trading, customer reaction and so on. The company executives will then begin to review the factoring market. Of course, if they have been recommended by their clearing bank, they will almost inevitably have discussions with the bank's factoring subsidiary. Relatively well informed people may contact the ABFD or other sources to obtain a list of competitive factors, but these will be in the minority. Others may read about the industry in the national press or possibly consult suppliers who already use the service.

Whatever they do, they will almost certainly receive the impression that all the factoring companies are providing very similar, if not identical, services, and that the objective is to achieve a financial facility at the minimum available price. These impressions will be reinforced by financial advisers and bank managers, who by and large are not themselves well informed on the subject. What will almost certainly not happen is for the company management to take a good hard look at their factoring requirement, in the light of their own business needs, coupled with some sensible analysis of what is actually on offer, so as to try and ensure that the best possible arrangement is made. Yet, as already noted, people who have been using the services will confirm that they are critically important for the well-being of the business under consideration.

CHOOSING YOUR FACTOR

The first rule is to choose your factor—don't let the factor choose you. Unquestionably, they will try. All factors have sales teams who, whatever their other deficiencies, are perfectly capable of presenting their services in a flattering light. A salesperson will be judged by his or her success in bringing in business, just as in any other industry. Frequently, part of his or her income will be commission-based. So the potential client should make no mistake that from the moment of the first telephone contact the factor is, or should be, selling!

Our potential client should not be in too much of a hurry to make that first telephone call. The first move should be to look inwards. Ask yourself and perhaps your staff some fundamental questions about the nature of the business, its needs, strengths and weaknesses. Initial motives for considering factoring will invariably have been based upon financial needs. Few small businesspeople give serious consideration, however, to the precise extent of this need, what other requirements exist and how they can best be met. Every business is different. The extent of business needs varies within the company as it develops. Bear in mind that not all factoring companies are the same. Like other businesses, they have their strengths and weaknesses, areas of particular expertise, areas of preferences and differing attitudes to businesses in different market places. The only way to establish these is by careful discussion and contact. Before any contact is made, the following issues have to be considered.

Financial facility
The need to set up a financial facility with minimum delay may well be very pressing. If this is needed to shore up a financially suspect business, it is unlikely that a reputable factor will wish to provide it, but in any event, it is best to endeavour to plan the requirement. Although improving, really good cash flow forecasting remains a fairly rare feature in British small business. The potential client should at least try to establish just how much money is needed and for what purpose.

A factor, just like any other provider of funds, will be much more impressed by a prospective client who produces forecasts based upon firm reality rather than the 'pie in the sky' figures very often provided. Try to establish with your management exactly how you see the next year shaping up in terms of sales revenue, gross margins, operating costs, new developments and the impact on your business of major external factors, such as price rises, raw material scarcity, the opening and closing of foreign markets, and so on. Show the assumptions made clearly and, above all, be conservative. Do not simply hand your auditor the task of producing a cash flow forecast in the abstract. Too many accountants' cash flows simply reflect their view of how they see the business developing. The consequence all too often is a row of rounded-off figures which bear very little relation to reality. Management should endeavour to produce realistic figures based on facts. You should look back to previous cash flows produced, compare the forecast with what happened in practice and assess the reasons for any differences.

The cash flow forecast will show quite clearly the level of funding required, but more important, will make it plain to the factor that here is someone who is trying to control his or her business on a professional basis. Also consider carefully what kind of financial facility is required. Many factors link the level of facility to the level of credit protection granted. If so, there is a risk that a decline in the perceived quality of the customer base may have baleful effects. First, the factor will come off risk; second, he or she will cut back on the level of facility offered to the client. Once negotiations have started, ask about the policy on concentration of risk. If the business is prone to occasional large sales to major customers, resulting in substantial debt concentration, this also could result in the holding of additional reserves on your factoring account. It is desirable for these issues to be brought out in the initial discussion, rather than after a factoring arrangement has commenced. Above all, be clear just why you require the financial facility and, if it is the primary requirement, make it clear to the factor that this is so.

Existing bank relationships
All small businesses have bankers, who will be aware, and hopefully supportive, of the intention to enter into a factoring arrangement. Bear in mind that from your bank manager's point of view, the trade debts probably constitute an important part of the security against which the bank is currently lending. They cannot be pledged both to the bank and to the factor. If a fixed and floating charge exists, the factor will need to obtain from the bank a form of waiver releasing the debts for factoring. Irrespective of the formal legal aspects, it is highly desirable for the management of the business to carry their banker with them and to negotiate with the bank, if at all possible, a continuing level of facility once factoring has commenced. Here again, a realistic cash flow forecast is critically important. It is obviously necessary to ensure that the total package, once renegotiated, provides additional funding for the business in line with the cash flow forecast. There is a tendency for bankers to use the commencement of a factoring arrangement as an excuse to reduce facilities to the extent that the effective level of funding available to the business remains the same, or is, in some cases, even reduced. This is obviously pointless.

Bank relationships throw up other complexities. As we have seen, most of the major factors are owned by clearing banks, and early in the factoring negotiation the client will need to decide whether or not to seek support from the bank's subsidiary, that of another clearing bank or from one of the independent factors. The decision may be finely balanced.

There are advantages in using banks' factors. First, the clearing bank factors are becoming increasingly adept at providing corporate clients with facilities which are designed to achieve the optimum level of funds for the company, which sometimes exceed those available through a bank overdraft or loan and a straightforward factoring facility. They are in a position to do this, of course, because if their factoring subsidiary takes over the company's debtors, they in effect achieve greater security and comfort than if the factoring lays outside the bank's organization.

Second, where relationships have been good, it is sometimes expedient to use the factoring relationship as a means of still further improving the branch banking arrangement and, if necessary, using the good contacts in the branch to ensure the best quality service from the bank's factoring subsidiary.

Both of these advantages, of course, rest on the assumption that the bank factor and the bank itself work quite closely together. Sometimes, the factoring company will request the client's permission to submit regular returns to the parent bank branch indicating, for example, the level of debtors being handled on an ongoing basis, the proportion of those debtors that are at factor's risk from a credit protection point of view and the proportion at the client's own risk. This report will also spell out any difficulties that appear to be occurring in the relationship and perhaps take a view on the strength of the client's debtors. The lending banker is therefore aware of the residual value of the client's debtors and can take a view as to the enhanced security available to the bank against any overdraft extended. This is fine as long as relationships continue well. Such arrangements mean, as already indicated, that the banks can sometimes extend larger and, possibly, cheaper facilities to customers who are placing all their eggs in one corporate basket in this way. What the individual business has to decide is whether the advantages derived from such facilities are worth the risk that flows from disagreement or disillusionment with the bank or the factor or both.

Each case must be considered on its merits, but in principle, it could be argued that the supply of finance, just like any other commodity, is best obtained from separate sources. In other words, consideration should be given to using a factor different from that owned by the clearing banker with whom the company is borrowing. The financial facilities available to a small business are often critical to its survival. But other issues are important. How important is credit protection to the business? What is the bad debt history? Is the business likely to be moving into a market within which credit protection becomes more important in the future? Factoring may offer opportunities for genuine savings in this area. At the very least, it may provide the opportunity to reorganize staff, moving a good operator into work which will have a direct bottom-line relevance to the business. It may be sensible to approach key customers, explain the reasons for contemplating factoring and ensure them that delivery and service, far from suffering from the arrangement, should in fact be enhanced, if only because of the increased facilities now available to the business.

How important is export to the business? Is it likely to be so in the future? Do currency rates give you sleepless nights? Is collection a problem? Would it assist you to generate more export turnover if you were able to offer open-account terms in certain markets? If so, then obviously it is pointless talking to a factor who is incapable of providing a full export service.

Even more fundamentally, the potential client has to make a choice as to whether to use a recourse or non-recourse arrangement. If credit protection is offered, the level of funding available may be linked to the factor's capacity to underwrite the risk. If credit protection is what is important, well and good. If funding is what is required, then the need to seek credit approval of new orders can be irksome and may be considered unnecessary. Possibly the kind of advice provided by one of the recourse factors will be sufficient to buy the peace of mind that is required and expand the business substantially.

On the purchases front, consideration should be given to the scope for renegotiating effective prompt payment discounts, so that the cost of the factoring facility may be dramatically reduced, or even eliminated. In dealing with suppliers, it is best to be quite open about the intention and reasons for factoring. Any rational suppliers should be easily convinced. After all, the business is going to receive an injection of funds and a continually expanding finance facility. This is being offered following a period of thorough negotiation and examination of the business by a company which itself specialized in credit control. There is no reason to hide the fact and, indeed, the support of the factor can be a worthwhile argument in negotiating better terms from suppliers.

Negotiations

Having reviewed these and perhaps other points, it is time to start talking to factors. First contact will normally be with a factor's sales office and a representative will call to establish whether they can be of assistance. It is clearly desirable to talk to more than one company, but it is counter-productive to spend too much time talking to too many.

GETTING BEHIND THE SALES PITCH
The sales pitch will contain assurances that the factor is owned by an impeccably respectable shareholder, committed to the factoring market place. It will emphasize that this particular factoring company has the slickest service standards in the industry and so on. Get behind the sales pitch. Try to determine just what it is that the factor can offer your business in relation to the specific needs that have been identified. Ask about the style of management. You will probably be assured that 'our reporting lines are short', and that a decision on a quotation can be made in a short time. You can put this to the test by working out a timetable on future visits, survey and quotation, to see how, in practice, effective response times are achieved. Can you have access to senior management or directors or other decision-makers, if not on a regular basis, in the event that problems occur? Is it the practice of the directors to visit their clients on a regular basis? If not, how do they maintain contact with the market place?

In relation to credit lines, it is prudent to ask the factor at an early stage of the discussion to credit-check a cross-section of your customers, as far as practicable, so that maximum credit protection can be obtained. Ask about the factor's capacity to reduce debt turn. Ask about the flexibility of the dunning and recovery systems and the attitude towards the collection of debts that are at client risk. Make sure that you are clear about the factor's policy on the possibly vexed question of payments where heavy customer concentrations exist.

Ask about contract terms, periods of termination, minimum service charges and their application. Get the representative to explain the obligations that you take on when you sign a factoring agreement. Ask for a copy of the factoring agreement early in the discussions. Read it and make sure you are able to meet all the obligations without difficulty.

It is a good idea for second meetings to take place, if geography and time permit, on the factor's premises. Once there, ask to be shown around. Seek information as to the basis on which sections or departments work. Get them to explain just how credit approval is granted, cash collected from customers, invoices processed. Operational staff and management are nearly always quite prepared to give this kind of information. Try to make an assessment of staff morale. Does it appear to be a happy, well organized company? Do the staff appear well trained? Ask, if you feel so disposed, about the company's training policy.

All of this will have a beneficial effect on the sales executive with whom you are negotiating. Play fair with him or her, indicate at the outset that you will be talking to more than one factor, but that you will not be going around the entire market place. Provide the factor with the information required to reach a decision and perhaps make an outline quotation. Audited accounts will be required, coupled possibly with cash flow forecasts. Go through the accounts with the salesperson, pointing out any special features. Answer the questions honestly; hesitation could mean that an offer is withheld. They are not bankers, but they are vitally interested in the financial security of your business and it is inevitable that they will wish to understand every detail of the operation and your plans for expansion.

WILL YOUR CUSTOMERS LIKE IT?

On the vexed question of customer relationships and customer attitudes to factoring, there are of course ways and means of avoiding problems. Therefore, a review of important customers will identify those who may misunderstand the reasons for the factoring move. As with suppliers, it is best to be open and straightforward. The customers in question should be approached and told that a factoring relationship is contemplated. They should also be told that this does not indicate financial weakness—quite the contrary. The factor has conducted a full survey of the company's financial position and operation and has made an offer, which the company is disposed to accept. In other words, the business is being supported by a factoring company well versed in selecting businesses.

The client should add that the additional finance could underpin his or her capabilities as a supplier and should make it easier to continue the provision of the high standard of service and product. Explain that it will not affect credit terms nor will collection be more stringent so long as track record of payments is sustained.

Such a review and discussion with customers is no bad thing in itself and can be a vital element in the smooth transition of the ledger from client to factor.

Prices

Many factoring clients place too much emphasis on the price of factoring. Once quotes are obtained, any major discrepancy in service or discount fee should be noted. In particular, it may be possible to negotiate a little on the service fee rates, at least to obtain a commitment from the favoured factor that the rate will be reviewed on a predetermined date, assuming all goes as planned in terms of sales expansion and the development of the business. By experience, however, prices quoted are rarely sufficiently diverse to justify being taken as the main basis for the decision. The cheapest quote is not necessarily the best. All of the above features need to be discussed and perhaps others should be weighed carefully in the balance and a decision made. Above all, the chemistry should be right. A factoring relationship is a close one and its success depends very much on the personalities on both sides of the arrangement getting on well. If you feel that one particular company has the edge in this area, then a slight difference in the cost makes very little difference in the longer run.

Confidentiality

Many factoring negotiations are plagued, sometimes aborted, by the fact that the potential client has fixed firmly in his or her mind the notion that the company requires a confidential invoice discounting facility. For reasons explained elsewhere, factors are sometimes reluctant to provide this, particularly to very young companies and, as a consequence, time can be wasted on both sides.

Very often, discussions wither on the vine because the potential client is convinced that nothing but invoice discounting will do. Sometimes this is right. Sometimes the business requires funding only, being perfectly capable of administering the sales ledger, and does not require credit protection. Occasionally, there may even be a real risk that customer relations might be soured by the commencement of a disclosed factoring arrangement.

These occasions are rare. Usually the risk to customer relations is negligible and is more than balanced by the advantages which a full factoring relationship may bring. For instance, very few businesses have the kind of credit control and collection skills in-house that a factor can bring. This becomes tangible when one examines the record of the factoring industry in reducing average debt-turn, that is, the average time taken by customers to pay. In its 1991 Annual Report, the ABFD draws attention to the fact that, even in the depths of recession, its members still managed an overall improvement in the average debt-turn of their clients from 65 to 64 days. This is no mean feat and represents an advantage that should not be lightly tossed aside.

Sometimes though, the analysis of business requirements will indicate quite clearly that what is required is a confidential invoice discounting facility. When all the various advantages offered by non-recourse or recourse factoring are considered, they are rejected because the prime requirement is for a line of debtor-based finance which will assist in securing the company's growth. Once this decision has been taken, a different set of considerations emerge so far as the choice of discounter is concerned.

A few of these are common to those considered for factoring. Clearly, the relationship with the company's bankers is paramount. The putting into place of a discounting facility will place the discounter on an equal or near equal footing, in terms of the volume of funds supplied, with that of the bank. It is self-evident that such a move must be considered carefully by both sides, and the question of whether or not to place all the lending eggs in one basket looms even larger.

But the choice of discounter will involve other considerations. The main issue is geared simply to the volume of funds that can be raised. Service is secondary. So it is essential to question the discounter closely as to the basis upon which funds will be made available. The discounting agreement will undoubtedly contain provisions permitting the discounter to withhold elements of payments in certain circumstances, where, for instance, there is a high degree of concentration of debt among customers. It may also provide for funding limits above which the level of facility will be 'pegged'.

In the first instance, it is clearly important to establish the policy on concentration of risk and to go into the arrangement with a clear understanding of the discounter's practical attitude towards it. No provider of funds likes excessive concentrations. But policies and attitudes vary, especially in relation to different industries, so it is worth while checking out the issue early in the negotiations. Similarly, although discounters are quite entitled to place investment or funding limits on business, their existence may mean that one of the prime advantages of a discounting line, namely its capacity to grow with sales volume, is nullified, and it is quite legitimate to try to negotiate arrangements that do not provide for them.

Once again though, discounters, like factors, will be most impressed with a potential client who comes into the negotiation with a clear idea of what is required to develop the business. A well developed business plan, supported by effective cash flow forecasts, will make it quite clear just what the clearly identified increased funding will be used for.

They will also regard the client's ability to maintain an effective credit control and collection system as being an indispensable element. Bear in mind that the discounter has to place complete trust in the client's ability to keep the cash flowing. Usually, clients are required to be able to point towards well administered computerized ledger and credit systems, plus the capacity to provide regular data upon collections and cash flow.

Are clients getting what they want?

There are very few published statistics on the factoring industry and its clients, except those to be drawn from the ABFD. Generally speaking factors will tell you that they are adept at maintaining client loyalty, and will talk about clients who have stayed with them for many years, increasing their business dramatically in the process. In fact, there is a tendency within the industry for factors to lose clients after two or three years' operation, simply because the client company outgrows the requirement for the factoring facility. In theory this should not happen, but in practice the company becomes attractive to banks after a few years' rapid expansion supported by factoring finance, at which point the temptation to cut costs through the elimination of the service charge becomes difficult to resist.

There is little formal market research into the attitude of factoring clients to their factors save that undertaken by Business Marketing Services Limited through Burson–Marsteller in 1988 on behalf of the ABFD. The researchers were briefed, among other things, to examine attitudes to factoring among existing and potential users. It concludes that 'existing users of factoring services are very satisfied with the service', supporting this contention with the statistics that 43 per cent of those polled responded that the service was 'excellent' and 39 per cent with the comment that it was 'very good'. Certainly this represents a very high level of satisfaction. Other groups of service providers—bankers, estate agents, transport operators—spring to mind, who would no doubt be delighted to receive such an accolade. On this basis, the factoring industry can feel quite pleased with itself.

Of course, the figures should be interpreted against the background that the survey was commissioned in effect by the factoring industry itself. The clients polled were put forward by the factors. It would strain credulity to suppose that factors would put forward the names of their dissatisfied clients for examination, and this suspicion is reinforced by a further statistic in the report—the 44 per cent who would unreservedly recommend factoring to someone else. 44 per cent is a very good response, but it is not 82 per cent, which is the sum of the 'excellents' and 'very goods'. For all these reservations, the survey does confirm that the overwhelming majority of factoring clients appear to be happy with the quality of the service they are receiving. It confirms what one would have expected anyway. Most factoring clients are growing faster than those not using the facilities. They experience fewer problems and restraints on growth. They see the service as an effective way of raising finance (some 69 per cent value the instant cash flow), and they have experienced a more effective reduction in debt turn than non-users. Most significant of all, and we look at this in greater detail later, factoring clients appear to be generally better managed than do similar companies who do not factor their debts.

These research findings confirm, in statistical format, the impression which many people within the industry have had for many years. It is possible that they are agreeably surprised in many cases at the quality of the service they receive, compared with what they expected. The survey confirms this widespread impression beyond all doubt, even going so far in its conclusions as to state that 'existing users could be the best salesmen for factoring'. Of course, this is true for most services, but given the level of prejudice around this is probably especially the case for factoring.

The factoring/invoice discounting checklist

The following checklist will be helpful to company managers seeking to conclude factoring or invoice discounting arrangements:

1. Our business—what does it need?

- Cash for expansion
- Enhanced cash flow
- Capacity to plan cash flow
- New markets—domestic and/or export
- Better use of management/staff
- Enhanced supplier relationships
- Alternative finance source
- Credit protection
- Credit advice

2. Which kind of organization?

- Bank's factoring subsidiary
- Non-recourse factor
- Independent factor
- Recourse factor
- Invoice discounter
- Export factor
- Several of these

3. The following are important to us:

- Close location
- High efficiency levels

- Friendly, communicative
- Top-level relationships
- Modern systems
- Tact with customers
- Helpful staff
- Quick decisions

The above checklist is by no means exhaustive, and every potential client will have different and perhaps additional priorities. It is designed merely to emphasize the point that the choice of a factor or discounter should be based entirely on some kind of objective analysis of the needs and future requirements of the business. The costs, while important, are by no means the overwhelming consideration. The factor's capacity to provide really critical support to the growth of the business is.

8. *Client relations*

The key to successful factoring

Few service industries pay so much attention to client relations as does factoring. This is an inevitable consequence of the detailed nature of the service, plus the fact that the factor takes responsibility for one of the most important areas of a small firm's business. Daily liaison occurs between factor and client. It is impossible to run a sales ledger on any other basis, and it is therefore sensible to pay attention to relationships with clients and to maintain one point of main contact with them.

This is not the sole reason why factors have developed the function. By now, it will be clear that they are in a risk business. They are exposed to loss through a variety of causes. The chief defence against the substantial losses that can be sustained is constant vigilance and understanding of the client's business. In this way, the signs which warn of potential loss can sometimes be spotted in time for the factor to protect his or her investment.

Third, and this is linked with the previous two points, it is essential for the factor to build into his or her business a mechanism which ensures the maintenance of service standards. Besides being important to the client, such arrangements are highly relevant to the factor. The more effective the operation of the factor's service, the better the client's cash flow and the less likely the client to suffer major loss through bad debt. A reduced risk to the client's business means better security for the factor. So quite aside from the desirability in general terms for any service to operate efficiently, there are other cogent reasons for an effective client relations function.

Structure and operation

THE SPECIALISTS' APPROACH

Faced with these requirements, some factors, especially in the early days of the British industry, established client relations departments managed and staffed by specialists, whose role was to control and monitor all aspects of the client relationship, including security, and to ensure that service standards were maintained. They got to know very well details of the client's business and, of course, the people involved in it. They were familiar with all aspects of the factoring service and thus capable of liaising effectively between the factor's operational staff and those of the client. They also ensured that the client cooperated on a day-to-day basis in the routines which are essential if the factoring relationship is to work.

There are flaws in this structure. The client relations function, while developing specialist skills, inevitably means that the people responsible for security and service are divorced from the everyday operations relative to credit and sales ledger accounting. For example, the client relations manager can explain to the client just why it is that a certain customer has not been approved for credit protection purposes, but he or she has no power to approve the item. More seriously, the client relations manager is responsible for the security of the factor's funds, but has no power to influence credit and collection practice upon which security ultimately depends.

The cell system
Recognizing these drawbacks, most factors now adopt varying versions of what is known as the 'cell system'. This involves the establishment of a unit within which all main functions are performed—credit collection, sales ledger administration and the client relations function. So the unit deals with the client and the client's customers, and the unit manager is invariably the client relations executive responsible for the variety of aspects which can impinge upon the client relationship, including, of course, security of funds. Upon this basis, client and customer risk can be managed within the same unit. Management and staff become fully conversant with the characteristics of a client's customer base, as well as with the needs of the client's business. Difficult decisions concerning the advancing of funds can be made in the light of detailed and up-to-date information. It is also more difficult for the dishonest client to pull the wool over the factor's eyes, since the people dealing with the client's account are in daily touch with the customers and making advances on the debts that the client is factoring.

Security of funds

The important role of personnel in factoring
Whichever structure is adopted, the client relations function is responsible for the security of the factor's funds advanced against debts. It can be seen that from the factor's point of view, although the loss of money through customer bad debt can be a problem and has been increasing in recent years, the overwhelming risk to factors arises through advances made to clients on account of debts factored. The root cause of these losses is attributable to two reasons: financial weakness and fraud. Sometimes these two elements are present in the same case, but the fact of the matter is that the instant a client company ceases to trade, the collectable value of the debtors declines. It is therefore imperative that the client relations person, in monitoring the security of the factor's funds, remains constantly alert for signs of financial weakness. Audited accounts help, but they are historic and generally out-of-date when produced. Cash flow forecasts can be requested and dutifully

studied, but they will invariably be produced with one eye on what the lender or factor wishes to see and may, *in extremis*, be totally unrealistic.

In this respect, the client relations manager is in no different a position to that of a bank manager supervising a loan. But he or she does have some advantages denied the banker. First and foremost in factoring, opposed to invoice discounting, the factor knows intimately the characteristics of the client's sales ledger. On one level, the sales ledger is not an exciting document; it merely records what customers owe, but a great deal can be learned from its operation, particularly if a factor's information-retrievable system is effective. Movements in turnover, spread of customers, payment patterns, level of credit notes and disputes—all of these elements, if plotted and projected effectively using computer-based information systems, can tell the client relations manager a great deal about what is happening inside the client's business. The reasons for customer disputes, for example, can point to a fundamental weakness within a product line or distribution system. When combined with a regular contact and visit programme, the persistent study of ledger-generated data can provide an extremely valuable insight into just how a business is currently performing in all aspects of its operation.

Regular visits to a client, properly recorded, build up a picture of the performance of a business and the people in it, enabling a view to be taken of the degree of risk to which the factor is exposed. For example, if expansion plans discussed at one meeting never materialize and the client is vague about the reasons for this, a dimension is added to the understanding of the business, and the management running it, which will never emerge from the study of audited accounts. If the client relations executive is also responsible for the operation of collections from the client's customers, he or she is in a unique position, in discussion with the client, to point out potential areas of difficulty or opportunity. The visit may reveal the reasons for any problems. Difficulties with production or distribution, sloppy sales administration, inadequate stock control, all these may emerge through discussion and intelligent assessment of the information available. Frequently, these are the root causes of cash flow problems, and if they are faced head on at an early enough stage, serious problems can be averted for both client and factor. In the course of the factoring relationship, an account executive, through visits and almost daily observation of customer payment patterns, will accumulate knowledge of the business which is second to none.

This 'feel' can be acquired in other ways. At the outset of a factoring relationship, it is usually necessary to educate the client and the client's staff in the comparatively simple operating procedures that are needed to make the factoring relationship work. At this stage, an impression is received, and probably recorded, of the ability of the staff within the business to cooperate effectively with each other and with the factor. This impression is reinforced one way or the other as time goes by and the relationship develops.

Small things indicate the quality of the business and the attitude of the people within it. Efficiency with which invoices are raised, for example. Are invoices issued in a timely way, clearly and accurately? Do they properly describe the goods that are being supplied? Do they relate to a specific order number or order confirmation? Are customers' names and addresses properly described and laid out? How comprehensive and accurate is the general quality of the paperwork provided? Even more fundamentally, does the client respond promptly to disputes that are raised by customers? Does he or she communicate well both with customers and with the factor and provide prompt responses to both? The lifeblood of a small business is its customer base. Any client executive who notes the slightest sloppiness or untidiness with regard to customer demands should be watchful, with regard to that client. Above all, the extent to which a client keeps promises in relation to undertakings given, information supplied or targets met, confirms the quality of the people running the business. Not only do positive attitudes in these areas make the account executive's life more agreeable, but they will provide the basis for an excellent relationship between the factor and the client, which in turn can lead to substantial business expansion for the client and a profitable account for the factor.

THE IMPORTANT ROLE OF PERSONNEL IN INVOICE DISCOUNTING

All of these elements are even more crucial in invoice discounting relationships. Here, the factor has to take a good deal on trust. Clients are dealing personally with customers on a day-to-day basis and they are not aware of the factor's involvement. The factor will require, usually on a monthly basis, information concerning the customer ledger, which enables him or her to monitor the quality of the asset, i.e. the debtors, which is being financed. Factors may well wish to discuss with their clients the reconciliation of the sales ledger and will cast a critical eye over the clients' collection performance, as evidenced by the aged analysis information provided. They may wish to conduct quite frequent audits of a client's business to ensure that the information provided on a regular basis is accurate and up-to-date. Visit programmes may be more rigorous than with factoring clients, and there will certainly be regular telephone contact, probably on a daily basis. Again, the promptness with which a client deals with problems or disputes will be very noticeable to the person running the account. In this context, the account executive is entirely in the client's hands. In normal circumstances, account executives are unable to make any regular contact with the customers and are dependent upon what the client tells them in assessing the extent to which the security offered, that is to say, the customer balances outstanding, is valid and collectable. If the account executive has a good feeling about the client's business, he or she will be increasingly disposed to be flexible in relation to such matters as client payment levels or additional facilities. For a good client, reduction or elimination of a reserve held against older debt or concentration can be quickly considered and can make a substantial difference to the amount of funds available to a business for expansion. Factoring management are well aware that the chief feature of their service is the base it can provide for cash flow and growth. If a client cooperates and is honest, he or she is more likely to receive additional funding to meet commercial peaks and troughs and to place his or her business on a secure footing for expansion.

The problem of fraud

Factors will tell you that a client's financial weakness can be contained in most cases. A client ceasing to trade is unfortunate both from the client's point of view and from that of the client's employees. It also poses a problem for the factor because he or she has to recoup funds very quickly from customers. Factors are skilled in this and very often emerge from situations with their funds intact.

It can be a different story where fraud is involved. We have already touched on fraud in Chapter 4. It is a longstanding hazard and very much more common than people realize. All factors suffer from it from time to time and there have been some spectacular cases. As long ago as the 1960s, a garment manufacturer in the USA, Irwin Feiner, took two major factors for as much as US $40 million by the oldest trick in the fraudster's book—false invoices. Since then there have been more instances, often less significant, but nevertheless very painful. At the time of writing, more than one UK factoring company is believed to be nursing wounds inflicted through fraud for very substantial sums indeed.

Rarely are frauds perpetrated on factors particularly complicated. They fall into one or two fairly simple categories. First and foremost, clients hang on to cash which belongs to the factor. Obviously, this can arise in invoice discounting accounts, but it is also perfectly possible for factoring clients to confuse customers by going direct to them, collecting cash which should have been paid to the factor.

Second, the raising of false or very early invoices, known within the factoring industry as 'fresh air invoices', is far more common than most people would believe. The fact that eventually such devices would be uncovered is little consolation to the factoring company, if they are sitting on a pile of worthless paper against which good money has been advanced.

Third, and this is even harder to detect, it is tempting for clients suffering severe cash flow problems to delay the raising of credit notes in respect of goods returned on accounts agreed.

Few fraudsters involved in the factoring industry are particularly creative in their approach. It is probably the case that 90 per cent of the frauds perpetrated fall within one or other of these categories. Mundane though they may be, from the factor's point of view, they are deadly. People outside the industry would probably be very surprised at the frequency with which factors have to contend with this problem. Fraud is common, it may be increasing and it is perpetrated by the most surprising people. All factors will tell you stories of the fraud they have discovered which was committed by a client with whom they have enjoyed for many years a trouble-free relationship. Suddenly, for whatever reason, the client has been put under pressure and has defrauded the factor. All too often, people slip into the practice. There is not much difference between raising invoices well in advance of the dispatch of goods and raising invoices which relate to no goods at all. If you convince yourself that the goods are to be supplied, it may not feel like fraudulent behaviour. However, fraudulent it is.

Client relations people in factoring companies are trained to watch for the signs and to anticipate trouble. Yet again, the behaviour of clients in dealing with disputes, the speed or slowness in passing over the factor's cash, serious administrative deficiency—all of these can provide signs. Much can be learned from customers. Factors learn to record diligently the myriad events that can occur on a client's customer ledger. By putting the pieces together, it can be established that all is not well. In doing so, and when the worst suspicions are confirmed, factors hope to have been able to build up a sufficient reserve on the account to weather the storm. Hopefully, there is enough 'clean' debt available for the factor to collect the funds out.

All factors, even those who have suffered severely from fraud, acknowledge that it is only a small minority who perpetrate such offences. However, the problem still arises as to how to distinguish the good from the bad. At the beginning of a factoring relationship, as with most agreements made in commercial life, all is sweetness and light. The client has been sold on the advantages of the service, and the factor has a new client, whose account he or she can, hopefully, operate at a profit. Rarely is fraud committed at this point, although it has been done. Sometimes months and usually years may pass before the fraud occurs. Usually it is triggered by financial weakness. This may have been detected by the client relations team, but in some cases it can be totally unexpected.

There is no real antidote. By careful policing of the account, factors try to anticipate the problem and keep their financial exposure as low as possible. Once it occurs, the collection effort gets under way and the non-fraudulent debt is identified and strenuous efforts made to collect. Client payments on account are, of course, suspended, and the factoring agreement terminated. Sometimes prosecution ensues.

In some ways, fraud hangs like a cloud over the factoring industry, which has developed a guarded, sometimes wary, approach to its clients as a consequence. Even though perpetrated only by a minority, it has to be constantly guarded against. Staff are trained to watch for the warning signs, and its very unexpectedness breeds a watchfulness that can easily turn into cynicism. If this occurs, it can do nothing to help the expansion of the industry nor the development of its reputation.

Client communications

One way of minimizing risk, of course, is good communication between factor and client. Factors do try hard to communicate effectively with their clients, partly for their own protection but also because in taking on the responsibility for the operation of the client's sales ledger, they effectively become part of the business. One of the main criticisms of factoring can be loss of control in a key area of business. Not surprisingly, clients wish to know a great deal about how their customers and the factor are performing. For instance, it is essential to be aware of the timing and the amount of customer payments, the extent of payments overdue, disputes, the degree to which sales ledger debt is becoming concentrated and so on.

There was a period in the early 1960s when some UK factors failed to recognize this need, believing that the quality of their service was such that clients should leave the day-to-day operation of the sales ledger to them, without bothering themselves with undue detail. This rested on the principle that if you are paying a factor to provide a service, it is counter-productive to attempt to run the sales ledger yourself. On this basis, the information provided to clients was minimal. Common sense and commercial pressures overcame this view in the fullness of time, and all factors now provide clients on a daily basis with full accounting information on both the sales and client account side. More conservative factors and clients stick to paper reports; however, the operation of a sales ledger can generate a fair volume of paper. Lists of customer payments, dispute and shortfall notices, the amendment of credit limits, the acknowledgement of invoices received for factoring and payments made on account, all of these require the raising and dispatch of items of paperwork. It gets worse. Some clients require sales analysis information. Others expect details of overdue items at the precise time they fall overdue. Some are concerned about maintaining an accurate and up-to-date list of customers. These kinds of pressures, coupled with increased costs, have persuaded factors to develop electronic communication systems, providing clients with the data they require through a telephone line. Most of the main factors operate these and those that do not will be forced to in due course by the pressure of competition and the sheer weight of paper.

FACTEL
Typical of the systems is Factel, provided by International Factors to its clients. A free service, provided via viewdata based upon the link between the telephone system and a television set, Factel offers International Factors'

CLIENT RELATIONS

clients a closed user group facility through which they can interrogate more than 40 screens of information about various aspects of the relationship between them and their factor. Thus, clients can use the service to find up-to-date details of their company's financial relationship with the factor, showing the total invoices outstanding and how much has been provided by way of prepayment and the extent to which bad debt protection has been offered. They can also, for example, obtain a summarized ageing of the sales ledger, a summary of the current position on each and every customer account, showing the amount of bad debt protection provided, and the stage the factor's collection procedure has reached.

The system provides information concerning the largest accounts which have been disputed by the customer, enabling better control to be put into effect. It lists accounts with the largest overdue position and shows historical information showing how the overall overdue history has changed in the previous 12 months. It is invaluable in enabling the client to keep control of the extent to which credit limits are up to date, and in this respect it goes some way towards solving the age-old problem of the need for clients to know when customers are getting close to their credit limit. To some extent, it also provides a communication system. By arrangement, International Factors enables clients to transmit schedules of offer and credit notes to them electronically and provide an acknowledgement of receipt. It provides a 24-hour message facility, and offers an immediate check on the progress of schedules of offer within the factor's system, so that the prepayment facility can be used to its maximum extent.

The system is impressive. From the client's viewpoint it is cheap; access is based on local British Telecom call rates. It is reasonably secure and, like all viewdata systems, easy to use. Of course, it suffers from the restrictions imposed by viewdata. Information provided cannot be manipulated; it has to be taken by the client in the format provided by International Factors, and the quantity of data which can be recorded on any one screen is strictly limited. Its use as a tool for management information purposes is also limited, simply by virtue of the technology that has been employed.

FACTFLOW

Another system, that provided by Lombard NatWest Commercial Services, International's competitor, is more advanced in this respect. Factflow, the client information provided by NatWest's subsidiary, is based upon the use of an IBM compatible personal computer, a modem and a telephone line. It is delivered to clients, either through on-line communication to Lombard's computer network for low-volume enquiries or as a database held on a personal computer in the client's office, updated daily by data transfer, for high-volume enquiries, and data manipulation.

Like International's system, once the equipment has been obtained the service is provided free apart from BT telephone charges. In principle, the information provided is similar. Client approval requests, client accounting, payment availability, all are there together with the facility to transfer invoice schedules. The difference, of course, lies in the technology employed. Viewdata, while user-friendly, cheap and ideal for straightforward movement of basic data, suffers from quite severe limitations in terms of the capacity to display large volumes of data, speed of access and, above all, the ability to manipulate information. The awesome power of the microcomputer provides Factflow with greater potential. It is possible for the discerning client to extract more information from a microbased rather than a viewdata system.

CENTURY LINK

Even the smaller factors, hitherto sceptical about the benefits of communication systems, are joining the trend. Century Limited, the factoring arm of merchant bank Close Bros Plc, have launched 'Century Link', giving clients access to data through a real-time system, which is updated continuously and which they claim is faster than that of the competition. Clients can interrogate their sales ledger or client account at any time during the working day in the full knowledge that the information they see is as up-to-date as possible. The service is free, save for the costs of on-line communication via the telephone network. It is simple to operate, no complex computer manuals are required and full operating instructions are provided.

The scope of the data available is also impressive. In addition to the sales ledger data shown in Appendix 5, there is a wealth of information, a small sample of which is summarized in Appendix 8. Century Link gives the client immediate access to his or her client account, to details of the last customer cash received by the factor, information about the 10 highest disputed customer balances, and much more.

At a stroke, systems like Factflow and Century Link eliminate one of the criticisms that has dogged factoring since its inception—that it removes from the client any practical control or supervision of the single most important part of a small to medium-sized business: the control of the customer base. As time goes by, it is certain that the number of applications will increase, and that the intelligent use of technology will transform the factoring business itself. It is not fanciful to predict that before very long, factors will be able to use the interactive qualities of the systems to provide business with an ever-increasing flow of commercial information and products, using the power of technology to help the client to develop his or her business, information skills and financial control.

It may be argued that there is little demand for such services. Most clients use factoring for the finance and are not particularly interested in high-flown computer-based information technology. But this is to ignore the trends in the world at large. Business is becoming more efficiently run, cost-conscious, and information-based. The lead, as always, is provided by the larger companies. But it is not, of necessity, the industrial giants who will always change the way things are done. Gradually, small business, too, is becoming more aware of the need for greater efficiency and the potential for improvement that technology brings. And the area of cash flow is one where there is great need for improvement.

Factors are in an excellent position to radically change the way in which small business operates and the standards to which it aspires. There is a long way to go but a start has been made.

9. *The factors*

Bankers all?

It does not require a Ph.D. in statistics for anyone looking at the list of factors shown in Appendix 3 to deduce that the factoring industry in this country is owned mainly by the UK clearing banks. In the past few years, quite considerable growth has taken place in the number of organizations providing factoring or invoice discounting services. The latest count indicates that there are some 40 businesses falling into this category, and although the recession has slowed the rate of entry, it is by no means certain that the market has reached maturity.

Nevertheless, the larger players are bank-owned. The ABFD statistics for the year ended 1992 indicated that nearly 72 per cent of total factoring and invoice discounting business was transacted by subsidiary companies of the 'Big Four', and that some 69 per cent of the cash advanced to factoring and invoice discounting clients came from the same sources. Of the remaining business, some 17 per cent is undertaken by such companies as RoyScot Factors and Kellock, themselves owned by the two Scottish clearers, or Hill Samuel Commercial Finance, whose ultimate parent is Trustee Savings Bank. The remaining factors and invoice discounters, while providing some variety and choice, cannot be said to have a serious impact in terms of market share.

So are the factors nothing more than an extension of the banking industry? Will the tendency towards concentration and uniformity that has taken place in the banking market place leave the factors in the same position? Does it matter if it does, and how will such a trend be best avoided? What about competition and service standards, innovation and product development?

This chapter looks at all of these aspects and attempts to place the industry in a wider context. It sets the stage for some of the discussion that comes later, especially with regard to the marketing of factoring. And it looks briefly at the factors themselves and their capacity to develop their business.

MARKET SHARE

Before doing so, one or two trends should be picked up. The dominance of the clearers does not mean that the market situation is entirely static. In the past five years or so, the market position has changed quite radically. As we have already noted, the product mix has altered as invoice discounting, and to a lesser but still important extent, recourse factoring, has forged ahead at the expense of full service factoring. But market shares have changed, too. In 1985, 58 per cent of the full service factoring offered was provided by a subsidiary of one of the Big Four with the then Credit Factoring, the NatWest unit, leading the market with some 22 per cent of the total market. By 1989, the renamed NatWest arm, Lombard Commercial Services, had been knocked off its perch as market leader by International Factors, but more significantly, the full factoring market place has consolidated to a quite extraordinary extent. No less than 90 per cent of the full service non-recourse factoring provided in this country is now offered by a subsidiary of one of the Big Four clearing banks, with International Factors enjoying market leadership and the hapless Lombard being overtaken by Griffin.

Why has this occurred? Is it part of a grand design by the big clearers to scoop the factoring market and exclude all others from providing a service? Not really. It simply reflects the fact that in providing the service, the big banks have one or two very important advantages. First, they have their branch networks who, whatever their deficiencies and problems, do provide them with market advantage. Over the years, some bank managers have been persuaded to regard factoring as a service worthy of serious consideration for some customers and so they recommend the customer to use the services of their bank-owned factor. Many believe that they do not do so to anything like the extent that they could or even should, but they do provide a considerable number of qualified new business leads. As in most financial services, credibility is most important when a consumer is considering a service, and the bank manager's recommendation still counts for something even in these jaundiced days.

SIZE OF FACTOR

But there is more to the trend, of course. Factoring is a business in which the economies of scale can be made to work effectively. If you are providing credit and collection services, the more customers you have in as many market sectors as possible, the better. You become better informed about the payment practices, strengths and weaknesses of different customers in a range of industries, your in-house credit information facilities becomes more diverse and powerful and, above all, the payment track record of many thousands of companies provides a basis for making quick and effective credit decisions that is not available to a credit manager, no matter how skilled, operating in a single industry.

In this context, size becomes important. The larger factors have the staff, the premises, computing capacity, the experience, information sources and the reputation to convince people that the service is first class. They can argue that they have made investments in people, technology and systems, that they are stable and permanent. The costs of entry into a market of this kind and of competing with such organizations are considerable.

So any company using a non-recourse factoring service is more than likely to be on the books of a subsidiary of a major clearing bank. Certainly, the service can be obtained elsewhere on both a cost-effective and efficient basis. But the clearers have taken over the market to a considerable extent. There is more to this than the mere economies of scale. The structure of the market reflects both the prejudices of those considering becoming clients and those providing the service. If you examine the characteristics of the companies that have joined the ABFD since 1985, this point becomes clear. Two of them, Hill Samuel Commercial Finance and UCB Invoice Discounting, have no non-recourse portfolio of any kind. Hill Samuel do a very small amount of domestic recourse business but, in reality, they are invoice discounters. UCB are invoice discounters pure and simple. Even the more broadly based *arrivistes* such as RoyScot and Kellock Factors do very little non-recourse business, with Kellock concentrating almost entirely upon domestic recourse factoring and RoyScot providing more than 34 per cent of their factoring business without credit protection.

The lone newly arrived practitioner of the more traditional service among the factors joining the association since 1985 has been Security Pacific Business Finance (Europe), who were rewarded for their pains by being taken over by Century Limited, a staunchly recourse-based house. All of these are signs that the factors are reacting more to market demand, or to its absence, than to anything else. They are moving away from the service elements of their businesses and towards the simple provision of finance. Yet paradoxically, the clearing banks, who in some ways have the most to fear from the large-scale development of invoice discounting or recourse factoring, have done more to keep the full service ideal going than has anyone else.

Growth and profitability

So it is clear that full service factoring is growing far more slowly than the industry, which in its public statements fails to distinguish entirely between non-recourse and recourse factoring, let alone invoice discounting, would have us believe. Far from being the core service, full and export factoring, by 1992, had reached the stage where it represented no more than 19 per cent of the total turnover of the members of the ABFD. In 1985, Alex Lawrie Factors, the Lloyds Bank recourse subsidiary, had no less than 69 per cent of the recourse factoring market to itself. By 1991, Lawrie, despite having turned in quite reasonable profits in the intervening period, had to share their hitherto specialist market niche with 10 other ABFD members, and had to content themselves with a mere 48 per cent of the recourse market. More to the point, the total recourse market had grown by a factor of some two and a half times in the six-year period, as compared with just under two times for non-recourse business. The growth of neither service, of course, rivalled that of invoice discounting but the move away from full service was underlined.

It becomes even more apparent when factors outside the ABFD are considered. During recent years, there has been an influx of new players into the market place, but there is little doubt that the vast majority of the comparatively small companies that have entered the industry are providing anything more than invoice discounting or at most, recourse factoring. The potential invoice discounting client is spoilt for choice. Companies requiring a full service, much less a factoring service that actually offers the facility to handle business in foreign markets, have far fewer options to choose from.

Allowing for these quirks in the statistics which underlie the performance of the industry, is growth satisfactory? The trends summarized in Appendix 1 look healthy but they are based upon invoice discounting and, to a lesser extent, the expansion of recourse factoring. Full service factoring, although growing, is developing far more slowly, and appears to be provided primarily by the clearing banks. It is hardly surprising that invoice discounting grew during a period of economic expansion when companies were seeking funds to cater for the working capital requirements which always emerge in such situations. Invoice discounting, compared with a static, security-based overdraft, has a number of important advantages for an expanding company, and with the choice available and the pressure faced by discounters in terms of rates in recent years, it can compare well on a cost basis. Factoring, with its mix of service and finance, is more difficult to sell, and as we shall see, has been substantially undersold in recent years. Both, of course, compete with the services offered by the parent banks and it is instructive to compare the extent of their use with other forms of lending.

Each year, the British Bankers Association issues an Abstract of Banking Statistics. If you take the figures for bank lending to the manufacturing and service sectors, and remove from them the areas of business quite clearly unsuitable for factoring, it is possible to obtain a rough yardstick of just how much progress the industry has made since those far-off days some 25 years ago. The Abstract shows that in 1985, for example, the total volume of sterling lending to UK residents by members of the Committee of London and Scottish Bankers, a group which accounts for a major proportion of the total of UK banking business, was £87 625 million. This figure does not include the funds advanced by factors, which do not constitute lending in the banking sense, in any event. It does include loans to such sectors as agriculture, forestry and fishing, construction, the finance sector, central and local government and several others which are not appropriate to factoring.

By pruning these from the statistics, one comes to an approximate total of what might be termed, for comparison purposes, comparative bank lending, of £22 138 million. In 1985, the ABFD statistics indicated that their members were advancing some £380.3 million at the end of the year. So the funds available to industry from factoring and invoice discounting represented, say, 1.7 per cent as compared with bank lending at that precise point in time. The same arithmetical process applied to the relevant 1990 figures demonstrates clearly the impact that the growth of invoice discounting had over the period—the comparable figure is 4.5 per cent—but it is still small, almost insignificant compared with the contribution made by the banks, and if the invoice discounting element were to be stripped out, it is probable that it would be reduced to the order of considerably less than 2 per cent.

The figures have to be read in context—banking has been around for a long time—factoring and invoice discounting are starting from a narrow base and are relatively new. Nevertheless, the claims of the industry to be the fastest growing financial service must also be seen in context, as must the respective contributions to the national economy.

This becomes even more pointed when the profits generated by the factoring industry are considered. In 1989, for example, the Association members turned in a total profit of just over £40 million. This reflected a period of relative prosperity before the recession began to bite and the culmination of the period of growth we have been examining. In the same year, the pre-tax profits of the eight members of the Committee of London and Scottish Bankers included no less than £404 million earned by NatWest and £692 million produced by Barclays (BPA Annual Abstract of Banking Statistics). The Yorkshire Bank turned in profits of £113 million and Clydesdale, £59 million. In other words, the entire profit of a whole industry is substantially smaller than that of any one bank! It could be said that we are not comparing like with like, that we are dealing with only one or at most two services, whereas these days banks provide a considerable range of corporate services to many companies. When all the objections are taken into account, however, it has to be admitted that the overall impact made by the industry remains small. Total performance in terms of convincing people to use the service and then making an adequate profit from the operation has been less than sparkling.

Factoring people

In situations of this kind, where an individual company is not performing, the finger is frequently pointed at the management, who apparently lack the will and ability to produce the drive and direction required to lift the business to the required level. So far as factoring is concerned, the managers are as competent and as hardworking as those elsewhere. They are only too well aware of the gap that exists between the potential for their service and their performance to date. The topic is a frequent one on the occasions when factoring people get together to swap experiences and problems. Nobody in the industry appears to have the formula which will succeed in raising its profile, getting rid of the mixed images that beset it and achieving real growth.

Many factors probably feel that progress has in fact been satisfactory. From their viewpoint it may have been, since their main role in life is to satisfy the aspirations of shareholders, and to date there are few signs that they have fallen down in this, since with the exception of Barclays a number of years ago, none of the clearers has withdrawn from the industry and even Barclays subsequently re-entered it.

Perhaps this is the key. With rare exceptions, hardly any of the people running the industry are shareholders of the companies they operate. Indeed, and perhaps this is most significant of all, none of the major factoring companies is run as a core business. All are contributors to group profitability, parts of larger organizations, whose broad role and strategy are likely to be very different from that of the factoring part. The profits produced by the factoring arm are not essential to the continued overall well-being of the group as a whole. Important and significant they may be, vital they are not. This is not the kind of structure which brings about the attitude to risk and reward that is essential to produce real growth. The management puts a premium upon solid competence. Risk taking is limited to those risks taken in making advances to clients, and these are contained within strict limits taken on a collective basis, as we shall see below. If, for their part, the shareholders are content with a relatively modest profit and a reasonable return on capital, who are the managers to argue? There is little incentive to go for growth with the risks and changes to lifestyle that such a process brings.

As a management style or philosophy, what does this approach sound like? It sounds, of course, remarkably like that of a bank. Generally speaking, however, people in the factoring industry would contest this view of their management style. They would argue that, whatever the names on the share certificates, their companies are run in a very different way from banks. And in many respects, they are clearly right. Even after many years of bank ownership, there are relatively few career bankers who have moved into the factoring business. True, senior bank management sit on the boards of their factoring subsidiaries. Sometimes these non-executive directors play an important role in achieving increased cooperation between the various divisions of the parent and the factoring subsidiary. But day-to-day affairs of the factoring business are left to full-time executives and staff who, for the most part, are not bankers.

It is certainly true that most people who work within the factoring industry have grown up within it rather than as bankers or, indeed, members of any other profession. Statistics do not exist for the proportion of factoring employees who have been trained in the industry, but it is probably quite high. Much of the work done is routine and dull—the processing of paper, invoices and cash is not an exciting task, although it is obviously important. As we shall see in Chapter 10, for a small industry, factoring has gone to not inconsiderable lengths to provide training opportunities for staff; and most of the bigger factors provide some form of training in-house, as well as encouragement to study for external qualifications.

In terms of location, like most British industries factoring has tended to become concentrated in certain areas. Factoring companies are overwhelmingly found in the south; indeed, they seem to have a penchant for moving as far south as possible. Several are based along the south coast; there are clusters in such areas as Haywards Heath and Croydon. Few of the major factors are based north of Watford. This may be considered somewhat surprising, since quite clearly a number of their clients are located in the industrial areas of the country.

It is very important, as we shall see later, to stay in touch with factoring clients, partly to ensure that the service provided is excellent and also to avoid undue risk to funds employed. This presupposes regular visits to clients by client executives and audit personnel. Quite clearly, if you have a major client base dispersed around the country this is expensive and difficult to organize. As a consequence of this, some of the factors have developed regional offices to whom they have devolved authority to deal with clients on a day-to-day basis. Most factors have offices situated in the principal centres of the UK. For the most part, these are sales offices whose function is purely to process new business enquiries and convert them into clients. Factors have been reluctant in the past to delegate the vital matter of credit control and responsibility for funds in use to regional offices, partly because of an innate fear that by enabling local staff to deal with the vital matter of client security the risk is increased. This tendency has been reinforced by the fact that heavy investments on centralized hardware and systems tend to mean that people are grouped at central points. The argument for local factoring arrangements are formidable, however. Reduced costs in terms of people, premises and communication can be achieved. There is, in reality, no loss of security so long as regionally based staff are well trained and sensible use is made in terms of accounting, data processing and other centrally operated functions of modern communications equipment. Above all, the prospect of developing new business is enhanced enormously where local offices are in operation. Experience indicates that clients prefer to work with people from their own region, and a satisfied client base is the most effective way of persuading new companies to use the service.

Some of the factors have recognized the merits of this argument. Alex

Lawrie Factors, for example, who in terms of client numbers have one of the biggest problems, have opened client service offices in Stockport, Edinburgh and Cambridge. H & H Factors operated an office in Stockport for invoice discounting purposes for many years without taking the plunge and transferring the whole of their northern factoring business there. There is no doubt that as pressure on numbers increases at the centre, more factors will be forced to consider establishing decentralized operations with real authority to deal with client problems. This is generally healthy and should assist the industry to grow. If they are astute, the bank factors will develop this trend, harnessing their technology and experience to local conditions, minimizing risk and persuading clients to work with a local unit. Such a policy could result in longer client life, better service, closer coordination and, last but not least, better promotion prospects for staff.

And what of management? So far, the impression has perhaps been given of solid competence and capacity rather than flair. You could argue that this is what is required in a factoring business whose stock-in-trade, after all, is cash, and where you do not require people to adopt the philosophy of a Wall Street bond dealer in choosing clients and in running them. Factors do not do this. The industry is not noted for its flamboyant characters, indeed, the prevailing characteristic is a certain moderation. Contrary perhaps to the impression given so far, factors are not dominated by their banking shareholders in the day-to-day running of their business. Major risks aside, they are left to make up their own minds about whether to provide facilities to clients and when to review them. They tend to execute these through the medium of credit committees or management boards meeting once or twice a week to consider presentations by business executives or client relations managers about new or existing business.

The qualities required are a good nose for business, sound risk judgement, knowledge of the foibles and tendencies of smaller businesses, an eye for detail and, above all, the ability to learn from experience. Sound people-management skills are required on the sales and operational sides of the business in order to get the best out of staff who are, not infrequently, called upon to provide a level of performance and commitment which would be considered exceptional in many industries.

I know of at least one clearing bank that regards its factoring operation as being one of the best managed within its very widespread group. It is that sort of industry. Let the day-to-day management get a little out of hand and chaos will follow, as some of the early participants found to their cost. Most factors have learned these lessons and, to a greater or lesser extent, run tight well organized operations.

Is this enough? Most people in the industry would probably reply in the affirmative. The clearing bank involvement has meant that standards of service are reasonable and a degree of respectability has been achieved.

Growth, while some way short of target, has been dynamic enough to enable the ABFD to produce impressive looking graphs each year. What is lacking from within the management of the factoring industry is a sense of the possibility of real achievement. Few of the factors' senior management have any feel for the prospects that could open up to the factoring company which shows a real sense of purpose and plays to its strengths. For the age of the small business is with us and it ought not to be beyond the wit of one of the factors to persuade its shareholder to permit it to become the unit within the bank's operation that spearheads the drive to do more for the small to medium-sized corporate sector. You would not believe it, reading the quite considerable press coverage that the banks' treatment of their small business customers receives these days, but the fact is that the factors are better equipped to provide an all-round service in this area than are other divisions of clearing banks.

The fact that this aspect receives no publicity and that, generally, banks appear to ignore the potential of their factoring operations is not the fault of the banks but of the factors. What is required here is not 'sound' management, good credit control and cautious client selection, but a little flair and, indeed, that overworked word, charisma. This is what is required to persuade senior bank management that the possibility exists of building something quite special, using some of the techniques developed over many years, in spotting and running good business in the small to medium-sized sector. This would probably involve changing and developing the factoring product in a way that the industry has not been capable of doing over the past 25 years, and it would perhaps require changes to the relationship between bankers and factors which could be quite dramatic and far-reaching.

10. *The marketing of factoring*

On 24 January 1989, introducing the main article in a *Financial Times* survey on factoring and invoice discounting, the newspaper's Growing Business Correspondent, Charles Batchelor, wrote:

> It is perhaps not surprising that demand for a service which can, at short notice, pay a business man up to 80 per cent of the value of his outstanding sales invoices should have expanded during a time of strong economic growth.

Yet two paragraphs later, Mr Batchelor, who had quite clearly spent some time studying the industry and the participants within it added:

> many business men resist the idea of employing a factor to handle their invoices for fear of what customers might think. Others use the service on a confidential basis so their customers never know a factor is involved.

These two quotations encapsulate precisely the position of the factoring industry. The potential is there; the funding, the quality of service, the expertise, all of this is available. Cases of successful factoring arrangements abound. Research indicates that clients are satisfied. Still, however, the industry does not completely fulfil its potential.

Why is this? The answer lies primarily in the way the service has been marketed. It seems to me that even now, many people in the industry, and perhaps more to the point, those controlling it, do not appreciate the size of the opportunity that lies before them. At the same time, the need to promote the benefits of the service on a much larger scale than has been done in the past is not fully realized.

This is not to say that no marketing takes place. All factoring companies, to some extent at least, market their service. Most spend considerable sums of money on quite well paid sales teams. Procedures for the selection of business are rigorous and are considered to be part of the selling package. Some market research has now been undertaken, and through the ABFD improvements have been made in public relations.

So all the elements of the marketing 'mix' are present. Why then, the continuing gap between promise and fulfilment? There is no one simple answer to this. As is always the case in business, the answer probably lies in a quite complex mixture of historical circumstances, people's attitudes towards their work, conventional wisdom and the relationships between the various organizations which compromise the market place.

In addition to reviewing the current arrangements, however, this chapter will endeavour to highlight ways in which the industry could progress more quickly. In doing so, however, I propose to reverse the normal order of the marketing 'mix', dealing initially with the industry's sales activities, then looking a little later at such issues as product, price, public relations and advertising.

Introductory sources

THE BANKING INFLUENCE

Most factors sell their services hard, sometimes quite efficiently. Nearly all of them these days have sales teams whose full-time occupation is to pursue business. The clearing bank factors use their parent banks as an important source of business. Consequently, the salespeople employed by these factors spend much of their time cultivating branch managers, or important introducers of business in the bank's hierarchy. As we shall see later, it is not always as easy a task as may be supposed. Bankers are cautious people and do not always readily yield any of their better customers to any subsidiary company of the bank, let alone the factor. It is all very well for the bank hierarchy to exhort its management to think on a group-wide basis; in practice it is sometimes difficult to achieve.

Moreover, the nature of the factoring business sometimes militates against close cooperation. As we have seen, not all business is suitable for factoring. Certain industries and commercial practices cannot be accommodated within the factor's arrangements. It is difficult to get this across to many branch managers, whose lending experience is based on security and balance sheet analysis and who are not necessarily restricted in their dealings to any one particular sector of industry. The consequence of this can be that the bank manager or area officer refers some business to the factoring company, which promptly turns it down. Unless communication is good at this point and the reasons for the refusal clearly explained, not just to the prospective business but also to the bank, this can result in a drying-up of future references.

Another area of difficulty can be the tendency of branch managers to refer their marginal business to the factor. This is based primarily on the belief that factoring is itself directed at helping companies which are in financial difficulty, but the attitude is in part understandable. Factors go out of their way to stress that, as compared with bankers, they are in a position to release more cash against the debtor asset by virtue of their closeness to the customer base and their understanding of collection. From the bank manager's point of view, therefore, it is perfectly natural when the lending ceiling has been reached in relation to the available security to refer the case to a factor. This is just what the factors require in many cases. But it is a narrow dividing line between such a situation and one where a worried manager tries to offload difficult accounts onto the factoring subsidiary.

THE MARKETING OF FACTORING

Many of these situations demand clear judgement and good communication between the two sides. This takes time to develop.

Comparison of the factoring and invoice discounting client numbers and the numbers of branches of the main banks bears this out. According to the figures produced in the BBA Annual Abstract, the main clearing banks have around 12 500 branches, and I estimate that the factoring companies within their groups have around 7900 clients. On the assumption that, say, 70 per cent of the factors' business originates from their parent bank (and this is probably on the high side) and assuming that the factoring clients 'turn over' on average every three years, it is clear that the bank are nowhere near the point where each branch is introducing even one piece of new business to its factoring subsidiary. Clearly, many of the bank branches are small and perhaps specialize in private business. But others are large and full of commercial accounts.

Comparisons are rough and ready, but the figures clearly demonstrate that there is a long way to go in persuading bankers to think in group terms, and to push good accounts their way.

INDEPENDENT FACTORS

The independent factors' salespeople have a tougher job than their clearing bank competitors. They are dependent on stimulating enquiry from a broad range of introducers, including, of course, accountants, finance brokers and competitive bankers and from contacts of existing clients. At least one of the independent companies has built up its business by the judicious use of mailshots. Generally speaking, advertising appears to produce relatively little by way of new business enquiries.

The scale of the problem is reflected in the size of the independent companies. Although the two independent leaders, H & H and Century, are both profitable businesses, the scale of their operations, as measured by client numbers, is substantially smaller than that of the main clearers. In fact, bearing in mind the lack of a branch network to draw on, they do disproportionately well in attracting new business. It is perhaps a pity that some of the sales skills they have shown over the years cannot be deployed within the clearing bank sector where the opportunities are very much greater.

The negotiation process

SELLING

Once the introduction is complete, most factoring salespeople will waste little time in getting in touch with the new business prospect. It is obviously essential that a professional approach is adopted. The main impression perceived by the client company will be derived from the contact with the salesperson.

Prior to and at the first meeting, the factoring salesperson will endeavour to obtain as much information from the new business prospect as is possible. It will be necessary to obtain a clear picture as to the history of the business, its management, profit record and financial strength. The details of the product or services must be explored and understood, the relationship between the supplier and the customer must be probed and assessed, and the prospects for expansion must be examined. Existing funding arrangements and the likely requirement for finance should be discussed and, to some degree, the competence of the management team must be assessed.

There will be considerable discussion on the operational aspects, some of them seemingly mundane. The factoring salesperson may seem to show unwarranted interest in the way in which orders are taken, invoices raised, collections of cash achieved and disputes resolved. The reasons for all this will by now be quite clear, but there is a skill involved in persuading businesspeople to talk about all of these issues and in obtaining as much of the basic information as is required in the course of one visit, or even an initial telephone call, without giving offence. Fortunately, this is not always too difficult. People like talking about their businesses, and after a little experience it is usually possible to guide the conversation in such a way that relevant data is obtained to enable the salesperson to quickly and efficiently ascertain whether the factor should be able to help.

Sometimes a salesperson will conclude that the characteristics of the business are such that it is unlikely that an offer can be made. He or she should say so at this stage, giving diplomatic reasons for this view. It may be possible to recommend an alternative means of meeting the prospect's needs. Factors have different criteria and are not adverse to passing business leads to each other if they feel they personally cannot help. Quite honestly, if a banking relationship is involved, it will be important to keep the bank appraised as to the reasons why the business has been declined.

Invariably, where the business is fundamentally unsuitable, the factoring salesperson may be hard pressed to proffer an alternative. He or she has been trained to sell factoring, not as a general business adviser, and his or her knowledge of business outside the factoring world may in fact be quite sketchy. Prospect companies are generally best served by seeking guidance or advice elsewhere in relation to general business matters.

When he or she is sure that the company can be supported, however, the salesperson will invariably be relied upon to produce, quite quickly, a proposal to the sales director or credit committee which will recommend the making of an offer. Certain information will be required prior to this. Unquestionably, the prospect's last set of audited accounts should be available, together with a breakdown of debtors and, inevitably, an aged analysis of debtors. Other items of specific information reflecting the characteristics of the business may well be required. Almost always, any quotation provided at this stage will be outline and non-contractual. It will certainly be conditional upon a detailed survey of the business and possibly upon the provision of further information. So long as the prospect company is prepared to provide the detailed information required, a negotiation can be brought to a fairly speedy conclusion within a matter of weeks, or even days, in cases of genuine urgency.

The quotation, when received, will always be in writing and will spell out the detailed terms of the offer. In addition to the standard items—level of service fee, cost of funds, percentage advanced, types of facility—there may well be other conditions, such as the provision of certain figures or details by the directors, before the factoring agreement is formally signed. A copy of the agreement should be requested at an early stage. Once the quotation is accepted and a start date agreed, the formal documentation is prepared for signature. At this point, the salesperson will normally hand over the account to a client relations manager and withdraw from the negotiation. He or she will, of course, have arranged for the quotation to be considered or approved by operational management, so that the people who run the account are at least aware of its existence, so no real difficulties in handing the matter over should arise. It is often a good move, however, for the client to ask that the salesperson who has handled the business negotiation should introduce his or her colleagues and perhaps be present while the formal documentation is signed and the day-to-day operational procedure is run through. This should ensure that any misunderstandings are short-lived.

The survey

During the course of the negotiation for factoring, a survey will be undertaken into the business. This will invariably be carried out by a specialist manager, although in smaller cases the salesperson may carry it out. Ideally, it should be carried out by specialists. The factoring salesperson has a vested interest in writing the business, and it is sensible from the viewpoint of both factor and client to have independent confirmation that the business is suitable and will benefit from a factoring or invoice discounting facility.

Normally, the survey should be completed in one day. The surveyor will undoubtedly go over some of the points already discussed by the salesperson, although these should be kept to a minimum. There will be some emphasis again upon the overall financial strength of the business. The surveyor will wish to examine such items as the company's bought ledger, VAT and PAYE records. The sales ledger will be scrutinized in considerable detail and sales ledger staff and management asked a number of questions. Survey staff will be on the look-out for such items as heavily overdue invoices, disputes, severe reconciliation problems, contra accounts, reservation of title, sale or return or any of the other inhibitors that prevent a factoring arrangement from working properly. They will probably wish to check bank statements, to verify any loan or leasing documentation and to examine any credit insurance policy that exists. If time permits, they may well wish to go through customer files or other records.

All of this may seem, and is, a little intrusive. Why, it may be asked, should not the factor request a copy of the company's last report and accounts, possibly some cash flow forecasts, interview the management and get on with it? This, after all, is what banks do, with varying degrees of attention to detail. And of course, this is the point. Factors are different from banks in their willingness to advance more money against debtors, but they do like to be reasonably sure that those debtors are, and will continue to be, a reasonable security for the advance. Most of the survey procedures are concerned with this point, hence the concentration on sales ledger administration and financial viability.

There are other elements, however. By the time the survey has been arranged, the prospect will have received a cost indication for the required service. Some of the entrail-gazing that goes on during surveys is an attempt to identify the data upon which that indication has been given. Here, the level of turnover, actual and projected, the number of invoices raised and the number of customer accounts, whether live or passive, are critical. Also, where a non-recourse arrangement is under consideration, the surveyor will pay careful attention to the quality and spread of the customer ledger, partly to ensure that an adequate level of credit protection can be given, but also to verify that the level of proposed advance is realistic from a factor's point of view. In short, the survey is directed at least partly towards ensuring that there is a degree of compatibility between factor and client. There is little merit in finding out too late that some credit or administrative issue exists that will divide the parties and cause friction. For this reason, if for no other, potential clients should cooperate in the survey process, and most generally do.

THE SALES EFFORT

The sales team is an important constituent of the factor's business. In terms of cost alone, it can be vital. Staff costs rival the cost of money as the biggest single item in the factor's budget. These days, the leading factors spend more than £5 million per annum on staff, and their sales teams account for a significant proportion of this expenditure.

Moreover, the factor is dependent upon the constant flow of new business, not just to sustain growth, but to replenish accounts which have terminated the factoring arrangement. Therefore, most factors employ substantial sales teams, usually spread around the country in regional sales offices. Frequently, salespeople are former operating staff who have transferred to the sales side, and have generally been attracted by the higher salaries earned there, coupled with what is perceived as being a more attractive, even glamorous lifestyle.

THE MARKETING OF FACTORING

After a few years in the sales role, staff tend to move to other factors after finding promotion is blocked, or again being attracted by higher salaries or better conditions. With the expansion of the industry, this tendency has degenerated, in some cases, into something of a merry-go-round, with people changing jobs at all too frequent intervals.

Salespeople in factoring companies attract other criticisms. They are accused, on the one hand, of pursuing marginal or even bad business at all costs, thus wasting the time of their operational or credit colleagues with cases that do not stand up to close examination or analysis. Sometimes their knowledge of the technicalities of factoring is limited. Quite obviously, it is not easy for a salesperson to acquire intimate knowledge of the entire factoring industry, and, indeed, that of small business, which operational staff glean from day-to-day contact with clients and customers.

They can also be accused, sometimes justifiably, of complacency and lack of drive in following up new business leads. Factors receive quite substantial numbers of enquiries for their services. Only a minority of these are both serious and of the quality that the factor requires. One of the key functions of the successful factoring salesperson is to distinguish the wheat from the chaff.

There is a danger, on the one hand, of pursuing business at all costs. Such salespeople tend to spend most of their time careering from one meeting to the next, possibly producing voluminous new business reports, but lacking the ability to politely terminate a negotiation which is leading nowhere. On the other hand, it is equally possible for salespeople to become too focused—to seek endlessly that perfect piece of business which will bring a gleam to the eye of the credit director and provide the factoring house with an ideal account.

As in most areas in business and in life, compromise between the two extremes is desirable. With experience, a good factoring salesperson will develop a 'feel' which permits the rapid assessment of good business and the capacity to politely turn away that which, for whatever reason, is unacceptable. This is assisted, of course, when the salesperson has received extensive training in the factor's requirements and criteria and has taken the trouble to work closely with operational staff in order to better understand their reasons for being sceptical about certain classes of business. Moreover, experience brings with it the capacity to make judgements about the people requiring the factoring or invoice discounting services. It is only too easy to make mistakes in this area, but the smart new business negotiator will take the trouble to keep in touch with business brought on in the past and to learn from mistakes. Where the client has failed, or particularly where the factor has lost money, it is frequently a salutary exercise to review the initial new business negotiation and assess whether any warning signs were present at the outset and were ignored. Above all, the factoring salesperson should endeavour to cultivate a broad business approach. It is too easy to fall into the trap of seeing all business from a factoring or invoice discounting point of view.

The appreciation of customer need is the first skill to be acquired by any salesperson in any industry. In order to accomplish this effectively, the individual selling factoring needs to understand business in the round. If he or she walks into a prospect's office and immediately commences a well rehearsed spiel on the virtues of factoring, little progress will be made. Far better to spend time talking with the managing or finance director about the business, their medium or longer term plans for it and the unique properties of the product or service. This approach need not be time consuming, but it must be informed. The salesperson should be able to demonstrate knowledge of the prospect company's industry or least genuine interest in learning about it. Once a rapport has been achieved in this way, it becomes an easy matter to test the fine detail of sales accounting, credit control and the quality of debtors.

Salespeople should also be well informed about all aspects of business finance, not just factoring. They should be trained to evaluate corporate financial needs and should be well versed in credit risk, besides understanding banking, investment and other rival commercial products. They should understand the principles of company law and the implications of a factoring relationship. In ideal circumstances, it would be desirable for factoring salespeople to have some experience of running a business themselves. Quite clearly, this is difficult to achieve in practice, but by temperament they should be people capable of understanding the pressures and difficulties faced by entrepreneurs in starting to develop a small to medium-sized business. They should also be well read and certainly well versed in current economic and financial news.

My experience indicates that most factoring salespeople are incapable of becoming involved in business with any international flavour (see Chapter 12). Ideally, they should be aware of and preferably have some experience of conditions in foreign market places as well as in the UK.

In short, they should be well-rounded individuals capable of leaving an excellent impression of their own company and the factoring industry with the people with whom they deal. This, taken together, constitutes a formidable job description. There are, in fact, some very competent people selling factoring services in the UK and it is probably only a minority who come close to meeting these standards.

Some Shibboleths

Salespeople are sometimes responsible for perpetrating some of the great factoring myths. Usually harmless, these assume, for example, that the commercial world is united in a giant campaign to do down and denigrate the factoring industry or, more specifically, the precise piece of business that the salesperson is trying to negotiate. The villains of the piece can be bank managers, legal advisers, accountants and even the operational staff within the salesperson's own company.

A more persistent and serious belief is the argument that the marketing and selling of factoring are in some way different and more difficult than for other products or services. According to this theory, the factor or invoice discounter is at a disadvantage as compared with people in other industries. This stems from the risks inherent in the provision of the service and the fact that not all businesses can use it. If only, goes the argument, factors were like paint manufacturers. They can simply go out and analyse their market place, produce and maybe modify their product, advertise and distribute it, and make a profit. Factoring is so much more complex than paint. Factoring clients require careful vetting. If you choose the wrong company or market sector you can fall foul of client loss or even fraud. Factoring and invoice discounting are therefore more complex, even mystical, and must be treated accordingly. The usual marketing principles put forward by business gurus and the business schools do not apply to factors.

The argument is, of course, total nonsense. It is true that factoring is a service which must be sold with full awareness of the risks involved, but it is by no means unique in this respect. Banking, insurance, lending of all kinds, all of these are services where the provider has to be selective and aware of the risks involved. All of these have grown to be multi-million-pound industries on an international scale. If factoring has not developed on the same scale, it is not simply because it is more complex or difficult to sell than any of these. Yet the myth persists. You hear people in the factoring industry repeat it all the time and although it is difficult to prove, it does seem that this feeling may well underlie some of the difficulties that the industry appears to experience in marketing itself.

A second Shibboleth may have an equal baleful, if unproven, effect. It is prevalent among credit staff, rather than salespeople, that all clients are out to get you. According to this viewpoint, the world is a wicked, woeful place, full of people whose main intent is to take and disappear with the factor's money. In consequence, each piece of new business has to be totally without taint. The debts to be offered are to be free of any encumbrance or contamination such as the various elements we dealt with in Chapter 4. Retentions, contra trading, reservation of title, any hint of residual contractual obligations—all of these, according to the pessimist, are death to the factor and must be avoided at all costs.

Of course, there is something in this. Any of these elements can, and do, weaken the factor's security and cause loss. We have seen the impact that fraud can have on the factoring business. It is clearly important that factors should be wary in considering all businesses and remain mindful of the risks involved. The fact remains, however, that only a minority of clients are, in fact, fraudulent. Where a business does contain elements which are unfavourable and weaken security, they should be considered as part of the business as a whole in relation to the company's total funding requirements. Moreover, it is frequently possible to take intelligent account of the strengths of a given business, as well as its weaknesses and the risks posed, and to construct a facility for it which is pitched at a level, or perhaps supported by security over and above debtors, that will permit the management to develop the business and the factor to handle the debtors in harmony.

Factors pride themselves on their commercial approach to business, sometimes contrasting this with the necessarily security-based approach of their colleagues in the banking profession. At its best, the industry is characterized by a 'can do' attitude towards the provision of finance. At its worst, its reason for being ceases.

Mixed messages?

These attitudes do nothing to help the development of the industry, but they are as nothing compared with the handicap that it has given itself in terms of its marketing posture in recent years. We have already discussed at length the question of the indifferent public perception of factoring. Despite the growth statistics, bank participation and so on, the belief is held by many that the factoring service is expensive and its use is an indication that a business is not soundly based. Allied to this is the feeling, still widespread, that the adoption of factoring by a supplier will inevitably cause harm to customer relationships. 'My customers will think I'm in trouble' is a fear which is widely expressed. Alternatively, there is the feeling that the factor will either press customers too hard for payment, thereby causing bad feeling, or be too lax or remote in collection performance. As we have seen, no-one really knows where these feelings originated and there are good arguments against them. They are still widespread, however, and deeply ingrained within the minds of many commercial people and business advisers.

At the same time, many people within the factoring industry will tell you that this problem no longer exists. Things have improved out of all recognition in their view and general acceptance, if not already here, is only a matter of time. I believe this to be pure fantasy. Since no reliable research into market attitudes around, say, 20 years ago was undertaken, it is by definition difficult, if not impossible, to measure the extent of any improvements in attitude. New evidence put forward to justify the improved position is usually anecdotal as was, of course, the original adverse reactions. Certainly, the ABFD research indicates that generally, the non-users polled were sceptical as to the claimed advantages of factoring. One exception to this was

THE MARKETING OF FACTORING

in relation to the financial facility, of which some 68 per cent of respondents agreed that they could make immediate use.

The most convincing evidence about the continued existence of negative market feelings comes from the factors themselves. In recent years, there has been a virtual stampede of factoring companies to drop the word 'factor' from their business or trading title, thus hopefully persuading potential clients, and others in the market place, that their company and its services are in some way immune from the anti-factoring disease. The thinking behind this is primitive in the extreme. If we do not call ourselves factors, the argument goes, our rate of enquiry for new business will not suffer because of anti-factoring perceptions. Our sales staff will be able to get in contact with potential clients and persuade them of the undoubted benefits of our service before they have had time to realize that the service in question is, in fact, factoring.

It is difficult to imagine a more misguided approach. It could, perhaps, be justified if the factoring company had evolved into a provider of a range of financial and other services which were being marketed to an identical sector of the market place. In such a circumstance, the argument could be put forward that factoring was only one of several services and should not therefore dominate the company's marketing policy or determine its name. Unfortunately, this is not the case with factors. They are still providing factoring as a core business. Eventually, even the most dim-witted client will realize that this is what is being sold to him or her. Moreover, cosmetic change of this sort does nothing to eliminate the image problem. On the contrary, it makes it worse, since change of this sort gives the impression that the company does not believe in its own product.

Of course, the position is made still worse when recent developments in terms of invoice discounting are taken into consideration. Seen from the viewpoint of the typical factoring company, the development of confidential invoice discounting is entirely logical. It can be easily provided, using funds available and an accounting system developed for factoring. Staff costs are lower, and properly managed it can be profitable, if risky. Surely one of the principles of effective marketing is to give the customer what he or she wants and needs. How can factors be criticized for doing that?

At one level they cannot. The managing director of a bank-owned factor, faced with the requirement to turn in a regular profit for his or her shareholders, can be forgiven for encouraging the taking of high-volume confidential business when the risk seems to be reasonable. But seen from the point of view of the industry as a whole, the position is far less clear. This is because, as the ABFD figures indicate, invoice discounting is, in fact, overtaking factoring as a prime product. People demand a confidential service for two reasons: first, because it is cheaper than factoring and because they believe they do not need the credit and administrative services; and secondly, because it is confidential and their customers will not know that they are using the services of a factor.

In these circumstances, is it any wonder that the market is confused? The factoring industry provided and promoted a service, similar though less comprehensive than its core business, and failed to differentiate between the two strands of the service. Every six months, the Association produces figures for factoring and invoice discounting, which are published to the world as though they were the same service. The growth rates of which the industry is so proud are based primarily on the expansion of invoice discounting. Invoice discounting is provided by companies which were, until comparatively recently, described as factors in their trading title and are still, essentially, factoring companies.

Why go on the defensive in this way? The answer will probably be put forward by certain of the bank-owned factors that the changes of name were required in the context of overall corporate changes or reorganization. That argument does not apply to the independent factors who have dropped the word 'Factor' from their title, and in any event I do not believe it was a prime reason for the move. Within any business there are always those who believe that change is by itself beneficial, and that a change in title or approach will necessarily achieve large and fairly rapid dividends in terms of growth. Frequently, younger management, wishing to make their name, are only too ready to put up ideas for the recasting of the company image. People on the sales side of the business do undoubtedly grow weary with having to account to the same old arguments from broadly the same groups of people, and it is therefore tempting to fall back on changes of description or image in order to make more immediate progress and to make life generally more agreeable. In doing so, I believe they have merely muddied the waters, mixed the message and confused their market place.

There is very little wrong with the basic factoring service that good marketing will not cure. There has undoubtedly been an improvement in public perception, notably among the professions in recent years. Elements of the old-fashioned attitudes still persist among business people, bankers and accountants, and there are very good arguments that can be put to these people. Sometimes, it is possible to change minds. It is a slow, laborious and sometimes painful process; nevertheless, it has to be done and cosmetic changes of name, coupled with failure to believe in the core service, do nothing to enhance the marketing process.

Marketing, not just sales

The first element of effective marketing is to understand your market place and your customer. Factors for many years have taken justifiable pride in their closeness and knowledge of the small businesses that, for the most part, comprise their market place. At the same time, there is evidence that for a long time there has been confusion in the minds of many in the industry between the concepts of marketing and sales. Mixed with this has been a leaning towards a kind of 'short-termism', which regards the achievement of this year's figures as being top priority, to the detriment of a more calculated market-led approach which has as its prime objective an understanding of what the customer requires and, just as important, what he or she will require in the future.

SURVEY OF ATTITUDES

Fortunately, there are signs that this is changing. For many years, the industry was content to rely upon intuition rather than systematic and hard analysis in evaluating its market place. In 1988, however, the ABFD, through its then public relations agency Burson Marsteller, commissioned Business Marketing Services Limited to conduct a survey into 'Awareness of and Attitudes towards Factoring' with the following research objectives:

1. To identify awareness and knowledge of factoring among UK companies and their advisers.
2. To inspect attitudes to factoring among existing and potential users and financial advisers.
3. To describe in detail the overall decision-making process.
4. To indicate preferred sources of information.
5. To deliver robust, marketable findings.

Results and recommendations

BMSL directed their attention at three audiences—existing users, potential users and financial advisers. The outcome of the research was very interesting, although perhaps not altogether surprising to many who had been associated with the industry for a long time. Essentially, the conclusions can be summarized as follows:

1. *Existing users* of factoring were very satisfied with the services they receive, which are perceived as making a major contribution to the improvement of cash flow and to increasing company efficiency.
2. *Potential users* (and to a lesser extent, financial advisers) were not sufficiently aware of the real benefits of using factoring; non-users of factoring do not fully understand it; factoring is seen primarily as a debt collection service and if companies perceive that they have no bad debt problems, they feel that they do not need the service.
3. *Non-users* associate factoring with companies that are in trouble. There is still a stigma attached to the service and many potential users see it as an admission of failure on their part, i.e. that they are unable to run the

company without outside assistance. There is also a very real fear that the use of factoring will upset customers.
4. UK factors have enormous market possibilities as the service is used only by a tiny fraction of companies.

By themselves, these conclusions provide the springboard for a potentially powerful marketing effort. These messages are crucial. If they are correct, and there is no reason to disbelieve them, it is in the interests of the industry to trumpet them to every corner of the land. The great discrepancy of views between users and non-users is by itself a significant finding, and goes a long way towards countering the criticisms with which the industry is beset.

So what have the factors done with this ammunition? So far, not much. Contrary to the cardinal marketing principle that the expansion of a business should be based upon perceived strengths, very little has changed, or appears to have changed, in the factors' stance to the market place. The world at large has been left in sublime ignorance of the BMSL findings. No noticeable shift has occurred in the quality or direction of the advertising carried out by factors. Certainly, none of the shareholding banks has come out with any kind of radical or startling statement in relation to its future intentions for its factoring subsidiary.

Here, we see the confusion between marketing and sales writ large. Year in year out, factors spend large sums of money on selling. The costs of direct marketing, salaries and overheads associated with the operation of sales teams and their support requirements are substantial. It is clearly vital for factors to write new business, and anyway, along the way, a good deal of information beneficial to the image of the industry is pushed into the market by the operation of the sales teams, even if their objectives are short-term and committed to the simple achievement of business. But here we have an industry which on the one hand suffers from an image problem, confirmed by the one piece of reliable research that has been done, yet on the other disdains the mounting of the full-scale communication programme required to correct the position and render more effective the short-term selling activities which are also necessary.

BMSL recommended that just such a programme should be brought into effect, with an educational basis, and aimed at making potential users aware of the real benefits of factoring finance for future development, improved cash flow, fewer and more effective staff, with an overriding message—factoring = improved profitability.

So far, this recommendation has been largely ignored by the industry. But one further important aspect that came out of the BMSL Report did receive attention. As a result of their research, BMSL gained a clear perception that the existing users of factoring appeared to be very well managed companies, offering at least as good, and perhaps better, more professional and more efficient business operation than non-users. The importance of this conclusion, if true, cannot be overemphasized. For if it could be demonstrated that companies which factor their debts are more effective than those that do not, then the perfect response to all of the negative criticism has been found. By definition, effective companies do not use a service that is expensive, upsets customers, or indicates that your business is next door to Carey Street. Efficient company management evaluate and measure the costs and benefits of any service that they employ; thus, the stigma is killed stone dead. Of course, the ultimate measure of efficiency in any business is return on capital employed. Therefore, in theory at least, it should be possible to compare and contrast the performance of users and non-users of factoring and invoice discounting and reach conclusions about their relative efficiency. The ABFD has attempted to do this. It commissioned another firm of researchers, Graham Bannock and Partners, to carry out a further study, 'Small Business Finance and the Role of Factoring', with a view to understanding the first systematic accounting-based comparison of users and non-users and so contribute to the knowledge of factoring and its role.

Their report, presented in February 1992, is a mine of useful information. It is based on comparison of a sample of matched pairs of independent companies, that is non-subsidiaries, with one member being a user of factoring and invoice discounting for at least three years up to August 1991 and the other, a non-user, being in the same line of business and of similar size, as measured by net assets or turnover. The final samples were 124 pairs of factoring users and non-users and 77 pairs of invoice discounting users and non-users.

The report makes a number of technical caveats in respect of the quality of the data available to its writers, and to the difficulty of its interpretation. Of particular note is the point that as the authors put it:

> The financial structure of a business reflects interplay of both the judgements of the providers of finance and the knowledge, resources and preferences of its owners. It is not always possible to determine from the analysis of accounts alone what mix of sources of finance will enable the performance of the business to be optimised.

For all that, Graham Bannock and partners make a very determined and credible attempt to establish whether there is any relationship between economic effectiveness and the existence of factoring or invoice discounting facilities. The conclusion is perhaps a disappointment to those who for years have assumed that there is a rationally based linkage. For the conclusion is that there is virtually no difference between the two groups in terms of the mean return on capital (defined as pre-tax profits expressed as a percentage of net assets). In fact, there was a slight superiority by the non-users of the order of 1 per cent for both factoring and invoice discounting groups. These differences are not found by Bannock to be statistically significant, however.

Moreover, the results of return on equity comparisons (pre-tax profits as a percentage of net worth) between the factoring clients and their non-user matches were exactly even.

So, in public relations terms we have something of a negative message. Or do we? For the fact is that the anti-factoring brigade have always implied that the situation is much worse than Bannock found it to be. Factor your debts on a disclosed basis, goes the message, and not only will your customers and suppliers assume that you are in trouble, but the sheer costs of the exercise will tend to put your business into difficulty if it is not there already. But if, in fact, there is little practical difference between companies who factor and those who do not, in the vital matter of return on capital employed is not that message completely undermined? I believe that it is, and that the industry should go to considerable lengths to promulgate the fact.

This is especially the case when one reviews the other main findings of the Bannock Report, which can be summarized as follows:

- users trade at lower net margins than non-users, have lower debtor to sales ratios, and are more highly geared, though with a greater ratio of short- to long-term capital
- a larger proportion of users of factoring than of non-users were growing in the period 1984–89
- fast growth companies, whether users of factoring or not, tend to be more highly geared because of their greater need of working capital

Bannock comments: 'These findings support our conclusion that factoring enables users with limited access to equity or long-term debt to sustain a higher level of trade than would otherwise be practicable, or even prudent.'

At first sight, these conclusions do no more than confirm the view that many have had for years about the factoring industry. Factoring equals growth, or at least the opportunity for it, mixed with a slightly risqué combination of over-borrowing and risk.

But surely, at the beginning of the 1990s after two major recessions, it should be apparent to anyone who thinks about it that what the UK economy needs, above all, is sustained economic growth based upon good products and services, preferably with an export element to them. Here is an industry which for years has proved to itself that it can help smaller businesses—the acknowledged engine of economic growth—to produce just that. Surely what is needed now is a coordinated campaign to get this message across. By efficient marketing, by the communication of this message to relevant sectors of industry, the sales effort can be rendered much easier.

And this comparatively recent trend through which the industry seeks to establish and analyse the facts can do nothing but good. What BMSL and

Bannock have to say may simply confirm, in somewhat more academic terms and language, what people in the industry have been saying for years. Nevertheless, the fact that in each case the outcomes were based upon independent research is itself important, and should supply the stimulus to marketing departments of factoring companies to make use of the research in their publicity efforts, and to commission further studies into areas of ambiguity.

Advertising and public relations

It will immediately be objected that, no matter what the advantages for a coordinated campaign, it cannot be afforded. The industry is still a small one, relative to say banking, insurance services and the like. The costs of advertising and public relations are huge. All that can be done has been done.

A marketing professional planning the communication requirements of the factoring industry, or even of an individual factoring company, would face a daunting task. Ideally, the industry should be addressing several audiences. It should, first and foremost, be putting out the message to the small to medium-sized company that factoring is a service which is appropriate to well organized and efficient businesses. This message will be linked to the association of factoring with business growth, but the prime aim of the campaign would be to address the negative feelings nurtured about the industry by so many small businesspeople and others.

Case studies would be an important element in this process, as would any tangible evidence that could be adduced to confirm the fact that factored businesses stay out of the clutches of administrators for longer periods than do those that are not, that they make more profit, that they grow more quickly and that they enjoy at least as good, or even a better relationship with their customers than do non-factored ones.

Data could also be used to appeal to other important groups, for example, accountants. Here, if anything, further research could be called for into the impact of factoring in terms of the effectiveness of reducing average collection periods, the level of bad debts suffered by factored as opposed to non-factored companies, and, in particular, the capacity of companies that factor their debts to pay for the cost of the service through debt-turn reduction and prompt payment to suppliers.

Another sector to be addressed would be the factors' shareholders. It might seem somewhat bizarre to mount a possibly expensive public communication campaign in pursuit of a group with whom you are in regular touch on a day-to-day basis. The evidence is, however, that bank managers as a group would certainly benefit from more information about the industry and its potential. Judging by the volume of business introduced through bank branches, they are not getting it at present.

Again, our marketing professional would need to consider how to influence the factors' own management and staff. The key objective to much corporate advertising is directed at the reassurance and motivation of staff, who are quite often more impressed with messages that appear in the media than with the efforts of their own management to tell them what is happening within the group for which they work.

Another important group to address would be the financial institutions who, while in some respects are in competition with factors, are interested in the development of the industry from a financial point of view. They lend the cash to the factors which is then passed on to clients; they also have strong influence in the moulding of commercial and industrial opinion which affects quite dramatically the way opinion-formers feel about a service or issue. Another group would be such bodies as the CBI, Institute of Directors, trade associations, chambers of commerce, trade unions and the multitude of interested groups that preside over and comprise the UK economy.

Finally, an important and obvious group would be the Government and opposition parties, members of parliament of all political tendencies and senior civil servants, especially those in key ministries such as the Department of Trade and Industry.

In addressing all these sectors, the marketing professional would face a number of difficulties. First and foremost, the data upon which his or her campaign should be based do not, for the most part, exist. It can be seen that research into factoring and invoice discounting has been extremely limited. Many people believe they know the answers that researchers would uncover if more studies were undertaken. However, questions still remain to be asked.

The second major difficulty would be the predictable one—money, or rather the lack of it. Campaigns on the scale described do not come cheaply. In mounting one, it would be necessary to plan expenditure carefully and to persuade people in the industry or the company concerned to be rather more generous in framing marketing budgets than perhaps has been the case in the past. Before going into the economics, however, it is worth while just considering what the industry does at present in marketing terms, as compared with the rather idealistic approach sketched out.

We have already noted that quite a considerable amount of sales effort is directed primarily at the achievement of business. Of course, the activities of salespeople spread awareness and go some way towards demolishing incorrect assumptions. All factoring salespeople talk to bank managers, accountants and potential clients. When they do so, how are they perceived? Inevitably, they are seen as having a vested interest. They are selling the services of the company for which they work and are interested primarily in short-term gain.

Moreover, because the industry has failed to research the raw data necessary to counter the main criticism made against it, the sales pitch is, to some extent, deficient. Anyone who has studied the principles behind the 'communication mix' will know that the sales representative, no matter how talented or dedicated, is to some extent at the mercy of the overall perception of the market place relative to his or her industry.

Studies undertaken in the USA tend to confirm that the reputation of a business in the market place is one of the key elements in persuading customers to give salespeople a positive hearing. Little known or badly regarded businesses have a much blunter sales edge than those that are well known and well publicized (Theodore Levitt, Industrial Purchasing Behavior—A Study in Communication of Facts, Harvard Business School, 1965). This fairly obvious conclusion is nevertheless important in viewing the sales and marketing activity of the factoring industry as a whole.

Here we have a situation where all the factors employ expensive sales teams, who spend a great deal of time convincing people that the service is a desirable one. At the same time, the industry, because of its attitude towards marketing as opposed to selling, fails to support these people with adequate advertising and public relations. In recent years, it has steadily increased the advertising and marketing 'spend'. I would estimate that, in addition to the sums spent on the direct maintenance of sales teams, members of the ABFD spend at least £1.5 million, probably more, on advertising each year. Of this, by far the greatest percentage is probably spent on press advertising. The sole experiment into TV advertising taken by Alex Lawrie has not so far been emulated by any of their competitors.

Compared with the money spent by the banks or other financial institutions, this is fairly low-key expenditure. On the other hand, it is a lot more than the industry used to believe was necessary. There is at least some recognition of the simple fact that unless you advertise your product effectively, people will rarely buy it, and certainly will not talk about it. But the real doubts set in when the context of factoring advertisements are considered. Take, for example, the advertising content of the *Financial Times* survey published on 1 May 1990. A number of the major factors bought space in the newspaper on that occasion to advertise their products. Virtually all the advertisements pounded away at the same themes—use the service and we will provide you with financial support and, inevitably, growth. The message received by the casual reader is overwhelming. This is a finance-based industry which is providing money to enable companies to grow. There is no mention at all of the conclusion unearthed as recently as the previous year through the ABFD's own research. There is very little reference to service standards, although in fairness, close reading of the advertisements does uncover references to services of various kinds.

For an industry which is constantly criticized for providing expensive finance, advertisements of this kind play into the hands of the critics and provide no differentiation between the various participants in the market place. Even more inexcusable was the total failure to emphasize the key finding, uncovered just over a year earlier, that factored companies are more efficient in business terms than non-factored companies. This point was not discussed in the narrative of the supplement, nor was it mentioned in any of the advertisements. Some of the advertisements were directed very clearly to obtaining new business enquiries for the factoring companies concerned. Experience indicates that advertising is not a particularly effective method of obtaining new business leads. Other methods, for example direct mail or regular contact with third party introducers, are far more fruitful as a basis of factoring enquiry.

This being so, one is forced to question critically the quality of the thinking that takes place in some factoring marketing departments. If advertisements don't pull business, why spend time and money producing advertisements at all? If, on the other hand, they can be successful in changing people's opinions about the industry and its products, why cannot they be used to do so? More fundamentally, given the known perceptions of the industry in certain sectors of the community, cannot some of the money be better spent conducting more detailed research into the practical effects of factoring? The outcome of this activity would inevitably, in due course, improve the advertising and public relations functions.

As usual, it will be objected that such an approach cannot be afforded by a small industry such as factoring. Research is expensive, as are broadly based communication campaigns. The answer to this is that if the factoring industry is going to grow as it should, it cannot afford not to promote itself more effectively. The 'what we can afford' approach to advertising rarely works. Far better is to quantify the objectives and seek to meet them on a planned and coordinated basis. Again, US research is instructive here. A major conclusion of a five-year study into some 67 television campaigns was that the quality of the campaign was far more important than the cash spent. So the problem lies not so much in the level of expenditure, but in just how it is spent and with what objectives. What is required is a somewhat longer term and rather more imaginative approach directed at converting large numbers of businesspeople with enthusiasm for the products of the industry.

The raw material is available. Case studies abound. Every factor and discounter in the country can point to numerous client businesses which would not have developed in the way that they have without factoring support.

In other ways too, the factors stand comparison with others in the financial sector. In an era where scandal has touched major financial institutions such as Lloyds of London, certain of the clearing and merchant banks, let alone such organizations as the Bank of Credit and Commerce International, the factors' record is without blemish. The emphasis has been placed on service to clients, the aiding of growth and providing help to small businesses at critical stages of development.

What does not happen is any real and purposive drive to broadcast the virtues to a wider market. In particular, the benefits that an effective factoring facility can bring to smaller businesses are understated. Until the industry succeeds in getting these over to a far wider public its own development will remain impaired.

The factoring product

PRODUCT DEVELOPMENT

This is not to say that the factoring product has achieved the very pitch of commercial perfection so far as the entire market place is concerned. Just like any other product, it requires development, branding and adapting to meet the specific needs of sub-groups within the market place. But anyone who, say, rejoined the factoring industry after an absence of 15 to 20 years would notice little basic difference in the service provided. Certainly the scale of the operation would be bigger. The balance between non-recourse and recourse business would have changed, and invoice discounting now plays a larger and more significant role. But the core product, in terms of scope and delivery, would have altered little. In a marketing sense, few changes have occurred; branding is non-existent, one factor marketing the service just like the others, and although prices have undoubtedly dropped, the method of charging remains the same.

Both services existed at the time that factoring was introduced into the UK. The early factors chose by and large not to offer invoice discounting on a large scale partly because this was not the way the service was offered in the USA and partly because it was considered, probably quite correctly at that stage, as being too risky. So effectively, the move towards the provision of a wider range of services to different market sectors does not constitute genuine product development. It merely means that factors and discounters are stressing differing aspects of their services. If anything, the move towards discounting has tended to mean that factors have been even less prepared to really develop their prime product.

Why is this, and does it matter? To answer the second question first, it all depends on your point of view. Just as many people in the factoring business will contend, in public at least, that the growth of the industry has been satisfactory, so it could be argued that there is no need to tinker with a perfectly sound product with which most clients seem to be quite satisfied. Moreover, they will point out that the factoring product is difficult to embellish, consisting as it does of a series of elements, each of which is designed to meet slightly differing requirements of smaller company management and which, if tampered with, could perhaps raise the level of risk, reduce service standards and be expensive to administer.

On one level, this is quite right. Management in the industry have enough on their collective plates—having to cope with the problems of growth, client failure, fraud and, latterly, the baleful effects of recession—to have any time available to deal with innovation.

On the other hand, there have been enormous changes in commercial life during the past 25 years. The development of the personal computer has transformed the way in which most businesses are operated. Political change has been more marked than in most comparable periods, and the shifts in political fashion as well as the emergence and decline of economic sub-doctrines such as monetarism have had great effects on business. The growth of feminism, and its effect on the modern family, have influenced the way business works. Business, large and small, has reacted to these changes, in ways which some find undesirable, but which are nevertheless necessary. Few industries have stood absolutely still in terms of the products they offer and the way in which they offer them. Businesses that have remained static often do not exist any longer, having been swallowed up by larger competitors or having gone to the wall.

So it is especially curious that in such a period of unparalleled change, the factoring product, directed as it is at the smaller business, in itself so characteristic of an era of developing enterprise, has altered little. Faced with sometimes ambivalent market reaction to its core product, the factoring industry's reaction has been to offer something else rather than to focus on the tedious but essential business of educating the market as to the virtues of its service and perhaps changing the manner and method of delivery to render it more acceptable to different people in different ways, and perhaps for different purposes. This is no easy task, but especially in view of the unwarranted but widely held adverse views held by many on the subject of factoring, it is one to which the industry should perhaps have paid more attention, seeking out the more precise requirements of different market segments and then satisfying them.

Easier said than done, I can hear my friends in the industry saying. Just how do you provide alternatives to meet diverse needs in the small business area, fraught as it is with risk and uncertainty? Well, for a start you have got to want to do it. You have to appreciate that a market is a mobile, changing thing, that public tastes and needs can change quite dramatically, especially in the modern world where communications and pressures are so effective. You also have to think, to use a somewhat overworked but relevant term, strategically—to consider business in terms of a future which will arrive quicker than we think. You have to be flexible, a little daring, and you probably have to raise both the skill level and the commercial awareness of your management and staff. There is no point in considering the development of a product without at the same time taking into consideration the ability of the people within the business to deliver it. This applies to the manufacture of widgets. It applies with even more force to a service business like factoring.

Packaged lending
There is little, if any, evidence that many within the industry are thinking in this way. But one company that has accepted the need to innovate is Hill Samuel Commercial Finance which is part of Hill Samuel Bank Limited, the corporate banking arm of TSB Group Plc. As members of the ABFD, Hill Samuel have developed a financial product which, while it has its roots in invoice discounting, is marketed on a basis which is completely distinct from either discounting or factoring. They have christened it 'packaged lending'. At first sight and for quite some time, I have to confess that I believed it to be just that—a package which wrapped up conventional services attractively and left the client in no different a position than would a simple invoice discounting line. Closer examination indicates that this is not the case.

In considering a packaged lending facility, Hill Samuel take into consideration the total assets within a client business which are available as security for financing rather than taking the conventional factoring or invoice discounting view and providing funding against trade debtors. They will provide advances against stock, plant and machinery and freehold or leasehold property. More specialized facilities and services are available for importers and exporters. The gamut of import facilities such as trade finance, letters of credit, supplier bonds, duty deferment guarantees and foreign exchange lending is available, as is overdraft finance from the parent bank.

All of this by itself is not especially unique. Some of the factors have been prepared to make funds available against assets other than debtors. It often makes good sense to do so, especially where freehold property is available, and it is not uncommon for stocks of readily disposable products to be used as security to provide extra cash and perhaps make the factor the main lender to the client where he or she wishes to assume that role.

Hill Samuel are the first to design and market this kind of facility on a systematic basis, however. Quite complex financial packages are organized, based on a very thorough review of the client's requirements, as expressed through a detailed cash flow forecast as well as the inevitable audited accounts, and a detailed discussion on the future plans for the business, and the quality and commitment of the management team.

Other factors take these elements into account when considering offering facilities. Hill Samuel have learned new tricks from their parent bank which are leading them into areas where judgement needs to be exercised in relation to the business as a whole, not just to the debtors. In turn, this means that the staff engaged in selling to the client and running his or her account after commencement need fresh skills. Apart from an understanding of business in the round, people need to be able to talk sense in the context of marketing, product and development. They need to understand just what it is that distinguishes the fast growing company from the plodder, the really ambitious management from the mediocre. Above all, they need an all-round knowledge of finance, to be able to distinguish a cash flow forecast that has been cobbled together by an auditor without really detailed knowledge of the business from the genuine article, prepared by an entrepreneur with a clear business plan who really knows where the business is going.

Packaged lending is directed at the larger company with the assets over and above its debtors to attract the size of facility that is worth while for the lender. It will be much more difficult to achieve the same effect with smaller businesses, the ones that provide the bread and butter of the factor. Just the same, Hill Samuel have shown that it is possible to innovate, using the skills and experience acquired in providing invoice discounting over a period of years. In doing so, they have departed somewhat from the original factoring/invoice discounting concept, but recognizing changing trends in the world and in the market place. They have developed a service which recognizes the particular needs of a distinct market segment. In so doing, they are behaving like any other commercial company in any other market place. They are also showing that it is perfectly possible for factors, like others, to evolve.

NEW TECHNOLOGY

Factors and invoice discounters do possess considerable corporate strengths derived from their closeness to and knowledge of the small to medium-sized business market. For its part, that market sector has well demonstrated needs and requirements: financial, managerial, information-based. Most small companies need help in many areas of their operations, and a variety of organizations exist, from business consultants through government departments and enterprise agencies to Training and Enterprise councils, whose role is to provide it. But large gaps remain unfilled, especially in the areas of finance and expertise.

The reason for this is simple. Small companies lack the resources to pay for the help they often need, or the assets to pledge for the funds they require. The services directed at their specific needs are often poorly coordinated or provided by organizations with no real knowledge of the customer's requirements. If the factoring and invoice discounting product could be developed to meet these requirements, the industry would be making a really invaluable contribution to the national economy. The problem is, of course, just how to do so and make a profit. There are no ready-made answers to this, but there are opportunities to make money.

Some of these are technology-based. As we saw in Chapter 7, factors have made some progress in communicating with their clients on an electronic basis. To date, the communication process has been one-way, with the factor giving out information to the client about the detailed position on the latter's sales ledger. The motives have been honourable but defensive, based primarily upon the factor's need to contain costs, reduce paperwork and keep the client informed and happy. Thus far, no factor appears to have considered whether there is potential for expanding business by means of drawing data from the client as opposed to providing it.

Yet in an age increasingly dominated by technology, it would seem probable, to say the least, that improved two-way information flows could be used as a basis for better services. Effective lending depends upon the availability of data. Through the ages, bankers and other lenders have become nervous at the point when the information stops to flow. When the promised audited accounts fail to materialize, the blood pressure rises.

In the context of smaller companies, effective asset-based lending becomes easier if real-time information is available. There appears to be no reason why an innovative factor or discounter should not develop a software package which could provide computerized accounting services for the client and make it feasible for data to be downloaded on to the factor's computer system, thus improving beyond measure the quality and timeliness of the accounting and commercial information available and rendering possible an expansion of both the service and perhaps the level of funding that could be released. Once the details concerning the client's surplus assets and liabilities, detailed cash flow, the innermost workings of the business, were available to reassure the factor, on a virtually daily basis, of his or her client's propensity to survive, it should be possible to provide finance and service lines well beyond the scope of those currently available.

I have not worked out the details of this, nor do I believe it my place to do so. What I do believe is that notwithstanding the fact that factors already make extensive use of technology, seen in the light of the changes that have occurred and that are taking place in the information technology world, there is a great deal more that could be done to develop and enhance services in ways which could transform the public perception of the industry.

Increasing awareness of labour skills

The importance of using consultants
If the factors were prepared to apply their already extensive expertise this capacity could be extended on an even broader front. Small to medium-sized businesses need consultancy help in all areas: production, marketing, finance, quality and administration. They don't get it because they invariably cannot or will not pay for it. Here again, the factors could have the high ground. They could, for example, make it a condition of the provision of

facilities in some cases that the client employs a consultant to improve certain weaknesses which had perhaps been identified at survey. These could relate to any area of the business—strategic, structural, marketing, production or financial control—any aspect that was holding back the progress of the company, the solution of which could reasonably be believed to be capable of unblocking the path to corporate growth and profit.

The exercise would need to be related to a well prepared business plan. It would also require skilled consultancy help. The factor need not employ the consultant, but could establish a multi-skilled network of approved people for the purpose, earmarking certain factoring funds for the payment of fees with the approval of the client. The spur to the client would be twofold. First, his or her business would be getting the assistance that it needed to lift it to a higher level of operation. Second, it would be feasible for the factor to link, with the perceived improvement in the operation, the increased availability of cash, in the form required by the client, either through factoring or invoice discounting.

An approach of this kind could achieve a great deal. Administered properly, it could play a part in helping many businesses to develop. All too frequently, small businesses suffer from a lack of basic management, marketing and business planning skills. Where these can be effectively provided, the impact, in terms of enhanced growth, is often considerable. The factors are well placed to be a catalyst in this respect, if they are themselves prepared, once again, to learn new skills and attitudes.

Nearer home there is the question of providing different forms of funding. Hill Samuel have already gone some way down this path. Improved communication links and the development of the capacities of the factor's staff and management might make it possible to experiment with other forms of finance. A particular hobby horse of mine has been to advocate the judicious application of equity investment, coupled with the taking of appropriate security as a means whereby factors could benefit from the kind of expansion that occurs during healthy periods of economic growth. This could raise problems in terms of the conflict of interest between factors as shareholders or investors and as financiers of debtors, but a truly innovative factoring company could overcome them, possibly with great benefit to its public image—the public relations advantages of building a bridge between short-term financing and venture capital could be considerable. It cannot be denied that the factors' market experience fits them for such experiments even if they would pose a quite considerable training need among management or the requirement to hire more people.

The adoption of ideas such as these, embryonic as they are, requires a total change of approach which is unlikely to take place. What can the factors do to make their existing product more attractive, credible and capable of being expanded? It can be argued that rather than attempting to be all things to all men, the way forward lies in providing a still better service through the core business or by producing the product at a lower, more affordable price. In terms of service standards, many in the industry would contend that all that can be done is being done. Service quality is high, most clients are satisfied, complaints are few and, after all, seen in the longer term, the business is expanding.

Total Quality Management
But once again, the world is moving on and there are signs that the factoring industry may be reacting slowly to external change. There has been a revolution in this country in recent years; it still has some way to go, but it is firmly established and it is about total quality. Thus far, factoring companies have not adopted formal techniques underpinning Total Quality Management (TQM), although its precepts are particularly relevant to the service concept that is at the heart of an effective factoring operation. TQM should not be equated totally with BS 5750, the National Standard which seeks to provide the basis for quality systems in the UK. There is no doubt, though, that the existence of the Standard has contributed greatly to the adoption of quality procedures in industry at large.

Research in the USA has shown that consumers want better quality and are willing to pay for it—as much as 20 per cent more for a better car, 40 per cent for a better dishwasher and 60 per cent for a better pair of shoes. There is little doubt that UK consumers do not differ from their US counterparts, nor that our factoring clients and customers are any different from anybody else's!

In addition, research shows that 96 per cent of dissatisfied customers never complain. On the other hand, in the late 1980s service operations received nearly twice as many complaints from customers as they did in the previous decade. Poor service is the major reason why companies lose customers who are five times more likely to leave because of poor service than because of poor product quality or high costs.

Many factors are rightly proud of the fact that few clients complain about the quality of the service they receive and that the number of complaints received from customers is very small compared with the total transactions involved. The simple absence of complaint does not in fact mean that everybody is happy!

More to the point, surely the TQM approach is highly relevant to an industry which stands or falls by the standards of service provided to its clients. There may be great benefit to be derived from the introduction of principles along the following lines:

1. Everyone in the organization is responsible for continuous improvement. Problem solving is not the responsibility of the management team alone.

2. Everything in the organization is subject to change in the pursuit of excellence.
3. There is no compromise in the search for total quality. The company sets out to be first class in every product, service and process.
4. Quality is defined by the client. Whatever does not meet or exceed their expectation is, by definition, not quality.
5. Significant excess costs are caused by poor quality. There will be a systematic campaign against unnecessary spending, waste, bureaucracy, meetings and office politics.

In short, the entire business is repositioned relative to the requirement to service the client at all costs. This means complete retraining and a fresh approach. TQM employees are capable of answering the following questions:

- Who are the company's major competitors?
- What makes the company unique, how does it differentiate itself from its competitors?
- What are the company's strengths and weaknesses against those of its major competitors?
- How do the company's costs for service compare with those of its major competitors?
- How is the company performing in terms of sales, profits and return on capital employed?
- What is the target of the company, the work group, the individual, in terms of achieving better results?
- How satisfied are clients with corporate performance and has this satisfaction level been monitored, recorded and disseminated?
- Finally, what is the role in your work group in helping the company to implement this overall business strategy and to expand as against the competition?

Every employee must have a genuine commitment to doing what is required to please and service the client. The successful management of a client relationship ensures that the overall dealings between the client and the factor arising from the factoring/discounting agreement are conducted in such a manner that the arrangement is mutually advantageous within acceptable limits of security and profitability.

Although BS 5750 touches upon the element of human performance so vital in any service industry, it is primarily systems- and procedure-based. The government, mindful of the need to raise the standard of training in British industry, has introduced a National Standard under which employers who wish to do so can become 'Investors in People', which will enable employers to embrace the concepts of clear vision, total commitment to people and continuous improvement, which ought to be the bedrock of any business, and certainly a service-based industry. Again, a National Standard has been established, against which in rather the same manner as for BS 5750, employers can submit themselves for assessment by a qualified assessor provided by their local Training and Enterprise Council. First, though, they must ensure that they meet the demanding standards set by Investors in People, which requires that the best training and development practice, based on first-class communication and commitment by the top management, prevails within the organization. Investors in People is central to TQM. It should lead to enhanced business performance, better customer relationships, and ultimately to improved bottom-line performance. Its achievement need not be prohibitively expensive, although its achievement will cost something, not least in management time and effort.

Indeed, the adoption of such a programme could well save money for some of the major factors. Staff costs are already high. Factors will constantly bemoan the fact that an increase in total business volume handled seems inescapably to lead to increased staff costs. There may well be scope for reductions in expenditure and in numbers as the industry becomes larger and, hopefully, more efficient. In the USA during the period 1983–88, factors were reported as having reduced the ratio of operating expenses to sales volumes from 1.03 per cent to 0.77 per cent. This had a startling and disproportionate improvement in terms of pre-tax return on total assets—1.7 per cent to 3.1 per cent. Reporting on these figures, Arthur Andersen Consulting, retained by the National Commercial Finance Association, commented: 'Technology investment kept pace with rapidly growing volumes and contributed to higher productivity.'

Clearly, the link between investment in more effective systems, investment in people, and bottom-line profit is hard to prove. It is also dangerous to generalize on the basis of trans-Atlantic comparisons. But it is a well known fact that in banking and service industries worldwide the linkage between well directed capital investment and lower or more productive labour is well established. There may be scope for similar savings on this side of the Atlantic, and if some of the cash saved were to be used in developing the skills and attitudes of the people in the industry, so much the better.

The way forward

Anyone reading the last few sections of this chapter in isolation could be forgiven for concluding that the prospects for the industry are dim. Here is an industry apparently confused about the nature and benefits of its own product, reluctant to develop it, unsure about the best way of promoting it, and perhaps worried by the persistence of negative feelings in the market place. On the one hand, it can point to impressive growth figures; on the other, the broader market still lies fallow.

Yet, in many ways, the opportunities have never been greater. The status of small to medium-sized business has never been higher, and there is an undisputed link between the factors' products and the capacity of small business to expand. The answer to the conundrum posed in the first section of this chapter still stands. The basic reason for the inability of the industry to fulfil its potential lies in the way that the products have been marketed, and this chapter contains a number of suggestions for possible improvement, some of which may be regarded as being controversial or unrealistic. In at least one respect, they are. For it is a fact that change on the scale that is required rarely comes about by the adoption of any one solution or prescription. The simple adoption by the industry of more effective advertising or public relations, desirable perhaps in themselves, will not bring about the degree of change that is required to ensure real development.

What is probably needed is a large number of smaller changes, themselves driven by changes in attitude or motive, which combine to lift performance. Take, for example, the changes for good achieved in recent years in Britain's airline industry. These did not come about because British Airways changed the livery painted on their aircraft or ran some interesting television adverts. The ads and the paint reflected a fundamental change that was occurring within the business, in thousands of different ways and through the efforts of thousands of people, in all kinds of jobs and at all levels. Before the new message could be put out through carefully chosen media, the reality of the performance had to be raised, underpinned and demonstrated.

I am not suggesting that there is chronic under-performance in the factoring industry. The people within it no doubt feel that they are performing perfectly well, and in many cases they probably are. But no doubt the same could have been said for many aspects of the services provided by British Airways before the undoubted transformation in service that that company achieved. Now that the business is, quite literally, operating on a different level, it is probably difficult for old hands to convince newcomers of the scale of the transformation that was achieved. But it is clear and obvious to those that use airline services, and they are the ones that matter.

In factoring terms, and in a strange way, the wheel has perhaps turned full circle. During the early years of the UK industry, there were zealots among the factors who argued that what the market demanded was a computer-based, super-efficient service that would provide for the small business the kind of streamlined and effective service that it could not possibly achieve for itself. Through this lay the path to greater efficiency, client security and growth, and ultimately the expansion of the factoring industry itself. The cash was a secondary element.

Realists argued that this was idealistic nonsense. At base, what was required was money, supported perhaps by an efficient service, but the service was merely a means of effective delivery of the cash, aided enormously perhaps by more efficient collection from customers, but based upon the simple capacity of the factor to finance a growing asset, through the acceptance of invoices. The industry, probably quite rightly, accepted the second argument, and factors to a greater or lesser degree based their operations and marketing upon it. An unfortunate by-product, as we have seen, is the fact that if you base your entire operation upon the principle of getting as much money to your client as possible in the quickest possible time, and charge a service fee as well as a money charge, you are open to the criticism that your money is expensive.

But the world is changing. In the broadest context, service is suddenly a key element. People, even the tolerant British, are less prepared than they were to tolerate poor standards in services as well as physical products. Suddenly, partly through government initiative, we are inundated with charters, codes of practice, undertakings of all kinds to a more discriminating public from those providing services, that the old ways will not do. This trend both reflects and influences the attitude of the public; its strength should not be underestimated, and it offers opportunities as well as risks. The factoring company which is the first to recognize and exploit the new mood will undoubtedly do well. This may involve changing the marketing of the service along the lines dealt with in this chapter. It may involve something completely different, which builds upon the individual strengths of the factor and enables the company to project itself and its services to advantage. The way forward may, and probably should be, different for each of the companies in the market place. Diversity is a strength in itself, and could be a key element contributing to the growth of the industry. What will not promote that growth is a bland, uniform approach which provides the same product in the same way every time. Enormous sums of money are not required. Some imagination and flair are.

11. *The Association of British Factors and Discounters*

Background

The Association of British Factors and Discounters, or ABFD for short, was established in 1976, around 10 years after the introduction of factoring services to the UK. The prime motives of those involved in the establishment of the Association appears to have been a desire to maintain standards of service. In those days, a strong strand of the conventional wisdom within the industry was that clients used factoring as much for the services provided as for the finance. This view has become a little outmoded as time has passed. At least two managing directors of factoring houses have said to me that 'they come for the money and stay for the service', and this is a fairly accurate summary of the attitude of most clients.

Nevertheless, the Code of Conduct adopted by members of the ABFD indicates quite clearly that the members should offer sales accounting and collection services of a high standard, and the Association is always on hand to receive and deal with complaints that their members have fallen down in this respect. The Code also prescribes that members should conduct their business in a professional way and promote the interests of the UK industry by maintaining high ethical standards of conduct. Moreover, they should charge fairly and openly for their services, leaving users and potential users in no doubt as to the total charges involved. Membership is open to registered companies or divisions in the UK which are engaged in factoring or, since 1990, invoice discounting, as their main business. A member's net tangible assets, or if it is a subsidiary, the consolidated net tangible assets of the ultimate holding company, must be not less than £1 million. This requirement, laudable in itself, is one that has caused a certain amount of controversy among the increasingly large number of factoring houses that have been formed in recent years, who, by virtue of this provision, are not eligible for membership.

On the other hand, the costs of membership are not particularly onerous. The entry fee is only £500 and members divide the costs of administering the Association between them, excluding the costs of certain training courses, which are paid for on a separate basis. In practice, this means that members of the Association will see change out of, say, £20 000 per annum for membership, which, considering the level of the public relations undertaken by it in recent years, would seem to represent good value.

Structure and activities

The structure of the Association is fairly conventional. There is a Council, which consists of one representative per member company, who is entitled to appoint an alternate. Members of the Council, which meets every two months, are invariably the chief executives of the companies that they represent. Then there are three committees, each normally chaired by a member of Council, with members in every case being drawn from member companies. A typical committee member is a middle-ranking executive of a member company specializing in the subject matter covered by the committee.

One of the most important committees, and one which has played a critical role in unifying attitudes within the Association in recent years, is the Education Committee. This is responsible, of course, for all training matters, in particular the Certificate and Diploma courses which the Association runs for aspiring executives within its member companies.

Then there is the Public Relations Committee, which as the name implies is responsible for public affairs and press relations. The handout which is issued to potential new members of the Association talks about a 'limited amount' of advertising, brochures, etc. This cautious approach is obviously designed to reassure existing and potential members that the Association is not run by a group of marketing-mad spendthrifts, who will spend all the profits of the constituent companies in wild advertising forays. More of this later.

The Public Relations Committee is also responsible for the organization of the annual dinner. Like those of most professional or trade associations this is a fairly elaborate affair, held normally in one of the Livery Halls in the City of London, where the executives from each of the member companies assemble to dine and to be addressed by representatives of the great and the good of British industry, who invariably go on at some length as to the contribution the industry has made during the past year to the well-being of British business. There is a certain cynicism about the usefulness of these occasions, but the fact remains that they do provide an opportunity for the perspective of the industry to be widened somewhat by contact with the worlds of politics, industry and other areas of commercial life.

Finally, there is the Legislation Committee, which as the name implies tends to look after the legal and other related matters which affect factoring or invoice discounting and to make representation to governmental or other bodies on such issues from time to time.

Naturally, the Association has a Chairperson, Vice Chairperson, Secretary and Treasurer. They are elected annually from among members of the Council, but the convention is that the Chairperson, like the Vice Chairperson, sits for a two-year period, and is succeeded by the Vice Chairperson at the end of that time. The Vice Chairperson is traditionally also the Chairperson of the Public Relations Committee. Effectively, therefore, these two people have the most powerful positions within the Association. Although responsible to the Council for their actions, they are the individuals charged with running the Association's affairs on a day-to-day basis. The formal and legal secretariat work is undertaken by a firm of solicitors, there being no full-time Secretary General to the Association.

A valuable aspect of the Association's work is, of course, the publication of statistics. Members are required to exchange information relating to the scale of their operations, which I have quoted extensively in this book, and this enables those interested to chart the course of the industry as it expands. A second 'non-statutory' function is, of course, the exchange of credit information. The existence of the Association enables credit managers from its various members to meet on a regular basis to exchange information concerning bad or doubtful debtors and to operate, in effect, as a credit club.

The need for training

As the industry expands there is, of course, a growing need for trained people. The education function of the Association is therefore well established, and for many years it has been responsible for a training course in which all member companies are allocated vacancies and through which successful candidates receive a Diploma in Factoring. Generally, the industry has run this course itself through the efforts of an appointed Director of Studies and Course Administrator plus those of a number of executives from factoring companies, who have given their time to training their colleagues and passing on their experience. A trainee emerging from this course, which has been conducted partly by correspondence and partly through a mixed residential course followed by an exam, would have received a good basic grounding in all aspects of factoring. Historically, pass rates have been high. In 1990, for instance, out of some 35 people examined, 28 passed (3 with distinction). The main problem, of course, has been that 35 people per annum is an insufficient number of trained people in relation to the needs of the growing industry.

As a consequence, the Association has reviewed its education policy and has produced a revised scheme whereby a Certificate course will be introduced to replace the Diploma. This will be based mainly on correspondence and will comprise 10 modules covering the whole range of topics needed to develop the necessary professional knowledge of the factoring and invoice discounting industry. Thus, students will emerge with knowledge of the industry itself, marketing and business development, client management, legal and accounting aspects of factoring, together with financial analysis and credit management. Each member company is required to appoint one member of staff, whose role is to act as a coordinator for all the students taking the Certificate within the member company. In addition, he or she is responsible for any practical problems a student may have and is backed up by external tutor support. Some 170 students are registered, so it is expected that the course will make an increasing contribution to training within the industry.

Moreover, standards have been raised. The Association has also established a Diploma course, which can be taken by those who have passed the Certificate course. The intention is to maintain the standard of the Certificate in line with the old Diploma course and to raise the new Diploma level quite substantially. Here again, the study will be part correspondence and part residential, but the intention is to broaden the students' experience. The subject matter covered by the Diploma is related to real corporate situations as opposed to the somewhat dry theoretical topics that have comprised a large proportion of studies in the past. Although some time will be spent refreshing the knowledge gained during the Certificate course, students will also be expected to undertake a project within their own companies, which will put into effect the knowledge they have acquired on a practical basis and in relation to the actual business situation within the employing company.

Quite clearly, of course, it will be desirable for the projects to have some practical use for the company concerned. In view of the likely confidentiality of this part of the training, it is planned that some of this work will be marked by the executives of the company concerned, supported by independent assessors to ensure the maintenance of standards and the elimination of bias.

This represents an important development in the Association's educational policy and practice. It is vitally important that, as the industry grows, it is able to draw upon a pool of trained people, who understand not just the theory of factoring, although that is important, but also how it should be applied in practice. Of course, perhaps unfortunately, the Association cannot insist that people who have received training are offered promotion within their individual companies, and no statistics exist for the number of people who have taken the exams and subsequently been promoted. By its nature, the new system may provide a more realistic basis for recognition of merit, involving as it does a more practical approach embodied in the project work, but it is quite clear that the extent to which the enlightened policies established by the Association result in practical benefits will depend very much upon the individual member companies.

Public relations

It would seem that the early days of the Association's public relations activity were dominated by two themes. First, a tendency on the part of certain members to see public relations as an expensive and rather peripheral activity, which generated little practical benefit or bottom-line return. Linked with this was the feeling that any expenditure should have a directly beneficial effect not just upon the image of the industry generally, but upon the profit and loss account of the individual member company. From personal and anecdotal experience, it has taken some time for members to recognize the existence of a greater good and a wider requirement for the whole industry to be viewed in a more positive light.

Recent developments have changed this somewhat. The Association has appointed a public relations agency of international repute. Not before time, some serious research into attitudes towards the factoring industry has been commissioned, and if the factors have not acted upon that information, then that is not the fault of the Association itself. In recent years, the industry has obtained far better press coverage than previously. Supplements on factoring abound. Not only the *Financial Times*, but other members of the 'quality' press—*The Times*, the *Guardian*, the *Independent* and the *Daily Telegraph*—have all run large supplements which, in addition to the advertisements, are bringing much needed revenue to the newspaper and contain a good deal of hard copy describing to the commercial public the progress which the factoring industry is making. The supplements are generally positive and informative and they represent a vast improvement on the kind of press the industry received a decade ago.

The biannual publication of the Association's statistics provides another opportunity to draw attention to factors' services, as do the comments of the Chairman of the Association when the annual report is produced, with regard to such matters as the level of bad debts being suffered, the growth of the industry or perhaps trends in the small to medium-sized business sector. These have been supplemented by TV and radio interviews on business programmes and many articles and items in various professional and trade journals.

Not all of these are prompted by the activities of the Association. Most of the main factors employ public relations people, who are assiduous in attempting to get coverage for the company they represent. But much of the enhanced publicity which has benefited the industry in recent years has been achieved through the Association's activities. Or put it another way—if there was no Association the level of publicity received would be considerably lower.

Publicity of this kind is difficult to evaluate, but in terms of newspaper space alone, the industry has had good value for money. The remarkably consistent and relatively high profile which the industry has achieved in recent years must have had a beneficial effect upon public perceptions, even if the level of increased awareness has not been scientifically measured.

So the conservative policy previously adopted by the Association has, to an extent, been changed. This has occurred mainly due to the efforts of a new breed of factoring managers, who understand the importance of good public relations and who have succeeded in gaining influence within the Association. Notable among these is Leslie Bland of Century Limited, whose period of chairmanship has been characterized by a degree of drive and enthusiasm which compares very favourably with the level of both qualities applied in previous years, and which has been mainly responsible for the higher profile which has been achieved.

Has enough been done and will the improvement brought about be sustained? The problem with hard-driving chairpeople is that they are sometimes succeeded by less energetic ones. People feel the need for a period of respite and calm or slower progress. More fundamentally, as has been argued throughout this book, the scale of the public relations and, for want of a better word, 'image' problem faced by the industry, is a substantial one and it is one which can only be solved by the industry itself. Contributions by individual factoring companies, though useful, cannot carry the weight that the industry can put across through the Association, nor, of course, is it realistic to expect one single company to finance the cost of the kind of campaign that is required.

What is required, in my view, is a continuing campaign addressed to the sectors and to the issues that we have identified in previous chapters. Such a campaign will build upon the research that has already been done and it will cause more studies to be carried out. It will use the outcome of that research to attack head on the prejudices that have been voiced about the industry and its services by various people over the years. It will need to use all forms of media and a variety of arguments. It will need to be broadly based and yet clearly directed at very well identified recipients. The message must be clear, based upon well researched facts and feedback must be thorough and acted upon.

I can already hear the question 'What about the cost?' People within the industry will put forward the argument that it cannot possibly afford marketing activity upon a substantial scale, especially when the benefit likely to be received is uncertain. A second reason for maintaining the current level of activity, or even reducing it, is the point of view that it is no part of the Association's business to mastermind and launch publicity campaigns. Nor is it equipped in terms of management, let alone finance, to do so.

In any debate, the arguments for doing little, or nothing at all, can always be put compellingly. At base, the response to this kind of proposal depends upon the view taken of the industry's progress to date. If you believe that it is already fulfilling expectations, that the progress made in terms of clients supported and the level of profitability achieved is adequate or even excellent, then there is a good case for doing little more than is being done at present.

If, on the other hand, you believe that there remains substantial scope for growth and that the industry has as yet scarcely started to show what can be achieved in helping businesses to grow, both domestically and internationally, then the alternative view is relevant. In Chapter 10 we examined the basis on which a public relations campaign could, and in my opinion should, be mounted. The one remaining question is whether it should be done by the individual members of the industry or by the Association.

In my view, it is unrealistic to expect any one of the individual factors to undertake the full financial burden of a broadly based marketing campaign. But there is a more compelling reason for the Association, rather than one individual company or companies, to be involved. What is required is a message to the market place indicating that 'Factoring is good for you', not necessarily a message that 'X factor's services are good for you'. This is not just because the services of X factor may or may not be the best available at any one moment, even if this business has the willingness and capacity to provide the marketing budget. The real point is that criticism of factoring, ill-informed as it often is, is voiced on a broad basis. The response must be equally broad in scope and must be seen to be putting forward what the industry can do for British companies across the board. As indicated in Chapter 10, the intention must be to counter the adverse publicity by hard, factual analysis, and this is best done by relating the benefits to the efforts of the industry as a whole.

As to costs, although quite clearly any increase in public relations activity will cost more, it is by no means certain that it is necessary to throw money at the problem. What has been achieved thus far in terms of increased awareness is due partly, at least, to the new attitude that has been applied to the problem among Association members and the substantial efforts of its officials. The next step need not necessarily be that much more expensive than the last. What is required is, perhaps, more imagination, drive and flair, rather than massive funding. Marketing history is full of examples where the prospects of products or services have been transformed without massive expenditure. For example, in recent years, people and governments worldwide have become increasingly aware of 'green' issues and of the way in which the environment must be protected. There remains a long way to go, but awareness has been substantially raised. It is highly unlikely that the original proponents of 'green' measures possessed vast marketing budgets or even particular marketing skills. Yet they have changed people's attitudes throughout the world.

The comparison may appear specious. Factoring does not have the same potential newsworthy impact as the greenhouse effect. It can call upon one or two quite good themes, however. In particular, the help it gives to smaller businesses, the assistance it can give to exporters and all of the issues which we have explored at length in this book carry within them the basis of a campaign which could quite effectively dispel the negative image which the industry still suffers from in some instances.

There is no reason in the world why such a campaign cannot be mounted by the Association, given the willingness among the members to put in place the necessary funds and, perhaps, to expand the staffing arrangements. I have no idea as to the extent to which the current Association budget would need to be increased for such objectives to be met. I do know that it is possible to organize and run effective public relations campaigns for sums of money which certainly should be well within the means of an industry which has developed to the level reached by the factoring industry today. Whether the banking shareholders will judge it to be a worthwhile investment in the context of the marketing spends incurred on their other services remains to be seen.

A wider franchise?

This leads, of course, to the criticism made quite frequently by people in the factoring industry, although not those employed by an Association member, that the Association is simply the mouthpiece of the bank-owned factors, a somewhat cosy club which, while it may undertake useful work from time to time, is constrained by virtue of its membership from any major accomplishment or radical move.

This is, of course, a very British criticism. The British love clubs, associations and groups of all kinds, and none more so than the powerful and the wealthy. Inevitably, those outside the charmed circle tend to resent those within it. Not infrequently, the criticisms made by outsiders have a germ of truth. The defenders of the system argue, on the other hand, that, notwithstanding its deficiencies, the system works.

Most of this criticism applies to the Association. As we have seen, nearly all its members are bank-owned, and they dominate the market to such an extent that the market shares of the non-Association members are insignificant. There would appear to be some case for increasing the Association's membership from among the ranks of some of the independent factors, bringing in new blood and possibly fresh attitudes. The vehicle for so doing already exists in the shape of the Association of Invoice Factors. Formed in 1978, this Association represents a group of 'independent' factoring companies, which are independent in the sense that they are not owned by clearing banks. In general, they appear to provide much the same range of services as do the larger factors, but the members, listed in Appendix 4, are smaller businesses, whose capital base would probably not generally meet the ABFD's requirements for membership. It seems likely that their combined turnover and client base is also substantially smaller than that of any one of the ABFD members.

The ABFD is prepared to consider sympathetically applications for membership from factoring companies which meet the minimum capital requirements of £1 million. It would obviously be foolish, particularly in the current climate, for the ABFD to reduce this requirement simply to meet the needs of smaller factors. It is very much in the public interest for the factoring industry to be able to claim a reasonable level of capitalization.

On the other hand, it is clearly absurd for the factoring industry to have two independent trade associations. This can only create needless confusion, or even animosity, and cannot be helpful to the factors themselves. It would presumably be of benefit for the Association of Invoice Factors' members to gain access to the education programme being developed by the ABFD. A common Code of Conduct, one complaints procedure and a wider sharing and publication of information would all be beneficial. For this reason, it would seem appropriate for some kind of associate membership status of the ABFD to be created and offered to the smaller Association's members. Quite obviously, this should also be offered to other factoring companies who are not members of the AIF. It is clearly essential to maintain standards, particularly those in relation to capital adequacy and performance. Associate status could be achieved by gearing minimum capital requirements to the level of funds advanced and by insisting on the maintenance of these relationships as the business is developed.

Staffing

Of course, such a policy would have resource implications. The performance and capital adequacy of the new associate members would have to be regularly monitored if the notion of applying consistent standards was to mean anything at all. This, coupled with any increase in the publicity programme, would inevitably lead to a requirement for a full-time secretary to the ABFD. This would replace the 'ad hoc' arrangements which currently exist, through which the ABFD is run effectively by the staff of whichever chairman happens to occupy office at any one point in time. This arrangement has the advantage of being inexpensive and so far has worked, but would hardly seem to be conducive to the effective management of a trade association to what should be a major growing industry.

It is difficult to conceive of any major industrial or commercial interest group operating without a full-time dedicated staff. One wonders how effective would have been the CBI, for example, if all of its officers had remained unpaid volunteers. Nearly all trade or industry associations have full-time staff, as do all professional bodies.

Again, the cost objection will be raised. It will be said that the industry is too small to be able to finance such expensive undertakings as a full-time secretary, a permanent office and, perhaps, a small supporting staff.

Here again, the argument is closely related to the different points of view as to the potential of growth within the industry. Those of us who believe that it has a substantial growth potential will argue that this is unlikely to be realized unless the ABFD plays a significant part and, in order to do this it must be properly staffed. Others will say that this is unrealistic and beyond the purses of the existing membership.

12. *International factoring*

Background

Modern factoring was conceived in an international atmosphere. Exported from the USA to Europe in the 1960s, it has now taken root in nearly 40 countries all over the world. During this period and especially latterly, there have been enormous economic and social changes worldwide. Improved communications, the reduction in the cost of international travel and, above all, the development of telecommunications has shrunk the world in a quite remarkable way. On a social level, the advent of mass tourism, while bringing problems of its own, has broadened people's perceptions and has probably, by and large, increased the ability of different nations and individuals within them to get along with one another.

In the business world, developments in Europe and elsewhere have made it easier for comparatively small businesses as well as the large corporations to operate on an international scale. The most recent development in Europe will almost certainly make it essential for them to do so and may well bring an era of unparalleled market opportunities for companies of all kinds. The growth of multinational business inevitably spawns smaller imitators. Better communications have made businesspeople alert to international opportunities and threats. The very availability and process of travel broaden the outlook and stimulate new ideas and fresh approaches.

Factoring and invoice discounting have not been untouched by these trends. The International Factoring Report of Factors Chain International (FCI), of which more later, states that 'more than 88 000 businesses used factoring to settle trade transactions with some 6 million corporate customers in 1990'. The list provided by FCI in Appendix 9 shows that some 507 factoring companies are operating worldwide. It is possible that even this understates the true figure—there were at least 40 companies providing factoring and/or invoice discounting services in the UK at the end of 1990, for example—so others may exist elsewhere in the world which FCI has not counted. The point is, however, that 500 is a substantial number and that the factoring service is widespread and is growing. The FCI annual report points out also that world factoring volumes tripled in the five years to 1990, and it adds that the benefit of factoring, especially international factoring, is quietly revolutionizing the way trade transactions are settled around the globe.

Of course, FCI has a vested interest to support in this respect—it is after all the main international factoring organization—but a glance at the turnover figures which the organization has produced and which are shown in Appendix 10 confirms the expansionary trend. The increases in world sales volumes, and the development of markets in places as diverse as Mexico, Spain, South Korea and South America, confirm the fact that factoring is firmly on the world map. Much of this growth has taken place in recourse factoring. As we have already noted, factors tend to commence operations by providing the service on a recourse basis, perhaps developing the full factoring service when their customer database and capacity to provide satisfactory credit protection have been developed. It would appear that the growth of invoice discounting is primarily a British phenomenon which will probably not occur on a worldwide scale. Later in this chapter we shall be reviewing the statistics in more detail and seeking to place British experience in a world context. We will consider the differing forms of international factoring and examine how cross-border factoring works. Above all, we will try to understand why it is that in an era of unrivalled international development, improved communications and the rest, export factoring, which appears to be particularly suitable for internationally minded businesses, has so far failed to realize its potential.

BANKING INSTITUTIONS
Anyone who walks through the streets of the City of London cannot fail to be struck immediately by two things. First, the immense wealth and therefore power of the place. The UK banks and financial institutions have a role in the UK economy which is proportionally greater than that of the corresponding entities in most other countries. The contribution of 'invisibles' to the UK balance of payments is proof of this, and there is no doubt that the banks, in particular, play an important part in the life of the nation at all levels. The second obvious feature is the internationalism of the City. There are hundreds of foreign banks in London, some of which are representative offices, but a considerable number of which are fully developed branches. They come from all corners of the earth and from countries of widely differing political or religious orthodoxies. There are, of course, other important financial centres—New York, Frankfurt and Tokyo rival London in importance these days—but what appears to differentiate London from other centres is the sheer range of organizations which have chosen to do business there. There are good historical reasons for this. The City became the centre of world finance during the nineteenth century when British imperial power was at its zenith. Bankers and financiers go where the business is, and during this period London was, without doubt, the place to be. By the turn of the century, London was financing a huge proportion of world trade. Sterling was the international medium of exchange in a way that the dollar was to become in due course.

So the influx of foreign banks continued until the present day. In 1959, the Redcliffe Committee (Report of the Committee on the Working of the

THE BUSINESS OF FACTORING

Monetary System) pointed out that one of their prime roles was to grant credit to finance the movement of goods between the UK and other countries. Since then, of course, the functions have expanded; the development of the foreign exchange markets, the emergence of Euro-currencies and new products such as leveraged buy-outs and venture capital have led to still more diversity. Nevertheless, it remains the case that much of the development of the City has been based on what can be broadly described as 'international trade finance'. The City is rooted in international business. As the world shrinks, this fact becomes more and more apparent. The banks have developed important international networks, sometimes by establishing their own branches in foreign markets, on other occasions by buying overseas banks. At the very least they have developed, over the years, tried and tested correspondent banks in virtually every part of the world where a British company wants to do business.

A high percentage of this business is related to short-term credit, that is to say, with sales terms of up to 180 days. Much of it has traditionally been transacted either 'on sight' by the presentation of specified documentation at a fixed future date or by the opening by the customer of a letter of credit. The latter probably remains the basis upon which most overseas trade is negotiated. In simple terms, it is an undertaking by the bank of the customer in the overseas market to pay a defined amount to the exporter so long as certain specified conditions are met. It is, of course, the customer who opens the credit through his or her banker who must have confidence that the importer, their customer, will have sufficient funds available in his or her bank account to meet the full value of the credit at the time the bank is required to effect payment under it. The credit can be confirmed by a bank elsewhere than in the customer's territory, normally, of course, in the country of the exporter. There is no doubt at all that a letter of credit confirmed by a London bank is the most secure basis on which to export goods since the bank, which has first-class status in credit terms, is assuming the obligation of the issuing bank, and providing the exporter can present documents which are completely in accord with the terms of the credit, payment will follow, either through the transfer of cash or by the acceptance and negotiation of a bill of exchange.

There lies the rub. Traditionally, and quite rightly, bankers have always insisted on stringent documentation standards in relation to the opening and payment of documentary credit. This is understandable, since the issue of a documentary credit by a bank effectively guarantees payments so long as the correct documents are presented. The banks deal in documents, not goods and they have to be certain that everything is as it should be. Nevertheless, the Department of Trade and Industry indicates that some 70 per cent of letters of credit are not honoured on first presentation, simply because of errors and problems on timing. Not surprisingly, stories are legion within the banking world of cases where international trading companies have made errors in the preparation of documentation, with disastrous results for the consignment in question. The process can be slow and cumbersome depending on the efficiency of the banks involved and the effectiveness of the exporter and the customer. The advantages of open-account credit when dealing with relatively well developed parts of the world are obvious.

Yet the risks remain. The mere fact that a potential customer speaks a different language, operates in a foreign market place, is subject to different commercial conventions, practices and laws means that the exporter must be on his or her guard. So the letter of credit lives on, even if its usage is declining (and I can find no reliable statistics on this point, although factors around the world tell me that it is the case).

Export Credit Guarantee Department

Another significant feature of the export scene is, or course, insurance. For many years the main player in this area has been the Export Credit Guarantee Department (ECGD). Established in 1919, the Department was perhaps the first coherent manifestation of the view that the Government should take an active part in encouraging companies in their export efforts. As is often the case with governments, the foundation of the Department appears a little half-hearted, a mere gesture towards this mercantalist point of view. It was established as a mere sub-department of the Department of Overseas Trade and consisted initially of a staff of 13 people, including 3 charladies!

Since these humble beginnings the ECGD has expanded apace, and has developed a comprehensive array of policies and schemes designed to assist UK exporters, existing and putative. In particular, and in recent years, the Department has expanded dramatically the volume of total export business insured. In 1960–61, for example, total export business declared was a mere £742 million. By 1989–90 this had expanded to some £15 729 million (A History of ECGD and ECGD Annual Reports and Accounts, 1989–90). These days, ECGD's 12 000 exporter customers can avail themselves of an almost bewildering range of insurance products. Cost escalation cover, bond support, cover for the unfair calling of bonds, all these are available. Exporter customers can take advantage of various buyer credit schemes. Most significant of all, from the factoring point of view, ECGD has over the years concentrated substantially on short-term credit. During the 1970s, more than 75 per cent of the Department's business was dealt with by its Comprehensive Guarantee Group responsible for short-term credit. In 1976, the Department provided further refinements by enabling exporters to obtain cover for currency sales, based on the exposure at the time of loss rather than the date of the Department's issue of its guarantee. In other words, exporters were able to protect themselves as far as was realistically possible against adverse foreign exchange movements.

Again, and perhaps yet more serious from the point of view of the factoring industry, ECGD continued until quite recently to work closely with the banks in providing exporters with finance at favourable rates under ECGD guarantees for short-term as well as for capital goods industries. This facility, available since 1954 for manufacturers of capital goods, marks the end of ECGD existence as an organization providing an insurance service pure and simple, and moved it firmly into the financial sector.

So by the time the British factoring industry got under way in the 1960s there existed a highly sophisticated range of insurance, financial and collection facilities to help the exporter. ECGD's initial drive into short-term export finance more or less coincided with the arrival of the factoring industry in the UK. Any British company with the wit and capacity to obtain export orders could get them insured, financed and collected through an organization which had been in existence for generations and whose expertise extended worldwide.

These circumstances, coupled with the fact that the very organizations providing a major part of these services in due course also came to control the factoring industry, has made it hardly surprising that export factoring had limited impact. When you take into account the relative costs involved, the fact that the new service had to sell itself into a market well known for its conservative approach and on the basis that it represented the new, modern way of handling exports, the failure to grow quickly becomes understandable. We will be looking at these aspects towards the end of this chapter, but for now we must concentrate on the mechanics and operation of the service and examine how effective it can be for the exporter.

Export factoring

We saw in Chapter 3 how a full service domestic factoring arrangement works. In principle, there is little difference between this arrangement and an export facility. In practice, the different conditions brought about by international trade do give rise to differences, both in structural and operational terms. The vast majority of international factoring is undertaken through the cooperation between an export factor who, not surprisingly, is resident in the country of the exporter, and an import factor who operates in the country of the overseas customer. There have been and there remain instances where direct export factoring takes place, but these are the exception rather than the rule.

The two factor systems can be illustrated in Figure 12.1. The system works like this. A client decides to factor export debts either on a purely export basis, or more usually as part of an overall factoring operation encompassing the domestic as well as the overseas business. During the negotiation, the factor will undertake precisely the same checks and enquiries as in

INTERNATIONAL FACTORING

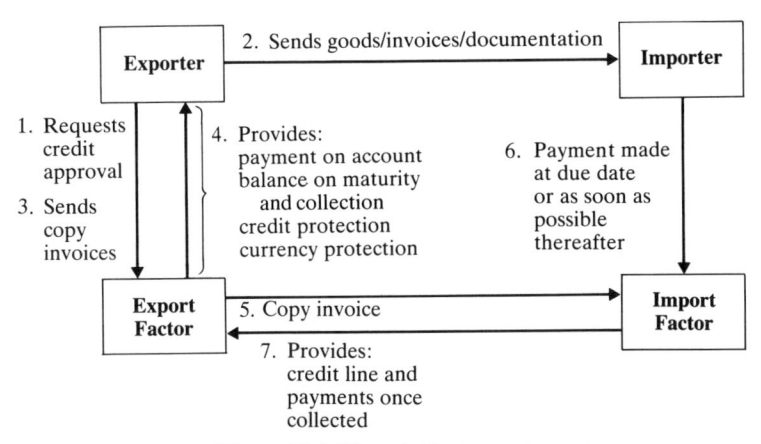

Figure 12.1 The two factor systems

domestic business. He or she will be careful to obtain full details of the following:

- the volume and type of export sales by territory
- the precise terms used in each export market place and, if necessary, from each customer
- the number and type of customers involved
- the likely pattern of future sales and credit exposures
- the number of invoices raised
- the level of disputes and the reasons for them

The emphasis at this point is upon the quality of the credit risk posed by the customer list. This is for the good reason that the next step is for the export factor to ask the import factor whether or not he or she is in a position to provide credit protection to meet the requirements of the exporter. Most export factoring is done without recourse, and it is essential in the early stages for the export factor to be entirely confident that the opposite number is capable or providing the level of service that is required. It is obviously important for this to be resolved at an early stage. The existence of two parties effectively cooperating to jointly provide a service means that the scope for misunderstanding is enhanced, and the fewer grey areas, the better. In addition, it is likely that the export factor, who is responsible for providing the financial facility, will, once the operation commences, gear the level of his or her facility, at least partly, to the level of credit approvals granted by the import factor. So this initial assessment is all-important.

In reviewing the credit requirements, the import factor has a number of advantages over both the client and the export factor. First and foremost, he or she is an operational domestic factor in the market place, at the most basic level, speaking the same language as the customer. He or she is aware of local commercial practices and conditions and is almost certainly engaged in granting credit and collecting from customers every day of the working year. The exporter's customers may well be known to him or her and may already be the customers of other locally based clients. The import factor will have access to sources of external credit information, not necessarily easily available to a foreign supplier, and should therefore be in a position to respond effectively to the request to set up credit limits.

Once the export factor has been notified by his or her import factoring counterpart that they are in a position to do so and that the costs of providing the service can be quantified, the export factor is in a position to submit a quotation to the exporter for the price of the service. Assuming that this is acceptable, the next step will be to complete the export factoring agreement. At first sight, this will not differ greatly from the corresponding document used for domestic sales. There will invariably be a separate factoring agreement for export turnover, however, and this will normally define the territories which the factor is prepared to handle as part of the arrangement. It may be, of course, that he or she is prepared to handle all export sales, in which case the agreement will relate to all debts becoming due from customers outside the UK. The client will be expected to provide the same or similar warranties as for a domestic factoring agreement, there will be provisions for such matters as the regulation of advance payments, for termination and the requirements to disclose information, all of which will be in line with the domestic agreements. More time may well be allowed in the factor's operating instructions for the resolution of disputes, bearing in mind the longer time lags in international business, and there will be provision for the basis on which the factor handles the question of foreign currency invoices and payments. There may be other minor differences, but in general the similarities between domestic and export agreements will be greater than the distinctions.

The factoring agreement

Behind this statement there do lurk one or two important differences, however. The factoring agreement will undoubtedly indicate that in case of dispute between the parties the provision of English law should be applied. This may well be acceptable so far as the relationship between the exporter and the export factor are concerned. But as regards the relationship between the export factor and the import factor, and more particularly where the exporter's customers are concerned, there is a certain amount of wishful thinking involved. If, for example, it becomes necessary to pursue customers to court and beyond in respect of outstanding debts, then in practice it is preferable to do so under the law of the country in question. Fortunately, and especially in Europe, most countries have well defined legal procedures for the recovery of debts. In countries where the factor is uncertain of his or her capacity to perform and where not represented by an import factor, the export factor will be more cautious before assuming the credit risk or advancing funds. In the early days of the European industry, it was inevitable that factors would forge relationships with other experienced factoring companies abroad, and the majority of those were found, initially at least, in Europe or North America. Thus, much of the early cross-border business was transacted within these markets. Now experience is spreading worldwide, and so are the prospects for ambitious, export-led companies who can use the skills of factors on a worldwide basis.

Another area of potential difficulty for export factors lies in the question of possible conflicts brought about by different systems of law relative to the assignment of debt. The assignment from the exporter to the UK factor will be accomplished in exactly the same way as for a domestic factoring agreement. Where the debt is to be collected directly by the factor or is reassigned to an export factor, however, any assignment will normally take place under the law of the import factor's country. In practical terms, this appears to work perfectly well, but there is the risk that under different legal systems the validity of the assignment could be challenged in circumstances where the client became insolvent. In spite of these uncertainties, cross-border factoring is developing. The existence of the factoring 'chains' has undeniably helped to reduce if not completely remove some of the commercial obstacles to international factoring, and the process of unification of European law, coupled with the continued development of international business, will undoubtedly assist further so far as legal issues are concerned.

From the client's point of view, all of this matters little. All he or she will know or indeed care is that once the factoring agreement has commenced it will be possible to invoice foreign customers and obtain up to 100 per cent credit protection so long as the client remains within the credit limits which have been stipulated by the import factor and adopted by the export factor. The client will raise invoices in the usual way and send a schedule to the export factor. Sometimes he or she will be required to send a second copy of all invoices so that this can be transmitted for working purposes to the import factor. Sometimes also the export factor may ask a client to provide more information than is customary in domestic business, including evidence of shipment, possibly even copies of negotiable shipping documents. Generally though, the procedure is similar to that used in domestic business.

TERMS OF SALE

One area where particular care has to be taken is the question of terms of sale. These vary substantially by country, even within industries. Factors, through their foreign contacts, are frequently well placed to advise novice exporters on the most appropriate sales terms, but, above all, they will stress the need for clarity. After all, there are a number of parties involved—the client, the customer, possibly sales agents, almost certainly forwarders and two factoring companies. The scope for misunderstanding, given possible language difficulties, undoubtedly exists. In certain markets and in certain countries it is essential to conform to the sales terms expected by the customer. There is little point, for example, in a UK clothing manufacturer seeking to sell a product into the US market without adopting the somewhat arcane payment terms which have been recognized in that market place for many years. Scandinavian and German department stores will invariably pay very promptly. Italian customers will require extended credit. Between the two extremes there is a variety of different sales terms which will probably have to be observed if the exporter is to operate effectively. Similarly, there has to be clarity on shipment terms—Free on Board, CIF, Franco-domicile and the like—which are fortunately clearly specified under the Rules of the International Chamber of Commerce and accepted worldwide. These must be equally clear if disputes are to be avoided.

Notice of assignment or factoring legend

Another detail to be considered by the export factoring client is the notice of assignment or factoring legend which appears on the customer's copy of the invoice. As we have seen, this will indicate to customers that the debt has been assigned, and in the case of export business, reassigned, to a factor and it will give clear payment instructions. In domestic market situations, it is a simple matter to print the notice on the invoice in a clear and prominent manner which is satisfactory from both the factor's and client's viewpoints. In multi-international business where several markets are involved, the payment instructions will differ by market as will the language, and so import factors provide export factors and their clients with sticky labels.

Export factoring clients should use the service as a basis for invoicing in the currency of the customer. This brings substantial advantages. Perhaps due to our Imperial past, British companies have been slow to realize the marketing advantages flowing from the use of customers' currencies. Even now, the absolute level of foreign currency invoicing with regard to UK exports as a whole is relatively low—around 30 per cent—despite the fact that it is difficult to sell at all into some countries, notably the USA, unless customer currencies are used. The development of the Single Market will accentuate this trend and the adoption, even by the insular UK, of a single currency will eliminate the problem completely, at least within Europe. Meanwhile, it is advantageous to use foreign currencies whenever possible, and factoring helps this process.

At the most basic level, even where a factor provides no specific foreign exchange cover, an export factoring facility at least makes it easier for an exporter. He or she can draw down sterling for a proportion of the sale, and depending upon the factor's track record on collection can more easily forecast the date of payment by the customer. This makes it easier to use the exchange market so as to obtain the necessary protection against foreign exchange fluctuations. Some factors will provide on-account payments in the currency of the customer, thereby mitigating if not entirely eliminating the foreign exchange risk inherent in export transactions. Quite clearly, where a client can achieve a matched funds position it can be advantageous to accept foreign currency advances, as European interest rates, in recent years at least, have tended to be lower than those for sterling. Other factors go still further and credit the client account on receipt of a schedule of invoices at the sterling equivalent rate ruling at the date of the offer of the debt for factoring. This effectively, of course, provides protection against currency fluctuation for the period of credit which must occur before the customer pays. This aspect of the export factoring service does not always receive the publicity it deserves—certainly, the factors do little to publicize it—and any serious exporter considering using factoring should give due weight to it, when choosing which factor to use.

Whatever the currency, the debts offered are accounted for, managed and collected in much the same way as are domestic items. The client will receive from the export factor an acknowledgement of the acceptance of the debt and will be able to draw down a payment on account in the currency specified within the factoring agreement and up to the agreed percentage as described above.

COLLECTION

Collection, on the other hand, is the responsibility of the import factor. Here, we must distinguish between credit-approved and non-approved debts. Individual transactions may fall within a credit limit which has been allocated by the import factor and for which he or she is responsible should the payment not be received due to the customer's inability to pay. The import factor will receive the benefits of the warranties and obligations taken by the export factor in his or her agreement with the exporter. In other words, the import factor will be comforted to the extent that both the exporter and the export factor confirm that each approved debt is represented by an actual bona fide sale and shipment of goods to the customer in question, who is liable for the payment of the amount stated in accordance with the invoice. On this basis, the import factor will normally guarantee a payment to the export factor on a specified due date—the FCI agreement, for instance, indicates that payment will be made under guarantee on the 90th day after the due date for payment by the customer. This is, of course, irrespective of whether the customer has in fact paid the import factor. If, of course, the customer pays before this date the import factor is obliged to pay the export factor the equivalent sum promptly after collection and if he or she does not do so, interest can be charged at an agreed rate. So far as approved debt is concerned, therefore, the import factor has every incentive to get on with the collection.

In the case of non-approved debts, however, the import factor will operate on behalf of the export factor on a collection basis only. The FCI Agreement uses the phrase 'best endeavours' in relation to the collection of such amounts, which takes place with the consent of the export factor being given before any expenses or additional costs are incurred.

From the client's viewpoint, an important difference arises between domestic and export business. In a domestic non-recourse arrangement, it is obviously in the client's interest to ensure, so far as practicable, that the factor provides a high level of credit protection. Inevitably, however, a situation will arise where the client's and factor's views on a given customer's creditworthiness do not coincide. As a consequence, there will frequently exist a proportion of unapproved debt on a sales ledger which the factor may or may not finance. In a domestic context, so long as the client is really satisfied that the unapproved customers will pay, and makes suitable provision for doubtful or bad debts, this is not the end of the world. The factor, who should be working closely with the client, may have advised against the sale, but the client has chosen to take the risk. Factor and client are both in the same country, speaking the same language, and it is in the factor's, as well as in the client's interest, that the unapproved portion of the sales ledger is accorded high priority in terms of the collection of outstanding debt.

The situation is not quite the same in an export context. The import factor will undoubtedly do his or her level best to collect—to use 'best endeavours' in the language of the FCI Agreement. But it is not in his or her interests to spend too much time and resources in doing so. After all, the import factor has given the necessary advice—that the debtor in question does not justify the level of credit which the supplier wishes to offer. There is no direct relationship between exporter and import factor. Any pressure on the latter to perform must be exerted through the export factor. The moral of this is clear. Exporting clients should think very carefully before ignoring the credit advice they receive through the service.

Finally, of course, there is the question of part approvals, that is to say, customer accounts where a credit limit is breached through further unapproved sales. Here, it is normal practice for the whole of the debt to be offered by the export factor to the import factor to enable him or her to handle the whole account on an effective basis.

Then there arises the question of customer dispute, where obviously the procedures between import factor and export factor must provide for notification either way when a customer raises some sort of claim against the validity of the debt because of inadequately supplied products or services. As we shall see later, most of the factoring chains have in place communication arrangements which facilitate the rapid transmission of information on all these issues. This is very important. A major drawback of cross-border factoring where two factors are involved used to lie in the duplication of accounting systems and procedures. In days gone by, it was not uncommmon for considerable duplication of accounting to take place, causing increased costs and inevitable bureaucracy and delays. The major factoring chains have now invested in automated systems and 'netting' accounting procedures, which to a large extent appear to have eliminated this basic problem.

Direct export factoring

There is a school of thought that it is preferable for cross-border factoring to be handled through one factor who has established a controlled network through which the export client can obtain the complete service. It is argued that the fact that there are, in most current arrangements, two different and distinct companies providing the service, must imply diminution of service quality, simply by virtue of the fact that communication lines are longer. In the first flush of enthusiasm among the factoring community back in the 1960s, there seemed to be a good deal of sense in the point of view that in order to establish a really effective mutli-directional international operation it was necessary to set up a network capable of serving businesses which was based on a single common service philosophy, common procedures, centrally trained and motivated staff and effective marketing. This would have the benefit of overcoming the potential difficulties mentioned above, coupled with the almost inevitable human problems that seem to occur whenever people of different nationalities and cultures seek to cooperate on any kind of commercial venture.

The main proponent of the direct export system was the then subsidiary of National Westminster Bank, Credit Factoring International, which established an extensive network throughout Europe, the USA and Canada based on a small but uniformly operated and controlled local office system which was staffed by nationals of the countries concerned. The concept, admirable in itself, failed. This was primarily because it proved impossible to generate sufficient cross-border business to cover the sometimes quite substantial costs which faced a sterling-based business in an era of continuous decline of the pound sterling against the US dollar and the main European currencies. This experience may well have had an inhibiting effect upon the factoring industry since, with one or two notable exceptions, most export factors now operate through the two-factor system. Lombard Commercial Services remains true to the spirit if not to the method of its original concept, preferring to operate directly from the UK through a team of people with language and operational skills based in their head office in Feltham. Lombard claims to have made a profit on this basis.

Of course, all factors have to consider direct export work from time to time. Business does not always come in ready-made chunks, designed to fit neatly into the network or chain to which you subscribe. Clients have the awkward habit of negotiating orders in more obscure countries and then requesting that the consequent sale be handled under the factoring agreement. Sometimes, depending on the risk involved, this request can be met. Factors can obtain bank or credit reports on the customer, together with the information on the country concerned, from any number of sources. They can then take a view and handle the business direct, using the bank system or an appointed collection agent to collect the money when the debt becomes due. Quite obviously in these situations much will depend on the territory concerned, the degree of political and economic risk involved and the factor's own ability to liaise effectively with the collecting agent. There is, in some circumstances, no reason at all why quite effective business should not be built up on this basis. It has to be said that direct export factoring is comparatively rare, and when it is offered the factor will not infrequently arrange for separate credit insurance to cover the risk of non-payment.

In recent years, import factoring has developed further. Indeed, the ABFD figures indicate that factors are now handling more import business than export! Here, the factor provides a service for the foreign exporter who is shipping goods into the factor's own country. This is, of course, a variant of the original factoring provided by US factors to European exporters. It lends itself naturally to maturity factoring where the exporter is buying the credit expertise, market knowledge and collection ability of the factor. Very often, the larger exporters enter into arrangements of this kind since it is clearly necessary to have sufficient sales volume in any given territory to justify the arrangement from both the client's and the factor's points of view.

Invoice discounting

Thus far in this chapter, invoice discounting, which is having so dramatic an effect domestically, has not really been mentioned. It would be quite possible to write a complete chapter on international factoring business without doing so. But it would be wrong, because invoice discounting does exist in an international context and will probably develop to a greater extent, albeit gradually.

At first sight, there is no reason why it should develop at all. In world terms, according to FCI invoice discounting is a minority activity, practised primarily by the slightly eccentric British, but by few others. The FCI statistics indicate that around 5 per cent of the total turnover relates to invoice discounting and most of it, if not all, appears to be UK-based. It may be, of course, that some of the recourse business referred to is also invoice discounting. A tiny proportion of this relates to the discounting of export business. To date, the overwhelming majority of invoice discounting deals relate to customers inside the UK.

There are good reasons for this. It is a fact that, for the vast majority of companies, if they export at all, their exports represent only a small proportion of their total business. Invoice discounting is a finance line pure and simple. If you require a financial facility that expands with your sales volume, it is obviously sensible to offer the sales which represent the greater part of your business.

From the discounter's point of view, the reluctance to get involved in taking foreign debtors as security is even more understandable. Confidential invoice discounting can be a risky business. If your client ceases to trade and the existence of the facility is declared and customers contacted for payment, a proportion may refuse to pay. As we have seen, the criteria for taking on invoice discounting business is more stringent, the risk greater and the potential size of losses larger. So why compound the risk and uncertainty by taking assignments on debtors, who, in the event of difficulty, are going to present more problems in collection terms than their UK counterparts? This understandable reticence has been further aggravated by competitive elements. Until comparatively recently, UK exporters could obtain what amounted to an undisclosed invoice discounting line from the bank by simply using the ECGD facilities already described. Of course, these facilities are no longer available on an organized basis and it may have been in anticipation of this new situation that a group of quite illustrious institutional shareholders established, a few years ago, the Export Finance Company Ltd (Exfinco). This business was committed to developing and exploiting the niche market represented by exporters who wished to finance short-term export sales secured by ECGD insurance cover.

At first, all seemed to go reasonably well. Exfinco, in something like a three-year period, achieved a sales level of some £350 million and a client base of 190. A management team with strong experience in export finance was developed, and the business seemed set for expansion. Unfortunately, it would appear that the expansion of the business was accomplished by offering the finance too cheaply. Exfinco clients were offered funds as low as 1½ per cent plus base rate, with minimal service fees. They also received protection against adverse currency movements at little or no cost. Not surprisingly, Exfinco failed to achieve impressive profits; in fact during the whole of its history it did nothing but lose money. This was bad enough, but worse was to come. In May 1989, Exfinco found itself in dispute with receivers appointed by the Welsh Development Agency and with the Agency itself in relation to the entitlement to sums due from foreign customers of a failed Exfinco client. This dispute hinged upon the respective rights of

Exfinco and the WDA as evidenced by Exfinco's master agreement with the client and a debenture issued by the client to the WDA.

The fact that the agreement preceded the debenture should have meant that the rights of the WDA under the debenture were postponed against those of Exfinco. The authority did not accept this, however, and commenced legal proceedings. The problem then became one of technical legal interpretation of the master agreement which was a complex, and to some extent a contradictory one, and provided for purchases of goods as opposed to the purchase of the book debts created by their sale. The Vice-Chancellor found that the Exfinco client contract was defective in that at the time the goods were sold by the client to Exfinco and resold by the client as agent, the sale to Exfinco depended upon whether warranties concerning the goods had been complied with and this, most unfortunately and somewhat paradoxically, could not be known at the time of the sale.

The consequence of this legal mess was that the Vice-Chancellor handed down a reserved judgment in March 1990 against Exfinco. The fact that this was subsequently overturned in the Supreme Appeal Court of the Judicature was insufficient to save Exfinco and its bold experiment with export invoice discounting. The company ceased trading. Does the Exfinco experience prove that export invoice discounting has no future? It certainly underlines the importance for factors and for discounters of getting the basic client agreement right and ensuring that it is simple enough to leave no doubt that the well established methods of purchasing book debts are employed. It also drives home just how vital it is for discounters to ensure that they are charging a sufficiently high level of fees for the services they offer. Given the risks involved, a 'spread' of funding is simply not enough, especially if you are providing foreign currency protection. But by itself this does not mean that export invoice discounting will not develop. The strength of demand for the domestic product is undeniable. No doubt ways will be found of applying invoice discounting to export business.

Already, International Factors provide the service, and claim that demand is steady and growing. Other major factors also do so. For example, Hill Samuel Commercial Finance, the asset finance subsidiary of Hill Samuel Merchant Bank, will consider including export debtors as a constituent of the assets they will finance as part of their 'packaged lending' approach (see Chapter 10). Already they will handle ECGD-backed debts on this basis, generally making currency finance available and perhaps also providing specialist trade financing facilities such as duty deferment, confirmation of letters of credit, supplied bonds or foreign exchange contracts.

Hill Samuel are also providing clients with credit protection for discounted export debt. The cover is provided 'on the spot' by discounters located in the market concerned, and is claimed to be competitive with that hitherto available to UK exporters. Of course, the insurance provided is primarily for the benefit of the discounter, as the quality of the receivable is enhanced considerably by the fact that the customer risk is covered. The Hill Samuel product is targeted at the slightly larger, better established business, which has the management and technical skills to undertake serious exporting as well as a good financial track record. It seems likely that it will be well received. Many companies will find a growth-based facility that underpins export performance of considerable interest. Undoubtedly, other discounters will develop similar schemes in due course.

The benefits of export factoring

It was Sir Harold Wilson who said: 'Exporting is fun'. He should perhaps have added 'after you have been paid'. Anyone with more than a passing acquaintance with most exporting business knows that is far from easy and risk free. The mere effort of persuading customers in other countries with different customs and practices to buy and pay for your goods is demanding. It requires understanding of people, effective marketing, patience and good judgement. It can demand organizational skills of a high order and it involves financial risk.

A well designed export factoring arrangement can do a great deal to minimize that risk and simultaneously assist the exporter to market his or her product or service. By definition, factoring is an open-account service and many overseas buyers require open-account terms. There are substantial advantages attached to open-account trading, always assuming, of course, that the credit risk will be contained and managed. Documentary complexities are minimized, payments can be remitted quickly. The arrangement is flexible and the volume of credit granted can be geared to the customer's credit standing and payment record. Above all, the customer is no longer compelled to tie up valuable working capital by ensuring that adequate funds are available to meet a letter of credit. As we have seen, it is far too early to write the obituary of the letter of credit or even the bill of exchange, but there is little doubt that as world trade develops and people and corporations become closer, the pace of international trading speeds up. This means that an open-account-based service will provide the exporter with a quality which is increasingly in demand these days. It means that the trade-off between the management of commercial risk and the requirements of marketing and selling can be more finely tuned. No matter what its other virtues, the letter of credit and other bank collection systems cannot match that overwhelming advantage.

But that is not all. An export factor who is doing his or her job efficiently can remove fear. By providing promptly and effectively a credit line on a customer in a far-flung market place and by collecting the cash that export sale can be effectively turned into a domestic one. Exporters can ship in the full and certain knowledge that provided they have met their obligations under the contract in terms of the supply of goods and services, they will get paid. Others can provide a measure of relief in this area. ECGD has been doing it for many years now. Insurance companies can provide credit insurance and can go some way towards reassuring the marginal or particularly nervous exporter. They have expertise in credit assessment, as does ECGD who also has a vast database and information upon which it can draw—it maintains information on some 150 000 customers throughout the world and has in-depth experience of many products and market places. But having extensive records and contacts is not the same as being directly represented in the foreign market place and having access to relevant and up-to-date payment track record information. Any credit professional will confirm that there is no substitute for personal contact with the customer, and this means being on the spot. Import factors are there on the spot in all of the world's most important markets and they should be in the position to compete effectively in terms of quality and speed with any credit insurer who is not.

Similar considerations apply to other aspects of the export factoring package. In collection terms, import factors should be able to perform as effectively as any bank or agent. After a period of trading they will get to know the customers. They will be in a position to write in the customer's own language. So long as communication is good between the two factors involved and the client, credit terms are clear and there is a clear policy on collection, there is no reason at all why a reduction should not be achieved in the length of time foreign customers take to pay. British factors claim impressive success in reducing their clients' average debt turn in domestic sales. No comparable information exists with respect to export factoring, but there would seem to be every reason to believe that a combination of effective credit assessment and systematic collection will have the same effect. Collection policy can be firm or relatively relaxed in line with the client's requirement. The satellite communication systems employed by the big chains through which export factors are notified very quickly of the receipt of funds by the import factor, coupled with the enhanced use of international telegraphic transfer of funds under systems such as Swift, must mean that the transmission of funds is quicker and must compare well with situations where exporters are forced to struggle with the complexities of the international banking system.

Then there is the financial facility. Most export factoring clients will require money on account in exactly the same way as their domestic counterparts. Factors will provide it in a manner similar to that described above, and its sensible use should generate corporate growth in exactly the same way as in UK business. The added advantage is that some factors will provide advances in foreign currencies, with possible cost savings.

All in all, it is a formidable package which removes a large proportion of the risk and difficulty faced by enterprising businesspeople who wish to develop export marketing capability. Potential exporters still have to research their markets, perhaps adapt or modify products, look into local legal and commercial practices and when customers are located, effectively sell and dispatch their products. But more than any other service, export factoring removes risk and uncertainty after the point of sale, it speeds cash flow, it enables the exporter to compete with effective and realistic payment terms and provides funding for future expansion. A good many of the obstacles to exporting are thus removed. At its best, export factoring is a superb service. Moreover, it should appeal to smaller exporters, and to the type of company that has considered exporting but has declined to become involved because of the obvious risks and logistical difficulties. There are many such companies in the UK.

So what about the costs? The pricing structure is usually exactly the same as for domestic business, with a service charge levied upon the client's turnover to cover the service element, and a finance or discount charge for the factor's funds utilized within the business. It is probable that service charges will be marginally higher than those for domestic business of comparable size and quality. The mere fact that the exporter is operating in a variety of different market places will, by itself, dictate that the cost structure will be different. Most people can see that this is a matter of common sense.

For all that, it is without doubt this aspect which has, more than any other, held back the development of cross-border factoring. All too often, factoring facilities which could have brought considerable advantages to client and to export factor have been nipped in the bud because of difficulties in reaching agreement on a realistic arrangement with an import factor or factors who were unable to provide a service at a rate acceptable to the export factor and his or her client.

Here again, common sense will indicate that commercial conditions will vary widely between countries, as do cost structures. The cost and degree of difficulty involved in obtaining a piece of credit information will vary between, say, Sweden and the USA. The costs of collection will differ in various countries, as will the effectiveness of differing judicial systems. These elements are part of the very reason why an exporter should wish to use a factor's service in the first place. They also affect the factors themselves, however, and they have made it very difficult for even the most committed international factors to develop their businesses cross-border.

The development of the factoring chains (see below), coupled with the growth of open-account trading and the increased awareness of the potential of foreign trade among smaller businesses, will gradually reduce this problem. The managers of the major chains would argue that the problem of pricing has been virtually eliminated as their membership and sales volumes have grown. This may be so. Certainly, one of the more progressive UK factors has indicated to me that their average service fee rate for export business is no more than 1.2 per cent. If that is the case, they have a very attractive product indeed. They are, in effect, providing their export clients with a quality and range of services substantially higher than that available in a domestic context. And the cost is only marginally greater, even bearing in mind the considerably more complex nature of export, as opposed to domestic, trade.

All in all, it is not a particularly expensive package. And, of course, it is a package. While all the facilities—credit advice and protection, cash collection and transmission, currency protection and, finally, expansion finance—are available individually from different sources, only the factor provides all of them. In the past, reasonably priced export finance has been available from the banks, based upon ECGD export insurance. But as we have seen, those days are gone. Some exporters remain wedded to the idea that letters of credit are the only secure way to work with foreign customers. They are entitled to their view; after all, it is literally their business. But surely most people will recognize the point of view that, in a shrinking, changing world it is necessary to move with the times, to recognize that foreign customers will not always beat a path to your door, and to do something to assist your customers' cash flow, as well as your own.

The fact is that nowhere can the exporter obtain the same breadth of service at an economic cost as is available through an export factoring agreement. The problem is, of course, that the factors, true to form, have failed to market their service in anything like an effective manner. The service has been shamefully undersold and growth has been stunted, to the point where it has become almost *de rigueur* in factoring circles to regard the export service as a Cinderella.

The international factoring scene

It is not fair, however, to direct this criticism exclusively at UK factors. A glance at the FCI statistics in Appendix 10 shows that their foreign cousins and competitors are, in general terms, little better at the complex yet easy business of helping clients to export. The FCI statistics make it clear that there is some way to go before international factoring can be regarded as being a serious competitor to the more traditional methods of financing foreign trade.

Historically, British factors have faced tough competition from ECGD and their parent banks. The fact remains that the meagre level of export factoring achieved to date gives comfort to those in the industry who have long argued that export factoring is a waste of time, and, more important, money, that it is difficult, even impossible to make a reasonable return on capital by providing the service, and that in any case there is a huge task to be performed in the domestic market, so why bother with foreign ventures?

The problem with arguments of this kind, of course, is that they are entirely circular. Until such time as a factor gears up to handle foreign business on a grand scale, we will not know who is right, the conservatives, or the progressives who, broadly speaking, put forward arguments such as those set out above. The reason for the apparent caution of European and other overseas factors is not hard to pin down. They, like their British counterparts, have found that it is possible, where local circumstances are appropriate, to expand their businesses within their own, known and established territories, on a basis that is satisfactory to their shareholders. For one thing is quite clear. Factoring is expanding worldwide. The FCI statistics make that quite obvious. And, unlike in the UK, it would appear that the service that is taking off is factoring and not invoice discounting. Seen in this context, and as illustrated in Appendix 10, it is quite clear that world factoring is indeed on the map and is capable of growing fast. But there are signs, especially in countries such as Italy where growth has been fastest, that continued concentration on the domestic market leads, through increasingly strong competition, to over-supply. Some British factors claim to have noted this trend in the UK.

An obvious and natural solution to this situation is to begin to look overseas. And especially in circumstances where developments such as the Single European Market are getting under way, this would seem quite logical. Even the most blinkered factor or banking shareholder will see the force of this in due course.

All of this is speculation, of course. What is a fact is that the opportunity for expansion on a global scale exists. Factoring is established in all of the world's major market places and quite a few of the minor ones as well. Yet to date, there has been little, if any, movement by the shareholders of the main factors to acquire businesses in the same industry but in other countries. Indeed, there can be few industries where the take-over situation has been so static, and, given the essentially international nature of the business and its potential for cross-border development, this has to be regarded as surprising.

An explanation for this may lie with the nature of the shareholders in question. In many parts of the world, as in the UK, factoring shareholders are banks or other financial institutions. Their innate conservatism may well be reinforced by the fact that, not unnaturally, if they think in terms of mergers and acquisitions at all, they probably think in terms of other banks. Factoring is perhaps simply too small beer to figure prominently in the strategic plans of many of the organizations which run the industry. Equally of course, and as we have already seen, the fact is that factoring, especially in its international manifestation, is in direct competition with other banking services, so there may be a natural reluctance to think too deeply or act over-enthusiastically in respect of its international development.

On the surface, there are few signs of any change in this attitude. British factors, currently preoccupied with the impact of the worst recession to hit these shores for years, have shown little interest in domestic, let alone foreign, acquisitions. There have been persistent rumours of possible moves into the UK market on the part of foreign banking groups, insurance companies and the like—none have transpired.

MAJOR INTERNATIONAL FACTORS

De Lage Landen

Perhaps there are straws in the wind. The Dutch purchase of ECGD may indicate increased Continental interest in the British financial services sector, which may in turn stimulate a reverse trend. More relevant from the factoring point of view has been the establishment of De Lage Financial Services Limited, which is the UK arm of the Dutch finance house, De Lage Landen (DLL), itself owned by the Dutch Rabobank Group. DLL offers a mix of factoring, invoice discounting and leasing services, and is able to handle multi-directional factoring business through established fellow subsidiaries in Belgium, France, Germany and Italy as well as in Holland. In addition, there is a factoring unit in Hong Kong whose main *raison d'être* is to develop export business from the Far East to Europe. The Dutch company is also a member of FCI and, indeed, is one of the principal players within that chain. This seems to achieve the best of two worlds: the effective use of an existing, and perhaps growing, network, combined with membership of one of the main factoring chains to provide spread and choice to clients. DLL's services are aimed very specifically at internationally minded and based businesses—companies which like DLL, regard the European market place as one unified playing field within which they can trade, confident that one trusted and known organization is providing finance, credit protection and collection services. Significantly, DLL has recruited an experienced international factor as managing director. Philip Black, the former managing director of Barclays Commercial Services and one-time chairman of FCI, is at the helm of the DLL in the UK. It is perhaps also notable that it has been left to a Continental European organization to blaze even a modest trail in the direction of a wholly owned and coordinated network operation. One would have thought that, even bearing in mind past difficulties, one of the British factors would be thinking along the lines of creating a Europe-wide network. After all, they have the experience and, ultimately, the resources. They are owned and supported by institutions who are themselves part of a rich international tradition. If the banks wish to, they can accelerate the pace of change and develop export-based services that will really benefit both themselves and the British economy.

Factors Chain International
For the moment, however, we must review the situation as it is. The fact is that the international factoring scene is dominated by two major chains of independently owned factors from a wide variety of countries who provide, multi-directionally, the export and import factor services dealt with above. The world market figures shown in Appendix 10 are produced by the largest of these—Factors Chain International.

FCI was established in 1968 with the objective of providing a framework within which factoring companies worldwide could cooperate bilaterally in export/import factoring transactions. It is a non-exclusive organization open to any factoring company that can meet the basic equity requirements of US $1 million. Members are required to have an active interest in international factoring and should be concerned to promote the services outside their own domestic markets. In countries where FCI is already represented, new members will still be admitted provided they can demonstrate that they will contribute a significant volume of international factoring business to the chain's worldwide volume.

A second main objective is to assist members through the executive body, the Amsterdam-based secretariat and the operating committees in their efforts to simplify and rationalize the work and routines connected with international factoring business. We have already touched on the importance of this work. A number of formal steps have been taken to assist the smooth flow of import/export transactions, but in addition FCI sets some store on the individual member companies helping each other by passing on information and expertise where appropriate. The FCI information brief describes the organization as a professional association, and its philosophy appears to be liberal in concept in the sense that the exchange of business between members operates almost on a market basis. For example, if an export factor wishes to write a piece of business in a given market he or she has the option of choosing one of the FCI member import factors resident in that country. The relationship thus established need not be applied to all of the business that the export factor wishes to do in that particular market.

This liberal policy is applied, however, within a fairly well defined framework, both in terms of the legal relationship between the chain and its members, and the communication system. When two factors cooperate through the FCI chain an inter-factor agreement is signed, under which each of the parties subscribes to the provisions of a 'Code of International Factoring Customer and Rules of Arbitration'. The Code is comprehensive, well written and clear. It deals with the basis of the arrangement between the two factors, stipulates that any disagreement should be dealt with under the arbitration system, lays down a procedure for the assumption of credit risk and sets out the obligations that the import factor has to meet in terms of payment to the export factor. It sets out detailed arrangements for the resolution of disputes and the warranties that exist between the export and import factors. In other words, it provides a complete basis for the relationship between the two sides. The rules of arbitration are similarly comprehensive.

Equally important to the smooth running of the FCI system is the FACT system, which is an advanced inter-factor accounting and communications system, the purpose of which is to transfer information accurately and quickly among members of the chain. It was developed by FCI during 1983–4 with the Geisco Company, and is the exclusive property of the chain and its members. It is operated on Geisco's mainframe, and members of the FCI communicate with each other using Geisco's satellite telecommunications network. Its main features are that it simplifies and regulates inter-factor communications, accounting and reporting. It provides a basis for 'netting' advice so that factoring companies who are trading together can effectively net off the amounts due one way or the other, and it generates the FCI statistics that are produced on world factoring and which are summarized in Appendix 10.

FCI claim that the system has two great advantages. First, the fact that all communications by any factor user are channelled through a central processing point means that there is only one computer connection irrespective of the number of parties involved. This in turn means that the different factoring systems and computer configurations used by FCI members do not constitute any obstacle to efficient operations. Each FACT user simply has to develop an interface in-house system, according to the standards stipulated by FACT. This, they claim, will eliminate all paperwork and related mailing from the international factoring operations and enables members to utilize something like 34 different transaction formats, each of which represents a document used in international factoring such as invoices, credit notes, payment advices, requests for credit lines and so on. Of prime importance, of course, is the fact that it renders unnecessary a separate book-keeping operation by the two factors. Thus, FCI appear to have eliminated one of the main difficulties faced by international factors in the early years.

The chain also pays some attention to the question of education and training. Regular meetings are organized on factoring-related topics and FCI has developed a correspondence course on international factoring for the staff of member companies. In the same way that the Association of British Factors and Discounters operates in the education area, the course material has been produced by factoring professionals around the world. The administration is based on the secretariat of FCI in Amsterdam and there is an education committee which organizes testing for all the participating students.

FCI also stresses the importance of members meeting on a regular basis to discuss technical and legal issues and to exchange views on the problems inherent in international business. Such matters as the transfer times of international payments, new opportunities for the use of telecommunications systems and marketing all occupy time in this area. FCI claim that, in addition to obtaining immediate access to a network of import factors in some 36 foreign countries, a member taps into the largest pool of factoring know-how that can be found anywhere in the world. There is, of course, some truth in this. FCI has succeeded particularly well in extending its network not just throughout Europe but into the increasingly important Pacific basin and into South America. Assuming that international trade continues to expand, the network could become a very important feature and could provide a basis for the long-awaited expansion of export factoring.

International Factors Group

FCI does not have the market entirely to itself, however. Its main competitor is the International Factors Group which was founded in the 1960s, again as an association of factoring companies with the prime aim of handling cross-border business. In 1974, a permanent office was established in Brussels, and in 1980 a management company was formed in Belgium so that members of the chain are now shareholders of International Factors Group SA.

The original intention was to allow one member per country, but that policy was changed in 1987 thus providing some element of choice for export factors requiring to operate in any given market. At the same time, as Bert Meerman, the Secretary-General, points out, there are a number of features of the Group's operation which differentiate it. First of all, it operates what Meerman himself says is a rather tight and solid set of rules and procedures for international business. Moreover and very significantly, the pricing or commission arrangements for the Group are fixed. In other words, each export factor knows, when talking to an export client, precisely what will be the cost of credit protection and collection arrangements in any given territory because the price to be charged by the relevant factor has been fixed in advance. This obviously saves time in inter-factor negotiation and is a valuable sales advantage.

International Factors Group also have a computer-to-computer communications system to allow electronic data interchange between its members. This was established in 1980 and since then IFDEX has provided the basis for standardized inter-member business transactions. Its use is mandatory for the members, who as a consequence have the benefit of one electronic system. It is seen as the backbone of the Group's structure and provides enormous advantages in running the quite complex operation which cross-border factoring requires.

The Group claims that it accepts members only if they can demonstrate a real and positive interest in doing cross-border business. The list of International Factors Group members and shareholders shown in Appendix 11 indicates a well spread network which, if not quite so far-flung as that of FCI, does provide most exporters with choice in terms of the markets they can address. Export volume handled within the International Group is of the order of SFr 1700 million per annum and an additional SFr 850 million is handled by members on a direct export basis. Direct comparisons with volumes for FCI are made difficult and tedious by the problem of currency exchange, but it is obvious that in any event, International Factoring Group is making a substantial and growing contribution to the development of international business. The UK member of International Factors Limited is the market leader in this country and has shown a positive attitude towards international business, especially in recent years. Their international turnover is divided roughly equally between import and export business, and I am reliably informed that the business they handle is profitable, thus giving the lie to the suggestion frequently repeated in some factoring circles that it is impossible to make a profit from international factoring.

Heller International Group
The third international group providing cross-border services is the Heller International Group. Heller International Corporation is a wholly owned subsidiary of Fuji Bank Limited, the major Japanese bank. Heller is based in Chicago and has operating subsidiaries, Heller Financial Inc and Heller International Group Inc, providing specialized financial services to businesses worldwide, particularly those in the middle market. The US factoring company, with an annual factoring volume in excess of US $6 billion, is among the market leaders in the USA. They operate their factoring services through a series of subsidiaries, either partly or wholly owned, in some 12 countries throughout the world. The policy has been to form alliances and joint ventures with commercial and banking interests in each of these territories. The spread of representation looks adequate, but it does not appear that the Group's international activity is particularly well developed. To date, Fuji Bank do not seem to have put any real measure of their considerable resources behind the development of international factoring, and the Group has not really achieved any coherence as an international business. The individual members quite frequently transact business through FCI.

Nevertheless, the fact is that exporters in an increasingly wide variety of countries do have a choice. There are at least three chains with whom they can operate, together with the individual factors who will handle direct exports or imports according to their individual view of the market. Obviously, from the point of view of the individual exporter, it is important to be sure when negotiating with an export factor that the factor is competent in the market in which the business is exporting or perhaps, more important, where it intends to export in the future. It is important to press the factor about the details of the competence of the import factor(s) that are used in any given territory. Potential exporters should not be frightened to ask for information concerning the collection ability of those factors and the likely level of credit protection that can be offered. They should also enquire about the basis on which rates are settled and reviewed, they should look into the manner in which the two factors are likely to communicate with each other and probe as to the quality of the staff on either side of the operation. In particular, they should be certain that the staff running the export factoring operation are genuinely committed to the business of international factoring and are well resourced and supported. With the better export factors, one finds an element of strong commitment on the international side of the business, particularly among middle management and staff. People know that they are in a 'difficult' area of the business and strive very hard to provide their export clients with good service. On the other hand, there are factors who pay mere lip service to international business, treating the export side of their business in particular as a necessary evil, something that must be done because the competition does it. In the absence of clear enthusiasm the potential exporting client should simply look elsewhere.

Major foreign markets

Before looking in more detail at the UK export factoring scene it is useful to examine the position in some of the key international markets. The FCI statistics make it clear that a very high percentage of world factoring volume goes through relatively few countries, as follows:

	US $ (millions)
Italy	71.2
USA	49.0
UK	29.2
Japan	14.8
France	14.3
	178.5

This represents something like 72 per cent of world volume, and the reasons for the differences in the rate of development between these countries are quite interesting.

Italy
For example, observers believe that the market in Italy may now have reached maturity after a period of very considerable growth. This has been

fuelled by one of two somewhat unusual elements. Italy is an ideal place for factoring in some respects since it contains a larger percentage of very small companies than anywhere else in Europe. The EC average is some 24 per cent of the total, whereas the Italians have no less than 40 per cent of companies in this category. At the other extreme, of course, Italy has a tradition of large, corporate businesses which dominate various sectors of the market place. This has also helped the growth of factoring, since 35 per cent of the market is accounted for by what is known as 'captive' factoring, whereby the large corporates, companies such as Fiat, Olivetti, Pirelli and Zanussi, established their own factoring businesses which provide a service primarily for their suppliers. This, of course, enables them to enjoy the lengthy periods of supplier credit to which they are accustomed, provides the smaller supplier with the finance that he or she requires and enables the large Group to make a profit on the factoring operation.

It does appear that the rate of growth of 'captive' operations is slowing (*Financial Times* survey, 4 April 1991). Nevertheless, this fairly ingenious and typically Italian device has had its effect. There are now something like 80 factoring companies in Italy who are either bank subsidiaries or 'captives'. Consequently, competition has become tougher and rates are increasingly under pressure.

A further reason for the development of the Italian factoring industry has been the fact that until 1988 the Italian Government laid down credit ceilings on bank lending. For various reasons, factoring advances were excluded from this and so the bank-owned factors inevitably pushed business rapidly towards their factoring subsidiary companies. The fact that the factoring volume in Italy is now one and a half times greater than that of the UK indicates what can happen if the banks really put their minds to it! At base, though, the main reason for the quite spectacular growth is cultural. Italian customers are simply used to expensive and lengthy periods of trade credit and so both the 'captives' and the banks have found a ready market for the services which they have developed. Italy also illustrates well the pattern through which factors provide recourse-based services initially, developing non-recourse facilities only with experience.

USA
We have already noted the failure of US factors to diversify into broader market sectors outside textiles and clothing. Despite this, the US factoring market place is a very large one and in spite of the decline in the number of factors involved in the market place—from some 35 factors to around 18—there remains considerable expertise and skill in the US factoring industry. In particular, US factors are highly skilled at assessing credit risks. Nearly all US factoring is done on a non-recourse basis. Indeed, US factors regard recourse factoring, as well as invoice discounting, as being a purely

financial service. As a consequence, the competitive position is based very much on a factor's knowledge of the market place and capacity to perform in terms of credit assessment. US factors sell their files of information and expertise far more aggressively than do their fellows in other parts of the world. Indeed, it is this aspect which has perhaps contributed more than any other to the failure of the industry to move outside its chosen sector. When you become an expert in a particular line of business it is sometimes difficult to consider others. As long ago as 1981, a report prepared by R. S. Carmichael & Co Inc for the National Commercial Finance Association pointed out

> the inability of factoring organizations to capitalize on new markets in the past seems as much a result of defensiveness on the part of factors themselves as actual resistance by the market place.

Nothing has changed in this respect and the position has, if anything, become more entrenched. The development of new financing techniques, and in particular the spate of leveraged buy-out activity that gripped the USA during the mid-1980s, has left the factors vulnerable and defensive. A number of their major customers, including the large retailing groups, have been the subject of leveraged buy-outs which have left them in a relatively weak and over-geared position, so that factors are faced with the problem of underwriting and financing the same volume of goods through business units which are nowhere near so financially healthy as was the case a few years ago.

Despite this, and perhaps because of it, US factors still seem unable to diversify, and some people are of the view that they are in exactly the same position as a business which is concentrating on too narrow a customer base. From the outside, at least, there would seem to be a strong and urgent need for the factors to act more strategically, to look hard at possible market niches where their services and highly developed skills could be applied successfully and to make more effective use of information and cross-marketing techniques. Easier said than done, particularly for organizations which have been in a particular groove for a number of years now. For all this, US factors have a history of profitability and good return on capital employed, and while it is possible that there may be some consolidation in the industry, there could equally be moves from outsiders, especially the Japanese. We have already remarked on the purchase by Fuji Bank of the Heller Organization. Fuji's competitor, Dai Ichi Kango, has also bought a controlling interest in CIT, Heller's main rival, so this process may have already started. What is also perhaps surprising is the fact that the major US corporates have not themselves thought of the idea of 'captive' factoring. This may itself reflect their conservative approach and the feeling that factoring is so closely related to the textiles and clothing business that it has little relevance to their own industry or situation.

Japan

The Japanese themselves appear to be taking factoring quite seriously after a period when there was comparatively little interest. Both FCI and International Factors Group have members in Japan, and it seems likely, given the nation's reputation for thoroughness and hard work, that they will in due course develop the factoring business in much the same way as they have paid attention to other areas of the financial services sector and to manufacturing. At present, of course, the volume of exports represents a tiny proportion of Japan's huge export volume, and it may well be that the important Japanese banks that have bought into factoring will concentrate on taking equity positions around the world. As we have already noted, their acquisition of Heller has not yet resulted in any dramatic movement, either in the USA or Europe, but increased Japanese involvement in the factoring business cannot be discounted.

France

For a long time, the factoring industry in France suffered badly from exactly the same kind of indifferent reputation that we have already discussed in relation to the UK business. In addition, the tradition in France was to discount bills of exchange or *traite* which were frequently attached to invoices. Once a customer had accepted a *traite*, it was a simple matter to arrange discounting with one of any number of commercial banks on a fairly cost-efficient basis, and so many French companies operated in this way for many years. Recently, there have been increased signs of growth in the market place, although the industry has by no means reached its full potential in France. There are some 15 companies in the market and the leaders, Facto France Heller and Société Française de Factoring, are both at least partially foreign owned. Facto France is 50 per cent owned by the Heller Group, while SFF is part of the Boston Overseas Financial Corporation. It may be that the French banks are somewhat ambivalent on the subject of factoring, although a number of them have now taken stakes in the factoring industry which does seem set to grow, particularly when the European Community dismantles the internal barriers on financial services.

Germany

At first sight, the performance of the German factoring industry is poor. The economic powerhouse of Europe appears to have passed the industry by. Cultural elements are again relevant. German companies traditionally pay their bills reasonably promptly, and so the demand for debtor-based finance is less pressing than in some countries. Again, one senses that the approach of some of the German banks is less than enthusiastic towards the factoring industry—some of the most severe comments I have ever heard on the subject have been made by German bankers, many of whom are not known for their progressive views. But the main reason for the failure of the industry to take off may well stem from the position in German law whereby companies are permitted to ban the right of a supplier to assign debts to a third party. This doctrine, known in Germany as *Abtretungsverbot*, has caused particular difficulties in relation to the German retail sector and the car industry.

Relief in this area may be at hand for the German factoring companies. Some years ago, the International Institute for Unification of Private Law (UNIDROIT) was established in Italy, with the difficult objective of assisting in the process of harmonizing business and commercial law. It turned its attention to the study of factoring law, particularly in relation to the possibility of achieving a standard factoring agreement. Given the complexity of this area, it was decided that this could not be achieved at one stage, but since then progress has been made on the question of assignment of debt. In 1988, at a conference initiated by UNIDROIT in Ottawa, representatives of some 60 countries met to finalize a convention, the object of which was to assist in the clarification of anomalies in national laws relating to factoring. Among the issues addressed was the issue of prohibition of assignment. As yet, the convention has not been ratified by any country other than France, but the point is that the passing of the convention lends some force to the arguments of German factors who, inevitably, are having to lobby quite hard with their own Government to achieve a change in the law. It seems probable that this will take place in due course, and once it does, Germany could become a powerful factoring nation, particularly in view of the recent reunification and the opportunities that are opening up in the eastern part of the country.

Worldwide, the industry should now be set fair to take advantage of the expansion of world trade that will occur once current recessionary conditions are replaced by expansion. Particularly encouraging is the development of factoring in such areas as the Asia Pacific region, which for a long time was an area in which documentary credit terms were the basis of international trading. There is a long way to go—the international sales volume represents only 5 per cent of the total factoring carried out in Asia—but at least a start has been made, and the presence of over 100 factors in the region should help to open up the situation further.

The export dilemma

Despite such progress, the fact has to be faced that the contribution made by factoring to cross-border business is disappointing. Only 5.6 per cent of the world factoring turnover in 1990 related to international business. Factors the world over prefer to stick to their domestic markets. True, there are some notable exceptions such as Turkey where, for some reason, 90 per cent of the business transacted is international, and countries such as the Netherlands and Germany, with around 30 per cent. By contrast, the more successful factoring countries concentrate primarily on domestic business.

The UK is not exempt from this general trend. Some 4 per cent of total factoring and invoice discounting turnover is international, but more than 46 per cent of this relates to import as opposed to export business. Since 1988, when the ABFD started distinguishing between import and export business in its annual collation of factoring statistics, the total international volume has expanded by around 25 per cent per annum, but the proportion of imports has amounted to about half and, if anything, is expanding faster than exports. Anyone reading the factors' publicity material would form the view that they are dedicated to helping the British exporter. They are not. Of all the ABFD members only three, Lombard Commercial Services (export sales around £75 million, and declining), International Factors (£107 million including recourse sales, and expanding) and Alex Laurie (£55 million, and static) are doing any export business of consequence. For the most part, the rest simply provide import factoring services which, apart from the fact that there is at least some contribution to the UK balance of payments through the service and discount charges earned by the factor, are essentially the same as UK domestic business.

Now there is no reason why export business is inherently more desirable than domestic. Factors are commercial organizations with responsibilities to shareholders. If the shareholders do not wish the export business to be developed, then they are entitled to take that view. The problem is, however, that over the last 25 years a number of misconceptions have grown up within the UK factoring industry concerning export factoring which are perhaps inhibiting development of the service. Factoring people will tell you that it is impossible to make a profit from export business. They will claim that it is risky and that, above all, there is little sign of a genuine market for the service. They will point to the problems that can arise in the daily operation of arrangements between import and export factors, particularly in relation to the question of rates to be charged for credit and collection services. Sometimes, these conversations take place against a background of genuine puzzlement. Some factors cannot understand why it is apparently so difficult to sell export services. There are, of course, elements of truth in these arguments but for the most part they are ill-founded. The reason why export factoring is not by now an important and well developed service for a large number of export businesses is, quite simply, because the factoring industry itself has failed to sell it. There are compelling reasons why it should do so. Much of this book has been devoted to the problems faced by the industry in terms of its image. One of the prime criticisms levied against factors is cost. The associated argument is that the service element of factoring is not worth paying for and, as we have seen, the suggestion is that client companies are simply paying a premium within the service charge for the privilege of using the factor's funds.

If there is one area where this kind of argument can be disproved beyond all reasonable doubt it is in export factoring. As we have seen, the export factor provides genuine added value in the form of a coherent package of services that is not available elsewhere. If factors want to disprove the critics, they need do no more than draw attention very boldly to their international capabilities.

It is also demonstrably possible to make a profit on export factoring. Once a satisfactory arrangement has been made with an import factor, he or she bears the critical costs of credit and collection. It is not necessary to maintain extensive credit and collection staff to operate export factoring. It may well be necessary to do so in order to handle the reciprocal import business which may occur through membership of a chain, but that is another matter and the costs will be met by the profit from the handling of the import business. In either context, export or import, what is essential is to negotiate realistic arrangements with factoring partners which cover the costs involved by both sides of the border, providing the import factor with a reasonable profit and enabling the export factor to do business effectively with the client. If, in relation to a specific piece of business, the characteristics are such that it is difficult to accomplish it within the chain arrangements, then the potential client will not receive a quotation for export factoring.

Then there is the question of the size of the market and the competitive situation. Many factors will point to a series of apparent obstacles to progress: the existence of the ECGD, the apparent fact that many major exporters are large businesses who, traditionally, do not require factoring, the suggestion that much of British export trade is committed to the export of major capital items sold on long terms of credit or the fact that many products are sold to 'difficult' markets, such as the Middle East. All of these arguments are regularly trotted out whenever the issue is raised.

It has to be admitted that most exporters are used to well tried methods of financing export sales, and unless compelling reasons can be put forward they are reluctant to abandon them. The point is, of course, that there are compelling reasons. The world is changing. It is no longer good enough for British exporters of all shapes and sizes and in all industries simply to expect to field requests from former colonial markets in a quasi-Imperial way, informing their customers that a product will be available just as soon as an irrevocable London confirmed letter of credit is opened in good time. Life is much more competitive these days. The balance of British trade has shifted fundamentally into Europe and will continue to do so. There are important reasons why exporters need to compete on an open-account basis and with efficiency and drive. The care for export factoring has never been stronger.

So far as ECGD is concerned, it is a fact that the arrival of factoring on these shores was in some respects ill-timed. Just at the time when ECGD was flexing its financial as well as its insurance-based muscles, and undoubtedly helping exporters with cheap funding, factors started to sell their export services. Inevitably, this proved difficult and the legacy of this difficulty has remained with a number of them ever since. But this excuse has now dropped away. No longer are the banks in a position to provide what is, in effect, subsidized funding on the back of an ECGD guarantee. ECGD itself has been through a period of travail, culminating in the sale by the Government of the short-term Insurance Service Group (ISG) to the Dutch credit insurance company NCM Holdings. There is inevitably considerable uncertainty as to just how this arrangement will work out in terms of the services provided for UK exporters. NCM is the world's fourth largest trade credit insurer, however, and whatever happens there is no doubt that in future at least ECGD short-term services will be provided on a commercial basis. The playing field will be a level one, and there is no reason at all why export factoring should not compete effectively. As we have already seen, provided properly, the service offers exporters a number of benefits which ECGD, or for that matter any other credit insurer, is unable to match.

All that is required is the ability to sell the service. It is a quite complex service; exporters are sometimes difficult to sell to, but then so are other people. Factors in some ways are in a privileged position in this respect. They have a client base of companies, most of whom are interested in expansion. Not all of them are exporters, although some of their products could perhaps be adapted for export markets. All they need in many cases is advice and encouragement to become exporters. The factor who adopts a prudent but aggressive approach among its domestic clients could in due course reap export benefits.

There is little evidence that many factors are adopting this approach. If anything, the reverse is probably the case. I believe that the real reason for the failure of export factoring to take off lies with the factors themselves and the banks that own them. We have already discussed the conflicts that exist in relation to bank shareholders and the development of domestic business. These are even more obvious in relation to exporting. The banks have well developed international services of all kinds, usually operated on a separate basis from their domestic operations but nevertheless working in competitive markets. The inhibitions relating to cross-selling that always exist in circumstances like these are certain to apply to export factoring.

Yet there are surely powerful reasons why the banks should promote export factoring. The range of services available to exporters from the banks and from other sources is complex and fragmented. The banks themselves, government departments, ECGD, chambers of commerce, export clubs and associations, and private organizations of all kinds proffer assistance to exporters in all forms. Few can provide the breadth of the package that the factoring service offers. The fact that various services in marketing, finance, transportation and so on are so fragmented should surely provide the factors and their banking shareholders with opportunities to present the service as one which is genuinely well coordinated and designed. Indeed, it is not fanciful for export factoring to be used as a base through which a complete export-based financial package could be mounted, using other banks' services together, if necessary, with those of other service suppliers. The combination of factoring, discounting, credit insurance and trade finance could be a powerful one if developed and promoted properly.

Little, if any, effort has been made to develop the marketing of export factoring upon these lines. Call into any chamber of commerce, indeed, call upon the Institute of Export itself, and you will find blissful ignorance of the services that are available and of the benefits they can present. This is not the fault of the recipient, of course. Blame must be laid fairly and squarely with the factoring industry and its shareholders. The critical comments made in Chapter 10 about the marketing of factoring apply even more especially to the export service for, among other things, they are missing an admirable public relations opportunity. Everyone, in principle at least, is in favour of exporting. British companies are supposed to be gearing up to meet the challenge posed by the development of the European markets. The banks and other financial institutions should be doing all they can to assist them in their endeavours. Few of the services already described can provide the essential cutting edge that the exporter requires to at once shelter risk and develop his or her international business. The factors and their banking shareholders should broadcast this fact to the world and do all they can to assist companies of all sizes to export.

There appears to be some doubt as to the total size of the market place represented by exporters. The Government does not provide figures for the total number of exporting companies and HM Customs & Excise say that they do not collate them. I have heard estimates varying between 6000 and 10 000 businesses that are supposed to be involved. Then there are the companies whose products would be suitable for development in the export market place if the businesspeople involved could be confident that they would be paid on time and would not suffer extensive bad debts at the hands of foreigners. No one knows the size of what could be called the 'tentative export market'.

A major opportunity is going begging. It is too easy to lay the blame wholly on the shareholders' doorstep, however. There is a need for a culture change within the factoring companies themselves. For many people within the industry, it has been achieving exactly what is required; year by year growth, profitability, gradually increased public awareness, all of these have been developed, In these circumstances, why venture outside the domestic market place? This point of view can be defended especially in terms of the requirement placed upon individual managers to turn in profit figures year after year. From the FCI statistics it is apparent that most of the factoring world feels the same way. My personal view is that this approach is short-sighted and unambitious. How many of the City's major institutions, banks, merchant banks and other insurance companies would have reached their present pre-eminence had they restricted themselves to operating purely in the UK market place?

The reluctance of many factors to get seriously involved in international business parallels the insularity of the British at large. The British Prime Minister has recently concluded negotiations with our EC partners at Maastricht, returning in apparent triumph with a deal which in many ways isolates the UK from her European partners. This has been widely welcomed in the UK and met with total incomprehension in most foreign capitals. There is little doubt that attitudes on the national level will have to change quite dramatically within the next few years as Europe develops and international trade increases. Attitudes within the factoring industry will have to change, too.

In practical terms, this means that the enthusiasts within factoring businesses who wish to pursue overseas work (and they do exist) will have to be encouraged. Sales teams, who in the past have rarely been expert in dealing with the special problems presented by export business, will need better training. Operational staff may well have to learn foreign languages or be specifically recruited for these skills. Above all, top management will have to regard the international side of their business as being, in potential at least, equally as important as the domestic.

Of course the service itself, good as it can sometimes be, may have to be changed if export factoring is to emerge as a real contributor to the international market place. This chapter has laboured the point that the service is broadly based, capable of fulfilling several needs. What no one appears to have done, outside the factoring industry as well as within it, is to look at the needs and requirements of the exporter in the round. Aside from any consideration of the effect of such an approach in terms of the national interest, there is no doubt at all that the exporter represents a well defined and discrete market sector. It is one that will grow and develop as the process of internationalization, touched on earlier in this chapter, gets under way. Given the imagination, factors are well placed to consider developing services which meet the increasingly diverse needs of exporters, actual and putative.

This will entail a complete change of approach. Traditionally, most business opportunities presented to factors are overwhelmingly domestic in respect of the split between UK and export business. The factors frequently take on export business almost as an addendum to the domestic, using the latter as a profit base. As conditions, particularly in Europe, evolve, it seems likely that this situation will change. British companies, faced with competition from Calais to Kiev, will be forced to adapt and to regard the customer in Europe in no different a light to the one in Birmingham. The only question is whether the factors will anticipate this change of approach or simply react to it. Those who have been preparing for this change are more likely to get their timing right, and those that get their timing right will almost certainly reap substantial rewards in due course.

13. *Boom, bust and boom again?*

Some people used to put forward the view that factors could be immune from the effects of the trading cycle. The argument went like this: when the economy was expanding, companies needed funds to finance growth and a service to control debtors, so they would naturally turn to the factors. If recessionary conditions prevailed, the factor might lose some money through customer bad debts, but would be more than compensated by the enhanced level of demand for finance from businesses whose overdraft facilities were being squeezed by the banks and who had, perhaps belatedly, realized the importance of credit protection in an uncertain world. This kind of argument was also used by those critics of factoring who saw the service as nothing more than a form of last-ditch finance, keeping alive companies which would, in the natural order of things, have gone to the wall. Consequently, the linkage which some saw between factoring and recession did the industry no good at all, perpetuating the image of a service aimed at propping up inadequately capitalized businesses rather than picking winners and growing with them.

The recession at the end of the 1980s put paid to this argument once and for all. It proved beyond doubt that recession is bad for factors, for the banks that own them, for their customers and for their clients. With the possible exception of insolvency practitioners, no one has done well out of it. Factors are cautious folk, and there has not been a great outburst of complaint at the way market conditions have affected their business. But they have suffered. On the most obvious level, corporate profitability has declined. Factors who, two or three years ago were turning in pre-tax profits of several million pounds, have seen these reduced dramatically. Even those who have retained a reasonable level of profits have found it harder to sustain performance. This is not hard to explain. The factors are in the front line of the recessionary battle.

Nowhere, of course, is this more true than in relation to client losses. There are no publicly available statistics covering this sensitive area, but scrutiny of some of the factors' accounts confirms the rumours prevalent in the market place concerning the large, sometimes very large, sums of money that some factors have lost through client failure, fraud or a combination of both. Quite obviously, recessionary conditions bring the risks to the fore. In the latest recession, the market for some small businesses has been slashed out of all recognition as larger organizations cut back on purchasing or cancel projects. This plunges the supplier into an immediate cash flow crisis, which can be solved only by finding new customers quickly or by retrenchment. The first option is often unrealistic, the second impossible as the business is already operating with minimum overheads. Such conditions make an increase in fraud almost inevitable, but it appears that many of the factors have been shocked this time around by the extent of the fraud committed, and in some cases by the identities of the people involved. Stories abound within the factoring fraternity of long-standing, apparently honest, clients who, when faced with the apparent option of postponing the demise of the business which they had worked so hard to develop, and attempting to defraud the factor who had helped to achieve it, chose the latter. Not unnaturally, such cases cause considerable bitterness. People within factoring companies take some pride in watching their clients' businesses grow—it is the most rewarding aspect of the service—and they feel personally let down when the inevitably messy and unpleasant aftermath of a fraud situation has to be dealt with.

Such situations, combined with recession-induced client losses which are attributable to other causes, weak management within the client's business or perhaps simple bad luck, induce a feeling of pessimism in the factor's operation which is difficult to remove. The feeling grows that things will never be the same again. The recession, having arrived and taken its toll, will never quite go away again. Of course, in a sense this is true. Dramatic changes in trading conditions do leave their mark. The risk is that the somewhat traumatic experience will leave the factor's staff with an enhanced sense of caution which, however justified in some cases, cannot be applied to all business situations if the industry is to continue to grow.

That this is not a fanciful analysis is borne out by the statistics produced on behalf of the member companies of the ABFD for 1991 (Appendix 1). Under the impact of the recession, for the first time factoring turnover failed to grow. The decline of around 6.5 per cent in domestic non-recourse business is hardly cataclysmic in the midst of the worst trading conditions which many in the industry have ever experienced. But it does undoubtedly reflect a setback, and one which in turn underlines the changes which are taking place within the industry and in its market place. Export factoring showed a decline of some 9.4 per cent, while invoice discounting continued its advance.

The trend may not continue. Better trading conditions may see a resumption of the scale of growth that the industry has come to regard as being normal. But the fact cannot be escaped: the factoring industry is now dominated by invoice discounting. It would be more appropriate, given the divergence in growth rates of the respective services, for the last two initials of the ABFD to be reversed. More to the point, the results drive home the remarks already made in Chapter 10 about the confusion which exists with regard to the marketing of factoring.

The path to real growth

A main theme of this book has been whether and how the factoring industry should and could expand to something like that which could be regarded as its true potential. In the light of these developments, is not this a mere pipe-dream?

On one level, there is no reason why an industry which accounts for only a minor part of the total bank lending to commerce and industry should be called upon to play a wider role. If the shareholders are content with the current situation, why change it? It can be argued that this is just the kind of situation where the operation of market forces indicates perfectly well what is desirable and what is not. If more businesspeople want factoring they will be prepared to pay for it, and it will expand commensurately, and vice versa. Much depends on your view of how market forces should and do work.

It is possible, however, to put this point in a rather different way. We are not in the perfect market so beloved by classical economists. This is not to say that no competition exists, merely that it is a fairly specialized form of competition in that the ownership of the industry is in the hands of organizations who tend to see the world from a particular point of view. Analysis of the turnover of the factoring subsidiaries of the main clearing banks, taking the combined total of factoring and invoice discounting turnover as being the defined market, indicates that, even after the advances made in recent years by 'smaller' banks such as the Royal Bank of Scotland and Hill Samuel, the subsidiaries of the 'big four' between them still hold more than 70 per cent of the total market share.

The 'free market' argument has to be judged in this context. There is no evidence that the clearers work together to stifle competition—indeed, there is every reason to believe that even the two Lloyds subsidiaries compete with each other. It is just that their dominating position, in an industry which can be regarded as being almost peripheral to their core business, means that none of the clearers have the incentive to develop their factoring operations.

Is there any reason why they should? And if the market potential and scope is so great, what is there to stop others from entering the market and addressing the 100 000-odd companies who could use factoring, and do not do so?

To deal with the second question first, the obvious answer is that, of course, there is nothing to stop anyone doing so, except the simple point that the performance of those factors without clearing bank support has hardly been spectacular over the past 25 years. True, the non-clearing bank sector is expanding in numeric terms. As we have seen, there is a large group of non-bank-owned factors, operating both inside and outside the ABFD, who fulfil the essential function of providing businesses with additional choice. None of them, including the biggest, have set the factoring world alight in terms of market share. Neither, it has to be said, have they been especially innovative or aggressive in marketing terms. One looks in vain at the independent sector for any evidence of the kind of original or creative approach that characterizes smaller, independent companies in other industries. If the commanding heights of the available market are to be scaled, it will require either a braver and more innovative independent company than has so far emerged, or a rush of blood to the head of one of the clearing bank subsidiaries.

This brings us to the first question—slightly rephrased—why should any of the clearing banks take the factoring industry seriously? Why, with all of the other problems that pile up on his or her desk, should a top executive in one or other of the clearing banks bother about a subsidiary which, while being profitable, in good years at least, and providing a reasonable service to bank customers, as part of a wide portfolio of products, provides a relatively meagre contribution to group profitability? To this slightly leading question one has to add the even more important point that the development of the service in question would probably be at the expense or even to the detriment of other bank services, notably the overdraft lending, which for a very long time has provided the core of the banking services used by most companies in the UK.

On the face of it, the response to this question is obvious. It is the response that the banks have been giving to anyone who has asked this question (although I am not sure that too many people have asked it) during the past 25 years. It is, of course, that there is no reason why they should. But one does not need to look too far back in history to find reasons why the banks should perhaps think again. For the fact of the matter is that, in some senses at least, the tide of events is moving towards the factors, not away from them. In the first place, there is a new awareness in this country about the importance of small business. Historically, the UK has lagged behind its main commercial rivals in the recognition and support provided for small and medium-sized companies as opposed to corporate giants. If, a quarter of a century ago, a government minister, senior civil servant or even perhaps a respected banker had been asked to define what was meant by 'industry' there is little doubt that the response would have involved associations with large-scale corporate business. Indeed, there was a period in British political life when conventional wisdom had it that one of the reasons for the apparent perpetual inability of British companies to continue to dominate world markets was the fact that the average size of our businesses was too small. Big was beautiful; it provided for economies of scale, for long production runs and permitted businesses to engage the level of resources that was needed to win market share.

As is so often the case, proponents of conventional wisdom overlooked that which lay under their noses. For the fact was, and is, that in many of the more successful European countries it was widely recognized that, while large conglomerates had an obviously important role to play, smaller business, too, could make a vital contribution. Even the Japanese, whose business units tended to be on the large side, were, among other things, busily devising techniques of management, the net effect of which was to break down units and processes to a human-sized scale so as to enhance worker participation and commitment to the organization.

Britain is a deeply conservative country and it took a long time for this message to gain acceptance. But it has now been absorbed by the Government, by its political rivals, by the Civil Service and last but not least, by the banks. Most of these organizations are apt to issue a plethora of statistics seeking to demonstrate beyond doubt the vital role small business plays in the UK and even in the world economy. Indeed, we may even have reached the point where the message has been repeated so many times that a degree of boredom has set in. Yet to date, the necessary connection has not been made, at official level or otherwise, between a service which is purpose-built to serve the needs of small business, and small business itself.

A very senior member of the general management of a clearing bank, with whom I spoke while researching this book, was, without question, a factoring enthusiast. He told me that were he in a position to do so he would, without hesitation, support the conversion of huge tranches of overdraft facility currently granted to the bank's customers to factoring or to invoice discounting. Such a move would, in conditions of economic stringency, render the bank immediately more secure by virtue of the factor's ability to monitor the facility.

The problem, of course, is that such a course of action is quite impracticable. It would meet entrenched opposition from the line management of the bank, from branch managers and, probably, from the customers themselves. We agreed that what was required was a gradual process of education and building of awareness among all the parties concerned. Brushing aside the point that the banks have had more than 25 years to get such an operation under way, why should they commence it now?

From the point of view of the banks themselves, there would seem to be some quite compelling arguments in favour of the positive development of their factoring subsidiaries. The clearers have faced some pressing problems in recent years, some of which are quite clearly connected with the market sector in which their factoring companies operate. First and foremost, the British bankers' pride and joy, the bank overdraft, has been seen to have certain limitations. It has one overwhelming advantage—its simplicity. But from the point of view of the small to medium-sized commercial customer, it has severe shortcomings, especially in terms of the level of security required.

Thus in many cases, especially where the bank manager is unable to countenance introducing the services of a factor, the lending takes place by means of an overdraft facility secured upon assets outside the business, generally, especially in recent years, the property of the directors or other participants in the business. This is all well and good until such time as the bank becomes uneasy about the continuing level of overdraft being extended. During recent recessionary conditions, this has been a not uncommon experience for many bankers dealing with small businesses. The entrepreneurs, in turn, have frequently been reminded, in no uncertain terms, that overdraft facilities can be called in without any period of notice, and that a bank which has taken a fixed and floating charge over the assets of a business can exert considerable power over it.

This is not to say that bankers habitually lend recklessly or deal with smaller customers in an insensitive manner, although some undoubtedly do so, and a fair proportion of the banks' public relations difficulties at the beginning of the current decade have been based on such beliefs. Nor is it suggested that all factors are perfect in dealing with their customers. The fact remains, however, that by any fair standards, a comparison between the two types of facility—bank overdraft and factoring—must allocate at least some points in favour of the latter. As we have seen, so long as clients stick to the provisions of their factoring agreement, which in practical terms means that they continue to offer to the factor valid and collectable debt, there is no reason why a facility should be curtailed.

This is not to argue that all bank lending should, in due course, be replaced by factoring or invoice discounting. Such a view is entirely unrealistic. What would seem sensible, however, and here we are considering the position from the point of view of the banks as opposed to that of their customers, is that there should be much greater emphasis upon the provision of joint facilities, and rather more enthusiasm on the part of the bankers for practical cooperation with their factoring associates than appears to take place at present.

This will probably pose the need for much more day-to-day cooperation between bankers and factors. As we have seen, the banks operate their factoring organizations separately from their mainline banking ones. You will not find a factoring representative at even the largest bank branches, let alone an operational factoring or invoice discounting unit. There are virtues in this approach. The banks have always regarded factoring and factors as being something distinct from mainline banking, and in many respects they are right. But if the intention were to really raise the profile of the service, and to go for the kind of growth that should be possible, given the size and development of the market, then the requirement to work together more closely would undoubtedly arise. Moreover, in an increasingly cost-conscious world, where the banks are judged at least partly by their ability to manage their branch networks on a controlled basis, there could well be opportunities to achieve greater harmony as well as to save money. It is by no means certain that the advent of such 'togetherness' would be welcomed universally by all those in the factoring business. Twenty-five years is quite long enough to develop individual corporate cultural characteristics and a certain unwillingness to face structural change, and no doubt some of the factors would not be over-enthused by the prospect of closer cooperation. But you cannot have things both ways. If people in the factoring industry really believe that their services are capable of being sold and operated on a wider stage, then they should be prepared to move with the times.

A degree of physical integration might bring benefits to some of the bank-owned factors in terms of a greater flow of business opportunities from bank to factor and a better understanding of their shareholders' viewpoint, and vice versa. Yet organizational change, even on a large scale, would be as nothing compared with the potential impact which could be brought about if the banks were to develop the factoring product in tandem with their own. Factoring, in product development terms, has virtually stood still for a quarter of a century, the bank overdraft for much longer, and the letter of credit for longer still. There have been great changes in recent years in the ways in which banks deal with large corporations, with governments and with each other. The City of London has faced more changes in the past decade through de-regulation than perhaps for a century. Yet the principles and practice of corporate short-term lending, especially where smaller companies are concerned, remain unaltered and based on the overdraft.

The limitations of this facility have already been mentioned. No statistics exist, but it is almost certain that the overwhelming number of cases for which the banks received criticism during 1990–91 related to situations where the proprietors had pledged personal assets, as well as those of their business, in support of a small company overdraft. It is possible that factoring, or the services and expertise of a bank factor, possibly in another guise, might have been useful to bank and customer in many of those cases. If a further dimension is added, and the thought entertained that some kind of marriage could be arranged between the two products, providing the advantages of both, and combining the skills and strengths of both bankers and factors, then it is entirely possible that heart attacks of a severe kind will occur in august banking parlours. On balance, it is preferable, however, that such seizures should occur among the bankers rather than their customers, and there is at least the possibility that a little creative thought in this area could bring forth some distinct improvements in banking services and assist the development of the factoring industry.

In many ways, the economic condition of the UK is ripe for just this kind of heretical thinking and for the development of factoring. The recession will come to an end, and when it does, businesses will require the right kind of financial support in order to develop. In view of their experiences during the period of difficulty, it is possible that the banks will be more cautious than hitherto, and this by itself may provide the factors with more scope. But there is more to the current economic scene than this. It is not always realized just how fundamental has been the decline in British manufacturing output during the past decade. During the 1980s, UK manufacturing output was overtaken by all of our main competitors. Whereas UK manufacturing output rose by some 6 per cent during the period, the OECD average was 35 per cent, and Britain was second from bottom, in terms of the growth of manufacturing, of all the OECD countries (*The Observer*, 'Unlucky 13 for the Economy', 5 April 1992). It is possible to read most things from statistics, but few would disagree that, whatever the benefits of the 1980s, the development of the UK manufacturing base was not one of them. Indeed, in the middle of the decade, there was apparently serious discussion among certain economists as to whether the economy could grow and prosper based entirely upon efficient service industries.

Such nonsense is now a thing of the past, and as is the way with such things, the trend is going the other way. People are considering ways in which the economy can be underpinned by an effective manufacturing sector, how people can be trained to develop and produce things, and how best we can compete within Europe and in world markets generally.

Factoring is not relevant just to manufacturing, but it can be highly effective in financing the growth of a manufacturing business. Moreover, the other chief feature of the past decade, the development of the smaller business culture, is, or should be, totally in line with what ought to be the strategic objectives of the factors. There is no doubt that the increased emphasis placed by Government in the 1980s upon smaller business—the 'enterprise economy'—had its effect in stimulating factoring growth in those years. The climate has changed for good. There is no evidence, however, that the factors have succeeded in any real sense in becoming identified with the change in mood.

Similar considerations apply to exporting. Recent economic history leads inevitably to the conclusion that the days of British insularity and nostalgia for an Imperial past are gone for good. Britain stands or falls in terms of her ability to compete in world markets with other industrialized nations and with the emerging ones. It is acknowledged that one of the prime reasons for smaller businesses, in particular, showing reluctance to export is fear of slow or non-payment. The factoring industry has a great opportunity here to provide the tool which could cure this problem once and for all and put factoring on the map. As has already been noted, the sale of ECGD's short-term export credit division to the Dutch NCM concern may well provide an opportunity for British factors to gain a foothold in the serious exporting market.

Will these opportunities, both domestic and international, be grasped? It has to be said that there are a few signs that they will. On 1 April 1991, the *Financial Times* published one of its periodic surveys of the factoring industry. Over the years, these have become an interesting barometer of the state of the industry, recording as they do the comments made by people within it to whichever FT journalist is producing the piece. In the lead article, Charles Batchelor, the paper's Small Business correspondent, under the by-line 'Time for fresh image', draws attention to the recent difficulties of the industry brought about by the recession, bad debts and declining profitability. He concludes the piece on a much more up-beat theme, pointing out the undoubted scope for the industry to increase market share. In support of this, he cites a recent survey by the Confederation of British Industry which found that only 2 per cent of companies had used a factor. In addition, he quotes two practising factors, one of whom estimates that the total market 'universe' for the factoring and invoice discounting industry is 150 000 companies, while the other indicates 250 000. With some 10 000 clients being serviced by factors and invoice discounters, he concludes, quite correctly, that: 'If the banks maintain their cautious policies for lending to small firms, the potential for factoring is enormous.'

Mr Batchelor is too polite to take the argument a stage further. Ignoring the fact that two senior people in the industry can quote such disparate figures as estimates for market size, and disregarding the marketing implications of this, it is plain that, as has been stressed throughout the latter part of this book, the main inhibitor to the development of the industry is the industry itself, and the policies of the organizations which control it. Put it another way, the clearing bank that gets the marketing of factoring right, relates it to its other services, and develops the business in a way that it is crying out for, will find for itself a very large number of new customers, however variously their total numbers are estimated. Whether one will do so, or whether one of the independents will gear up to exploit the opportunities that are available, only time will tell.

Appendices

APPENDICES

Appendix 1 *Association of British Factors and Discounters: Members' annual combined sales 1986–1992*

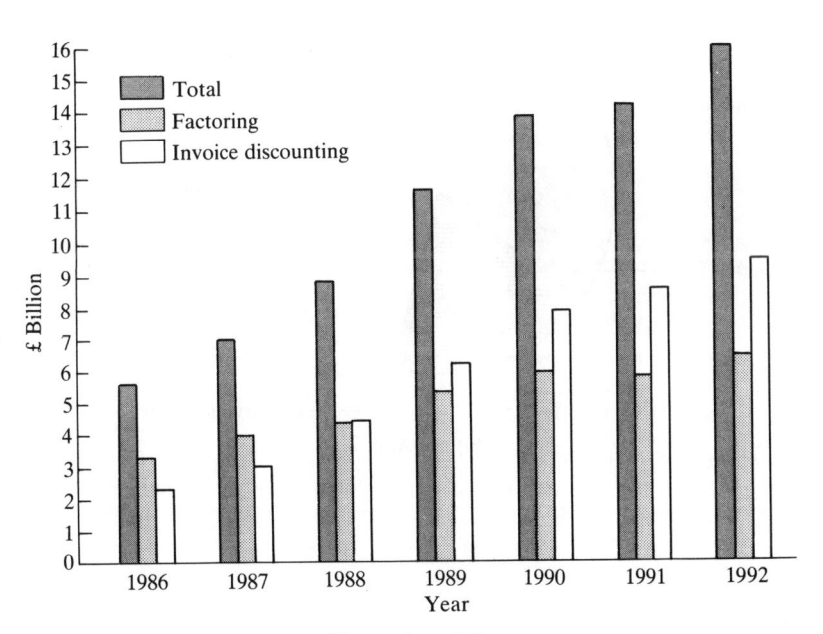

Figure App. 1.1

Appendix 2 *Association of British Factors and Discounters: Factoring and invoice discounting clients—industry sectors 1990*

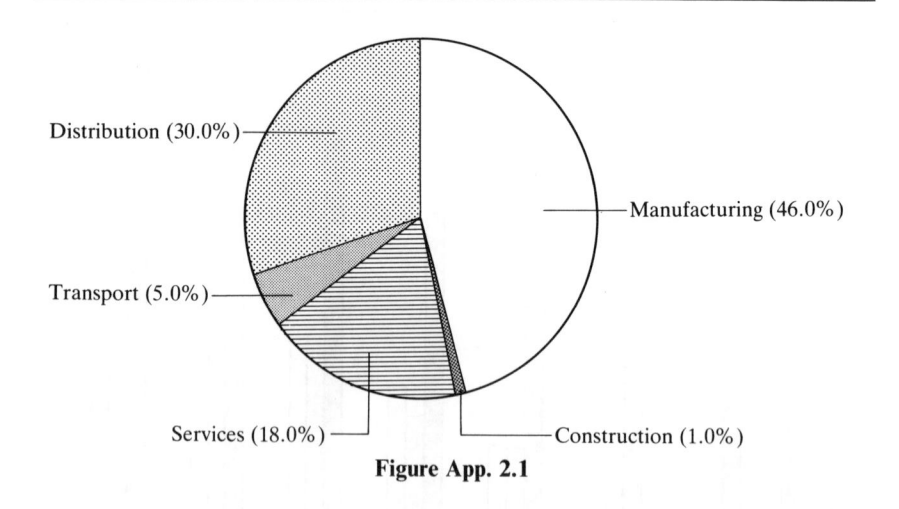

Figure App. 2.1

- Distribution (30.0%)
- Manufacturing (46.0%)
- Transport (5.0%)
- Services (18.0%)
- Construction (1.0%)

Appendix 3 *Association of British Factors and Discounters: Members and services*

Alex Lawrie Factors Ltd.

Beaumont House, Beaumont Road, Banbury, Oxfordshire OX16 7RN
Telephone 0295 272272
Telex 83627 Fax 0295 271634

Shareholder
Lloyds Bank plc 100%

Services offered
Factoring—recourse
Invoice discounting—whole turnover, export services

Approximate minimum client turnover
£100 000
Also new ventures and management buy-outs

Total volume of business
£1 652m

Regional offices

Banbury	London
Basingstoke	Maidstone
Birmingham	Manchester
Bristol	Newcastle
Cambridge	Newport
Coventry	Plymouth
Edinburgh	Southampton
Hatfield	Stockport
Leeds	

Client service offices

Banbury	Edinburgh
Bristol	Stockport
Cambridge	

Barclays Commercial Services Ltd.

Aquila House, Breeds Place, Hastings, East Sussex TN34 3DG
Telephone 0424 430824
Telex 95450 Fax 0424 427322

Shareholder
Barclays Bank 100%

Services offered
Factoring—recourse, non-recourse,
invoice discounting, confidential and disclosed—whole turnover.

THE BUSINESS OF FACTORING

Appendix 3 (*continued*)

Selected accounts and bulk import and export services—direct or through Factors Chain International

Approximate minimum client turnover
£100 000
Also new ventures and management buy-outs

Total volume of business
£1 130m

Regional offices
Birmingham   London Western
Bristol   Manchester
Haywards Heath   Northampton
Leeds   Reading
London   Southampton

Century Ltd.

Southbrook House, 25 Bartholomew Street, Newbury, Berkshire RG14 5LL
Telephone 0635 31517
Fax 0635 31703

Shareholders
Close Brothers Group plc 95%
Management 5%

Services offered
Factoring—recourse, non-recourse
invoice discounting—whole turnover, selected accounts import services

Approximate minimum client turnover
£100 000
Also new ventures and management buy-outs and acquisitions

Total volume of business
£167m

Regional offices
Birmingham   Newbury
London   Leeds
Manchester

Griffin Factors Ltd.

21 Farncombe Road, Worthing, West Sussex BN11 2BW
Telephone 0903 205181
Telex 87102 Fax 0903 214101

Shareholder
Midland Bank plc 100%

Services offered
Factoring—recourse, non-recourse
invoice discounting—whole turnover, seasonal, selected accounts
export services—through Factors Chain International

Appendix 3 (*continued*)

Approximate minimum client turnover
£100 000
Also new ventures and management buy-outs

Total volume of business
£2 140m

Regional offices
Birmingham   Leicester
Bristol   London
Cardiff   Manchester
Croydon   Milton Keynes
Leeds

Hill Samuel Commercial Finance Ltd.

Boston House, The Little Green, Richmond, Surrey TW9 1QE
Telephone 081 940 4646
Fax 081 940 6051

Shareholder
Hill Samuel Bank Ltd 100%

Services offered
Invoice discounting
stock and other asset
financing, export and import

Approximate minimum client turnover
£3 000 000
Also new ventures and management buy-outs and acquisitions

Total volume of business
£820m

Regional offices
Birmingham   Luton
Bristol   Manchester

International Factors Ltd.

PO Box 240, Sovereign House, Church Street, Brighton, Sussex BN1 3WX
Telephone 0273 21211
Telex 87382 Fax 0273 771501

Shareholder
Lloyds Bank plc 100%

Services offered
Factoring—non-recourse
invoice discounting
export services—through International Factors Group

Approximate minimum client turnover
£100 000 for domestic factoring
£250 000 for export factoring
£1 000 000 for invoice discounting

THE BUSINESS OF FACTORING

Appendix 3 (*continued*)

Also new ventures and management buy-outs

Total volume of business
£2 751m

Regional offices
Birmingham   London
Brighton   Manchester
Bristol   Nottingham
Cambridge   Poole
Glasgow   Reading
Leeds

Kellock Ltd.
Abbey Gardens, 4 Abbey Street, Reading, Berkshire RG1 3BA
Telephone 0734 585511
Fax 0734 502480

Shareholders
Bank of Scotland 95%
Management 5%

Services offered
Factoring—recourse, invoice discounting, export factoring—recourse, non-recourse
trade finance
venture capital

Approximate minimum client turnover
£250 000—for factoring
£2 000 000—for invoice discounting
Also new ventures

Total volume of business
£985m

Regional offices
Birmingham   Leeds
Edinburgh   London
Glasgow   Manchester

Lombard Natwest Commercial Services Ltd.
Smith House, PO Box 50, Elmwood Avenue, Feltham, Middlesex TW13 7QD
Telephone 081 890 1390
Telex 22593 Fax 081 751 3367

Shareholder
National Westminster Bank Group 100%

Services offered
Factoring—recourse and non-recourse
special service for small businesses
invoice discounting—confidential or disclosed, whole turnover or selected accounts
option with bad debt protection
services for exporters and importers

Appendix 3 (*continued*)

Approximate minimum client turnover
£75 000 for factoring
£1 000 000 for invoice discounting
Also new ventures and management buy-outs

Total volume of business
£2 466m

Regional offices

Bedford	Leeds
Birmingham	Manchester
Bristol	Nottingham

Royscot Factors Ltd.

Exchange Court, 3 Bedford Park, Croydon, Surrey CR0 2AQ
Telephone 081 686 9988
Telex 932211 Fax 081 680 1799

Shareholder
The Royal Bank of Scotland plc 100%

Services offered
Factoring—recourse, non-recourse
invoice discounting, confidential or disclosed, whole turnover, selected accounts

Approximate minimum client turnover
£200 000

Total volume of business
£357m

Regional offices

Birmingham	Leeds
Edinburgh	Hemel Hempstead
Glasgow	Manchester

Security Pacific Business Finance (Europe) Ltd.

Edge House, 42 Bond Street, Brighton, East Sussex BN1 1SE
Telephone 0273 321177
Fax 0273 326914

Shareholder
Close Bros Group plc

Services offered
Factoring—recourse, non-recourse
invoice discounting—whole turnover, selected accounts export services

Approximate minimum client turnover
£250 000 for Factoring
£2 000 000 for Invoice Discounting
Also new ventures, management buy-outs and buy-ins

Total volume of business
£270m

THE BUSINESS OF FACTORING

Appendix 3 (*continued*)

Trade Indemnity-Heller Commercial Finance Ltd.

Park House, 22 Park Street, Croydon, Surrey CR9 1RD
Telephone 081 681 2641
Telex 27348 Fax 081 681 8072

Shareholders
Trade Indemnity Group plc 50%
Heller Europe Ltd 50%
Heller Europe Ltd is ultimately owned by The Fuji Bank Ltd

Services offered
Factoring—recourse, non-recourse
invoice discounting—whole turnover, selected accounts export services—through Heller Overseas Network

Approximate minimum client turnover
£200 000
Also new ventures and management buy-outs

Total volume of business
£671m

Regional offices
Birmingham	Leeds
Bristol	Stockport
Croydon	

Client service offices
Croydon
Stockport

UCB Invoice Discounting Ltd.

Wren House, Sutton Court Road, Sutton, Surrey SM1 4TE
Telephone 081 770 1688
Fax 081 307 7740

Shareholder
UCB Group plc 100%

Services offered
Confidential invoice discounting—whole turnover
commercial mortgages

Approximate minimum client turnover
£1 000 000
Also new ventures and management buy-outs

Total volume of business
£417m

Regional offices
Birmingham	Manchester
Leeds	Sutton

(*Source: ABFD Annual Report* 1991)

Appendix 4 *Association of Invoice Factors: Members*

Anpal Finance Limited
P.O. Box 37
Kimberley House, Vaughan Way
Leicester LE1 9AZ
Telephone   0533 516066

Bibby Factors Limited
Kenwood House
77A Shenley Road
Borehamwood, Herts WD6 1AG
Telephone   081 207 1554

Clifton Mercantile Company Limited
115 Gloucester Place, London W1H 3PJ
Telephone   081 486 0541

Gaelic Invoice Factors Limited
Finlay House, 10–14 West Nile Street
Glasgow G1 2PP
Telephone   041 248 4901

KCH Limited
The Computer Centre
Benmhor
Campeltown, Argyll P28 6DN
Telephone   0586 54488

London Wall Factors Limited
Barkhill House
Chorleywood, Herts WD3 5NT
Telephone   0923 285199

Maddox Factoring (UK) Limited
Argent House
15 Progress Business Centre, Whittle Parkway, Slough
Berkshire SL1 6DQ
Telephone   06286 68706

Metropolitan Factors Limited
4 Heath Square, Boltro Road, Haywards Heath
West Sussex RH16 1BL
Telephone   0444 415081

Ulster Factors Limited
7 North Street, Belfast BT1 1NH
Telephone 0232 324522

Appendix 5 Sample sales ledger record

							Open item enquiry	
SFS21301		S.P.B.F. (Non-recourse)						
Client 0003		Any Client Limited			Domestic STG		AFC 001	
Debtor 0001072		A. Customer plc			Currency STG		AFC 001	
Credit limit		75000 Funding limit			9999999999 0%			
Balance		4810.70 Disappr (F)			0.00 (C)	(0.00)		0.00
Contact		A. Payer (Ph: 081 999 9999)						D1

Item	Type	Ref	Due Date	Apply	Doc Date	Amount	Balance	F C
00002	TINVOICE	4066	90292	00002	100192	368.01	0.00	
00003	TINVOICE	4097	130292	00003	140192	313.73	0.00	
00005	INVOICE	4382	50392	00005	40292	587.50	587.50	
00006	INVOICE	4383	50392	00006	40292	158.63	158.63	
00007	INVOICE	4384	50392	00007	40292	368.01	368.01	
00008	INVOICE	4720	290392	00008	280292	763.75	763.75	
00009	INVOICE	4721	290392	00009	280292	173.90	173.90	
00010	INVOICE	4730	290392	00010	280292	94.00	94.00	
00011	CASH			00011	30392	681.74−	0.00	
00012	INVOICE	4772	50492	00012	60392	1840.05	1840.05	
00013	INVOICE	4778	50492	00013	60392	158.63	158.63	
00014	INVOICE	4976	190492	00014	200392	313.73	313.73	

(3) Last (5) Next (6) A/c totals
(7) Debtor maint. (8) Brief debtor enq.
(23) More options (16) Exit

Figure App. 5.1 (*Source*: Century Limited)

Appendix 6 *Sample client accounting: Debts payable on maturity*

Ledger 000—12345 FIGURES AT CLOSE OF BUSINESS 01/01/92
CLIENT CURRENCY U.K. # 01/01/92

THE ACME TRADING COMPANY LTD.
Account executive J SMITH / KH

PAYMENT AVAILABILITY
Maturity period 75 days

		Ledger Balance	1231503.33 DB
Debts Purchased Acct	1261581.85 CR	'F' Risk	997110.53
Deduct I/E Disputes	0.00	'C' Risk	240140.11
I/E Excess C/L	0.00	Credits	5747.31 CR
=	1261581.85 CR		
		No of Customer A/Cs	144
P O/A facility 75%	946186.39 CR	— Active	62
LESS Client Account	878279.79 DB	— Inactive	82
		— Disputed	8
Amount Available	67906.60 CR		
		Value of Disputes	68604.33

**The amount available may be subject
to variation under the terms of the Concentration Limit   100%
Factoring Agreement   Value of Excesses   0.00

DEBTS PURCHASED ACCOUNT   CLIENT CURRENCY U.K. £ 21/08/92
                                    Account Balance: 1261581.85Cr

Date	Mat Date	Ref Nmbr	Tran	Amount	Conversion Details Ctry Curr Amount
02/08/90	15/10/90	94872	0552	42138.70Cr	
02/08/90	15/10/90	94873	0552	3946.38Cr	
02/08/90	15/10/90	94871	0552	6775.07Cr	
03/08/90	16/10/90	94874	0552	14653.99Cr	
31/07/90	13/10/90	94839	0552	187.60Cr	
06/08/90	19/10/90	94875	0552	32443.95Cr	
07/08/90	20/10/90	94876	0552	19839.78Cr	
08/08/90	21/10/90	94877	0552	21540.97Cr	
09/08/90	22/10/90	94878	0552	30210.75Cr	
10/08/90	23/10/90	94879	0552	39766.15Cr	
13/08/90	26/10/90	94880	0552	18201.80Cr	
14/08/90	27/10/90	94881	0552	14215.18Cr	
10/08/90	23/10/90	94879	0552	147.66Cr	
14/08/90	27/10/90	15996	0552	904.66Cr	
15/08/90	28/10/90	94882	0552	10464.22Cr	
17/08/90	30/10/90	94883	0552	10199.48Cr	
17/08/90	30/10/90	94884	0552	12441.89Cr	

Select a menu choice > > > >   F1-HELP
Menu B-Pay.avail End item First item G-clientacc Next Previous

Appendix 6 (*continued*)

CLIENT ACCOUNT

CLIENT CURRENCY U.K. # 02/01/92
Account Balance: 878279.79Dr

Date	Ref Nmbr	Tran	Amount	Conversion Details Ctry Curr Amount
15/08/90	94882	0103	78.48	
15/08/90	94882	0190	11.77	
15/08/90	259117	0101	28000.00	
15/08/90	259117	0135	15.00	
15/08/90	259117	0173	52.93	
15/08/90	80158	0634	1396.56	
16/08/90	259316	0101	10000.00	
16/08/90	259316	0135	15.00	
16/08/90	259316	0173	18.90	
17/08/90	94883	0103	76.50	
17/08/90	94883	0190	11.48	
17/08/90	94884	0103	93.31	
17/08/90	94884	0190	14.00	
17/08/90	15979	0502	3277.04	
20/08/90	259744	0101	42000.00	
20/08/90	259744	0135	15.00	
20/08/90	259744	0173	79.40	

Figure App. 6.1   (*Source*: Lombard Natwest Commerical Services Limited)

APPENDICES

Appendix 7 *Case study—Cash flow forecasts*

Table App. 7.1(a) Forecast A: Without factoring facility

£000	1	2	3	4	5	6	7	8	9	10	11	12	Total
Sales	88	90	91	102	98	110	115	118	120	122	130	135	1319
Debtors	205	208	209	223	230	242	267	283	297	304	316	333	–
Cash	85	87	90	88	91	98	90	102	106	115	118	118	1188
Purchases	38	40	43	49	45	50	49	59	60	59	51	56	599
Operating costs	44	43	40	49	41	55	52	60	56	55	45	51	591
Cash flow	3	4	7	−10	5	−7	−11	−17	−10	1	22	11	–
Overdraft	52	56	63	73	68	75	86	103	113	112	90	79	–

Table App. 7.1(b) Forecast B: With factoring facility

£000	1	2	3	4	5	6	7	8	9	10	11	12	Total
Sales	88	90	91	102	98	110	115	118	120	122	130	135	1319
Factoring prepayments	0	0	150	70	70	80	75	70	75	75	70	80	815
Cash	85	80	0	0	0	0	0	0	0	0	0	0	165
Drawings at maturity	0	0	0	20	25	25	30	33	37	42	45	45	302
Total cash	85	80	150	90	95	105	105	103	112	117	115	125	1282
Total costs	82	83	83	98	86	105	101	119	116	114	96	107	1190
Cash flow	3	−3	67	−8	9	0	4	−16	−4	3	19	18	92
Overdraft	52	55	0	0	0	0	0	0	3	0	0	0	–
Cash at bank	0	0	12	4	13	13	17	1	0	0	19	37	–

Appendix 8 Century Link: On-line reporting to clients

```
SFS10121                              (Non-recourse)                      Daily balance summary
Client   0003                        Any Client Limited                    Rating   C5    MEMO

────────── Sales Ledger ──────────         ────── Current Account ──────
Invoices MTD              89627.63         Opening balance              142233.77
Credit notes MTD           2874.63-        Cash receipts               107397.73-
Adjustments MTD               0.00         Advances to client           82000.00
Reassignments MTD           324.30-        Service charges               1344.42
Cash receipts MTD        107397.73-        Other charges                    0.00
Sett. discount MTD            0.00         Current balance             118415.75
Net change to S/L         20320.43-
Opening balance          221838.35         Client review limit         250000.00
Current balance          201517.92

────── Funding Disapprovals ──────         ────── Accrued Charges ──────
                                           Due from client             118415.75
 — Contra                     0.00         Client balance               83102.17
 — Dispute                  511.13
 — Others                 16566.94         Available @ 80%              29136.13
                                           Available fund               29136.13
Disapproved balance       17078.07
Approved S/L              18439.85         Collectability %                   99
 (7) Acct. enquiry    (8) Payments         (11) Client maint.    (12) Client anal.
(13) Advances        (14) Payment rpt      (23) More options             (16) Exit
```

Figure App. 8.1 Daily balance summary (*Source*: Century Limited)

```
SFS10302                S.P.B.F. (Non-recourse)                 Daily cash enquiry
Client A/C:   0003      Any Client Limited
              Domestic  STG
                        Cash received: 23/03/92

                                                  Dr Curr         Cl Curr
   Curr      Debtor     Name         Item   Type  Amount          Amount
*  STG       0001189    R. Small & Co.   00010  CASH  2209.00-    2209.00-
*  STG       0001269    A. Corporate plc 00005  CASH  2730.00-    2730.00-

                                             Total: 4939.00-     4939.00-
                                      PF7 – Previous day  PF9 – Item details
                                                              PF16 – Exit
```

Figure App. 8.2 Daily cash enquiry (*Source*: Century Limited)

```
SFS21321                                              Account enquiry - totals
Client 0003         Any Client Limited    Domestic STG              AFC 001
Debtor 0001072      A. Customer plc       Currency STG              AFC 001

Credit limit              75000  30/10/91 Expiry date              25/06/92
Funding limit        9999999999            Expiry date
                             0% (0.00)
Highest balance       4810.70 23/03/92    Payments this year              2
Highest payment        681.74  3/03/92    No. of items                   13
Last payment           681.74  3/03/92    No. of open credit items        0
Disc. allowed MTD        0.00             Days O/S                      365
Recourse balance      4810.70             Last movement            23/03/92
Non-recourse bal.        0.00
Unallocated credits      0.00
Last reminder         1114.14 17/03/92
                      ─────── CURRENT AGEING ───────
             A/c Balance   Not due                Due now        30 days o'due
Total         4810.70      3696.56  77%           1114.14  23%      0.00   0%
Unapp            0.00         0.00   0%              0.00   0%      0.00   0%
                         60 days o'due         90 days o'due      > 90 days
Total                       0.00   0%              0.00   0%       0.00   0%
Unapp                       0.00   0%              0.00   0%       0.00   0%
(1) Month-end ageing   (9) Debtor maint.          (17) Debtor memo pad  (16) Exit
```

Figure App. 8.3 Customer account enquiry (*Source*: Century Limited)

```
SFS10201              (Non-recourse)              10 Highest disputed balances
Client A/C: 0    Any Client Limited
                 Domestic                         Balances as at 20/03/92

                                                    % of
                                      Balance       GD's                STG
   Debtor       Name
 * 0001163      Short Pay Limited     511.13          0
```

PF1 – Gross debtors   PF3 – Contra   PF4 – Overdue
PF5 – Unapproved   PF7 – A/C enquiry   PF16 – Exit

Figure App. 8.4 Highest disputed balances (*Source*: Century Limited)

Appendix 9 *Worldwide factoring: Members of Factors Chain International*

For further details, please contact:
FCI Secretariat
Keizersgracht 559
1017 DR Amsterdam
The Netherlands
Telephone + 31 20 6270306
Telex 11261
Fax + 31 20 6257628

Country	Members	City	Principal shareholders
Australia	ESANDA FINANCE CORPORATION LIMITED	Melbourne	Australia and New Zealand Banking Group Limited
	SCOTTISH PACIFIC BUSINESS FINANCE PTY. LIMITED	Sydney	Bank of Scotland
Austria	INTERMARKET FACTORING GESELLSCHAFT m.b.H.	Vienna	Girozentrale und Bank der Österreichischen Sparkassen AG GKI-Holding Gesellschaft m.b.H.
Belgium	ACE FACTORS S.A. / N.V.	Brussels	ASLK-CGER BANK Société Nationale d'Investissement
	BELGO-FACTORS N.V.	Turnhout	General Bank Heller Overseas Corporation
	CERA FACTORS N.V.	Brussels	Cera Bank
	DE LAGE LANDEN FACTORS N.V.	Zaventem	De Lage Landen B.V.
Canada	ACCORD BUSINESS CREDIT INC.	Toronto	Privately held Canadian Corporation
	CANADIAN FINANCIAL CORPORATION	Montreal	Privately held Canadian Corporation

Czechoslovakia	TRANSFINANCE LIMITED	Prague	Transakta Zivnostenská banka Ltd. Girozentrale und Bank der Österreichischen Sparkassen AG Bayerische Hypotheken- und Wechsel Bank AG Factofrance Heller S.A.
Denmark	FORENEDE FACTORS A/S	Copenhagen	Den Danske Bank A/S
Ecuador	FACTURINSA S.A.	Guayaquil	Banco Holandes Unido S.A. International Finance Corp. Private Shareholders
Finland	FINNISH CORPORATE FINANCE LTD.	Helsinki	Union Bank of Finland Ltd.
France	BANQUE SOFIREC CCBP-FACTOREM FACTOFRANCE HELLER	Paris Paris Paris	The Edmond de Rothschild Group Banques Populaires Heller Overseas Corporation Compagnie Financière de Suez Crédit Industriel et Commercial de Paris
	UNIVERSAL FACTORING S.A.	Paris	Compagnie du Crédit Universel
Germany	DEUTSCHE FACTORING BANK	Bremen	Bayerische, Bremer, Hamburgische and Hessische Landesbank Landesbank Rheinland Pfalz, Landesbank Schleswig-Holstein, Norddeutsche and Westdeutsche Landesbank
	DISKO FACTORING BANK GmbH	Düsseldorf	Dresdner Bank AG 45% Hermes Kreditversicherungs-AG 45% Diskont und Kredit AG 10%
	GEFA Gesellschaft für Absatzfinanzierung mbH	Wuppertal	Deutsche Bank AG

Appendix 9 (continued)

Country	Members	City	Principal shareholders
Hong Kong	OTB INTERNATIONAL FACTORS LIMITED	Hong Kong	Overseas Trust Bank
Hungary	INTER-EUROPA BANK Rt.	Budapest	33 Hungarian Foreign Trade Companies Instituto Bancario San Paolo di Torino Hungarian Foreign Trade Bank
	HUNGARIAN FOREIGN TRADE BANK LTD.	Budapest	Hungarian Ministry of Finance and other enterprises
Iceland	LANDSBANKI ISLANDS (The National Bank of Iceland)	Reykjavik	Republic of Iceland
Indonesia	BANK INTERNASIONAL INDONESIA	Jakarta	Privately held Indonesian Bank
	PT SALINDO PERDANA FINANCE	Jakarta	Bank Dagang Negara (State Bank)
Italy	BARCLAYS FACTORING S.p.A.	Milan	Barclays Bank plc
	C.B.I. FACTOR S.p.A.	Milan	Istituto Centrale di Banche e Banchieri together with 72 other private banks
	CENTRO FACTORING S.p.A.	Florence	Centro Leasing S.p.A. Banco di Sardegna I.P.A.C.R.I. S.p.A. More than 70 Casse Di Risparmio
	FACTORIT S.p.A.	Milan	29% Banca Popolare di Novara 18% Banca Popolare di Milano Balance among 92 Italian Popular Banks
	MEDIOFACTORING S.p.A.	Milan	54% Cassa Risparmio Provincie Lombarde-Cariplo 30% Banco Di Sicilia 10% Istituto Bancario Italiano 6% Reale Mutua Assicurazione Torino
	MONTEPASCHI FACTOR S.p.A.	Turin	Gruppo Monte dei Paschi di Siena

Appendix 9 (continued)

Country	Members	City	Principal shareholders
	SANPAOLO FACTORING S.p.A.	Milan	Instituto Bancario San Paolo di Torino Banco Lariano S.p.A. Banca Provinciale Lombarda S.p.A. Gefina S.p.A. (Gruppo Generali) Cassa di Risparmio di Prato Finanziaria Tessile Investimenti e Partecipazioni Srl
	SPEI FACTORING S.p.A.	Rome	99% Spei Leasing S.p.A. 1% Edilspei S.p.A.
Japan	DAI-ICHI KANGIN FACTORING CO., LTD.	Tokyo	The Dai-Ichi Kangyo Bank Limited
	DIAMOND FACTORS LIMITED	Tokyo	Mitsubishi Bank Limited
	SUMIGIN GENERAL FINANCE CO., LIMITED	Tokyo	The Sumitomo Bank Limited
	THE CENTRAL FACTORS LIMITED	Nagoya	The Tokai Bank, Limited
	THE HYOGIN FACTORS LIMITED	Kobe	The Hyogo Bank, Limited
Korea	CENTRAL INVESTMENT AND FINANCE CORPORATION	Seoul	The Dongkuk Group and others
	DONG-A INVESTMENT AND FINANCE CORPORATION	Seoul	Daelim Industrial Co. and others
	GOLDSTAR INVESTMENT AND FINANCE CORPORATION	Seoul	The Lucky-Goldstar Group and others
	INDUSTRIAL BANK OF KOREA	Seoul	The Government
	PUSAN INVESTMENT AND FINANCE CORPORATION	Pusan	The Lucky-Goldstar Group and others
	SAM HEE INVESTMENT AND FINANCE CORPORATION	Seoul	Korea Explosives Group

Appendix 9 (*continued*)

Country	Members	City	Principal shareholders
Malaysia	SEOUL INVESTMENT AND FINANCE CORPORATION	Seoul	Commercial Bank of Korea Bank of Seoul
	ARAB-MALAYSIAN MERCHANT BANK BHD	Kuala Lumpur	Private Malaysian shareholders The Tokai Bank Ltd.
	MBf FACTORS SDN BHD	Kuala Lumpur	MBf Leasing Sdn Bhd (80%) Others (20%)
Mexico	BANAMEX FACTORAJE S.A. DE C.V.	Mexico	Banco Nacional de Mexico, S.N.C.
	FACTOR QUADRUM DE MEXICO, S.A. DE C.V.	Mexico	Quadrum, S.A. de C.V.
	FACTORING SERFIN, S.A.	Mexico	Banca Serfin, S.N.C.
Morocco	WAFABANK	Casablanca	Private Moroccan Groups Indosuez—Paris
Netherlands	B.V. DE FACTORIJ, Factorbedrijf van de Algemene Bank Nederland	Amsterdam	Algemene Bank Nederland N.V.
	DE LAGE LANDEN FACTORS B.V.	Eindhoven	De Lage Landen B.V. (wholly owned by Rabobank Nederland)
	FMN FACTORING	's-Hertogenbosch	Verenigde Spaarbank N.V. (VSB)
Norway	ELCON FINANS A/S	Oslo	Gjensidige Group
	FACTORING FINANS AS	Oslo	Den norske Bank
	UNI STOREBRAND FACTORING AS	Ålesund	UNI Storebrand Finans AS
Portugal	BNP FACTOR	Porto	Banque Nationale de Paris Group Union des Assurances de Paris
	NACIONAL FACTORING, S.A.	Lisbon	Banco Comercial Portugues and others

Appendix 9 (*continued*)

Country	Members	City	Principal shareholders
Singapore	DBS FACTORS PTE LIMITED	Singapore	The Development Bank of Singapore Limited
	KEPPEL FACTORS PTE LIMITED	Singapore	K Investment Holdings Pte Limited
	OUB FACTORS PTE LIMITED	Singapore	Overseas Union Bank Limited
	SINGAPORE FINANCE LIMITED	Singapore	Hong Leong Finance Limited
	UNITED OVERSEAS BANK LIMITED	Singapore	Public Listed Company
South Africa	NEDBANK COMMERCIAL SERVICES LIMITED	Johannesburg	Nedbank Limited
Spain	BANSABADELL FACTORING, S.A.	Sabadell (Barcelona)	Banco de Sabadell S.A.
	CATALANA DE FACTORING Catalana de Cobros y Factoring, S.A.	Barcelona	Banca Catalana
	HISPAFACTOR, S.A.	Madrid	Corporación Financiera Hispamer (Banco Hispano Americano)
	SANTANDER DE FACTORING, S.A.	Madrid	Banco de Santander, S.A.
Sweden	GOTA-FINANS AB	Stockholm	The Gota Group
	SVENSKA FINANS AB	Stockholm	Svenska Handelsbanken
Switzerland	AUFINA LEASING + FACTORING AG	Brugg	Union Bank of Switzerland, Zurich
Taiwan (R.O.C.)	CITC CO. LIMITED	Taipei	CITC Investment Co. Limited
			China Leasing Company Limited
			Others
Thailand	SIAM GENERAL FACTORING CO. LTD.	Bangkok	Siam Commercial Bank Limited, Group
			GF Holdings Co. Limited.

Appendix 9 (*continued*)

Country	Members	City	Principal shareholders
Turkey	AKTIF FINANS FACTORING HIZMETLERI A.Ş.	Istanbul	Vakifbank, Türk Eximbank, Garanti Bankasi, Finans Leasing, GSD Foreign Trade, Vakif Leasing, Güneş Insurance
	FACTOFINANS ALACAK ALIMI A.Ş.	Istanbul	Aksoy Group
	TÜRKIYE IŞ BANKASI A.Ş.	Ankara	Undersecretariat of Treasury and Foreign Trade The Employees' Pension and Mutual Aid Fund Individuals and Corporate Bodies
	TÜRKIYE KALKINMA BANKASI A.Ş. DEVELOPMENT BANK OF TURKEY	Ankara	State owned bank
UK	ALEX LAWRIE FACTORS LIMITED	Banbury	Lloyds Bank plc
	BARCLAYS COMMERCIAL SERVICES LIMITED	Hastings	Barclays Bank plc
	CHANCERY FACTORS LIMITED	London	Chancery plc
	GRIFFIN FACTORS LIMITED	Worthing	Midland Bank plc
	KELLOCK LIMITED	Reading	Bank of Scotland
	SECURITY PACIFIC BUSINESS FINANCE (EUROPE) LIMITED	Brighton	Security Pacific Eurofinance (UK) Limited
USA	BNY FINANCIAL CORPORATION	New York	The Bank of New York
	C & S/SOVRAN COMMERCIAL CORPORATION	Atlanta, Ga	C & S/Sovran Corporation
	ROSENTHAL & ROSENTHAL, INC.	New York	Rosenthal Inc.
	THE CIT GROUP/FACTORING MANUFACTURERS HANOVER, INC	New York	60% Dai-Ichi Kangyo Bank Ltd. 40% Manufacturers Hanover Corp.
Yugoslavia	GENERALEXPORT	Belgrade	Employees of Generalexport

Appendix 10 *Factors Chain International: Worldwide factoring business*

Table App. 10.1 Accumulative turnover figures for all FCI members in millions of US Dollars compared to worldwide factoring turnover

	1986	1987	1988	1989	1990	Increase 90/89
Invoice discounting	2 706	4 957	6 328	9 690	12 989	34%
Recourse factoring	13 930	18 852	21 207	25 745	31 710	23%
Non rec. factoring	16 722	24 607	28 310	36 884	41 662	13%
Collections	1 456	2 736	3 237	2 792	5 748	106%
Total domestic Factoring FCI	34 813	51 152	59 081	75 110	92 109	23%
FCI export factoring	669	903	1 030	1 281	1 827	43%
FCI import factoring	669	903	1 030	1 281	1 827	43%
Direct export	748	1 238	1 462	1 946	2 380	22%
Direct import	342	672	669	877	795	−9%
Total international Factoring FCI	2 427	3 715	4 192	5 384	6 829	27%
Grand total FCI	37 240	54 867	63 273	80 494	98 938	23%
World domestic factoring	97 782	131 067	151 522	179 198	230 564	29%
World international factoring	6 000	8 744	8 884	10 826	13 763	27%
World total	103 782	139 811	160 406	190 024	244 327	29%

Table App. 10.2 Factoring turnover by country in 1990 in millions of US dollars

No. of companies	Geographical area	Domestic	International	Total
EUROPE				
3	Austria	1 525	180	1 705
8	Belgium	2 762	690	3 452
1	Czechoslovakia	0	135	135
7	Denmark	952	346	1 298
5	Finland	4 920	110	5 030
17	France	13 325	1 000	14 325
14	Germany	7 665	2 678	10 343
5	Hungary	0	130	130
1	Ireland	200	10	210
1	Israel	0	4	4
80	Italy	70 000	1 280	71 280
1	Luxembourg	10	1	11
6	Netherlands	7 000	3 000	10 000
10	Norway	2 850	150	3 000
6	Portugal	1 490	79	1 569
18	Spain	2 530	255	2 785
15	Sweden	5 171	195	5 366
2	Switzerland	60	40	100
3	Turkey	6	56	62
34	UK	28 040	1 194	29 234
237		148 506	11 533	160 039
AMERICAS				
8	Canada	1 900	159	2 059
17	USA	48 212	800	49 012
70	Mexico	7 200	40	7 240
1	Dominican Republic	2	0	2
30	Brazil	200	0	200
1	Chile	20	0	20
4	Ecuador	57	0	57
131		57 591	999	58 590
AFRICA				
2	Morocco	0	3	3
5	South Africa	600	20	620
7		600	23	623

Table App. 10.2 (*continued*)

ASIA

3	Hong Kong	35	110	145
3	Indonesia	50	7	57
43	Japan	14 387	459	14 846
15	Malaysia	440	10	450
2	Philippines	50	1	51
20	Singapore	1 150	280	1 430
15	South Korea	4 000	206	4 206
1	Taiwan	0	25	25
7	Thailand	235	5	240
109		20 347	1 103	21 450

AUSTRALASIA

20	Australia	3 500	100	3 600
3	New Zealand	20	5	25
23		3 520	105	3 625
507	Total world factoring volumes	230 564	13 763	244 327

Note: *estimated as at 31 December 1990

THE BUSINESS OF FACTORING

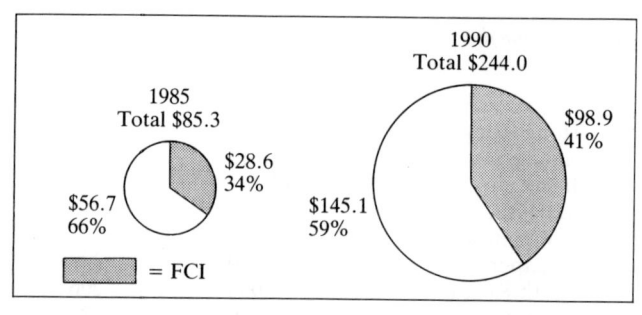

Figure App. 10.1 (a) Total factoring volume worldwide, US$ billions

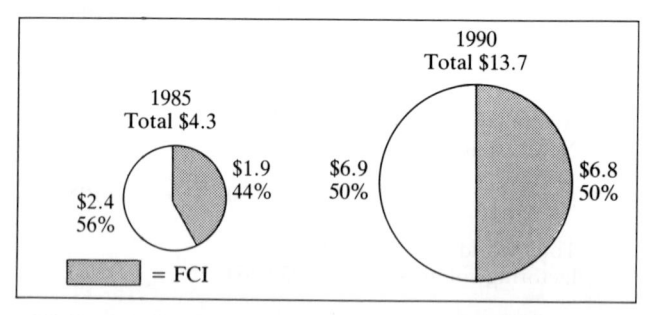

1985 Total $85.3
$56.7 66%
$28.6 34%
= FCI

1990 Total $244.0
$145.1 59%
$98.9 41%

(b) International factoring volume worldwide, US$ billions

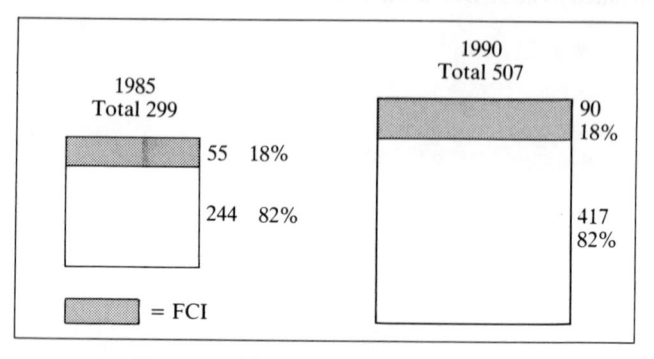

1985 Total $4.3
$2.4 56%
$1.9 44%
= FCI

1990 Total $13.7
$6.9 50%
$6.8 50%

(c) Number of factoring companies worldwide

1985 Total 299
244 82%
55 18%
= FCI

1990 Total 507
417 82%
90 18%

232

Table App. 10.3 Index of factoring volume growth for:
(a) Total world (base = 1980 in US$)   (b) Total FCI (base = 1980 in US$)   (c) 14 major FCI countries (base = 1980 in local currency)

		1980	1981	1982	1983	1984	1985	1986	1987	1988	1989	1990
(a)	World	100	103 +3%	103 =%	113 +10%	120 +6%	143 +19%	175 +22%	235 +34%	270 +15%	319 +18%	361 +13%
(b)	FCI	100	100 =%	96 −4%	106 +10%	108 +2%	159 +47%	207 +30%	304 +47%	350 +15%	445 +27%	481 +8%
(c)	Austria	100	138 +38%	131 −5%	129 −1%	132 +2%	133 +1%	138 +4%	153 +11%	166 +9%	176 +6%	196 +11%
	Belgium	100	95 −5%	122 +28%	160 +31%	201 +26%	229 +14%	274 +20%	279 +2%	324 +16%	401 +24%	502 +25%
	Canada	100	105 +5%	102 −3%	91 −11%	95 +4%	120 +26%	137 +14%	144 +5%	138 −4%	185 +34%	185 =%
	Denmark	100	95 −5%	126 +33%	140 +11%	170 +21%	159 −7%	163 +3%	166 +2%	205 +23%	286 +40%	373 +30%
	Finland	100	144 +44%	185 +28%	230 +24%	273 +19%	316 +16%	305 −4%	320 +5%	372 +16%	399 +7%	348 −13%
	France	100	147 +47%	195 +33%	211 +8%	240 +14%	248 +3%	294 +19%	379 +29%	480 +27%	585 +22%	690 +18%
	Germany	100	115 15%	110 −5%	115 +5%	120 +4%	133 +11%	161 +21%	184 +14%	177 −4%	191 +8%	235 +23%
	Italy	100	207 +107%	396 +91%	600 +51%	958 +60%	1 475 +54%	1 935 +31%	2 920 +51%	4 076 +40%	5 890 +44%	7 424 +26%
	Japan	100	112 +12%	103 −9%	202 +98%	213 +5%	172 −23%	180 +5%	173 −4%	258 +49%	259 =%	404 +56%
	Netherlands	100	105 +5%	116 +10%	155 +34%	188 +21%	228 +21%	262 +15%	278 +6%	346 +24%	372 +8%	482 +30%
	Norway	100	127 +27%	145 +14%	160 +10%	192 +20%	211 +10%	253 +20%	326 +29%	264 −19%	208 −27%	214 +3%
	Sweden	100	109 +9%	124 +14%	128 +3%	120 −7%	121 +1%	103 −17%	86 −20%	94 +9%	81 −16%	107 +32%
	UK	100	104 +4%	120 +15%	152 +27%	196 +29%	255 +30%	313 +23%	395 +26%	522 +32%	643 +23%	762 +19%
	USA	100	108 +8%	106 −2%	117 +10%	132 +13%	132 =%	141 +7%	157 +11%	160 +2%	165 +3%	173 +5%

Appendix 11 *International Factors Group: Members*

Company	General manager	Chairperson
Esanda Finance Corporation Ltd. Factoring and Business Services Dept. 436 St Kilda Road P.O. Box 5173 Melbourne 3004 AUSTRALIA Tel: 61/3/863.32.00 Fax: 61/3/863.32.33 Tlx: 154226	Mr. G. Dartnell Manager International	Mr. G. Dartnell Manager International
Factor-Bank GmbH P.O. Box 34 A-1014 Wien AUSTRIA Tel: 43/222/53.31.77.60 Fax: 43/222/63.81.33 Tlx: 115433	Dr. L. Binder-Degenschild	Dr. H. Schoeller Generaldirektor
International Factors S.A. Avenue de la Couronne, 358 B-1050 Bruxelles BELGIQUE Tel: 32/2/645.39.11 Fax: 32/2/646.06.89 Tlx: 22941	Mr. O. De Bouvere	Mr. J. Gielen
Crédit Lyonnais Eurofactors S.A. Avenue de Tervuren, 273 Boîte 10 B-1150 Bruxelles BELGIQUE Tel: 32/2/773.19.11 Fax: 32/2/772.28.19	Mr. Vic Verbist	Mr. Alfred Bouckaert

Appendix 11 (*continued*)

Company	General manager	Chairperson
Unifactoring A/S - International Factors A/S Helgeshoej Alle 23 DK-2630 Taastrup DENMARK Tel: 45/33/33.44.44 Fax: 45/43/71.13.07 Tlx: 27560	Mr. J. Becher	Mr. E. Lunderskov
Bikuben Finans A/S Rathsacksvej 1,3 DK-1862 Frederiksberg C DENMARK Tel: 45/31/23.08.33 Fax: 45/31/23.08.80	Mr. J. Storm Hansen Managing Director	Mr. K. Brandenborg
Finnish Corporate Finance Ltd, Siltasaarenkatu, 14 A SF-00530 Helsinki FINLAND Tel: 358/0/772.81 Fax: 358/0/772.84.98	Mr. L. Nybergh	Mr. K. Kouppala
SFF International Factors France Tour d'Asnières F-92608 Asnières Cedex FRANCE Tel: 33/1/47.91.70.00 Fax: 33/1/47.91.99.94 Tlx: 6310139	Mr. F. Rougeot	Mr. M. Billy Président Directeur Général Mr. Y. Delarue Chairperson of the IF-Group
SLIFAC-Société Lyonnaise d'Affacturage S.A. Rue Salvador Allende, 123 F-92000 Nanterre FRANCE Tel: 33/1/46.98.22.00 Fax: 33/1/46.98.01.17 Tlx: 616095	Mr. Ph. Pencrec'h Direct Fax: 33/1/46.98.05.36	Mr. J.-C. Irrmann Crédit Lyonnais-D.F.S.E. Rue N-D des Victoires, 40 F-75002 Paris FRANCE Tel: 33/1/42.95.09.56 Fax: 33/1/40.28.02.88 Tlx: 615310

THE BUSINESS OF FACTORING

Appendix 11 (*continued*)

Company	General manager	Chairperson
DG Diskontbank AG P.O. Box 160247 G-6000 Frankfurt/Main 1 GERMANY Tel: 49/69/74.47.04 Fax: 49/69/23.16.32 Tlx: 4170681	Mr. K. Herbert Direct Fax: 49/69/23.53.61	Mr. K. Herbert 'ad interim'
Crédit Lyonnais Factoring GmbH Postfach 370 247 G-8000 Muenchen GERMANY Tel: 49/89/51.49.90 Fax: 49/89/51.49.91.36	Mr. Joachim Ost	Mr. J.-C. Irrmann Crédit Lyonnais - D.F.S.E. Tel: 33/1/42/95.09.56
OTB International Factors Ltd. 12A OTB Building 160 Gloucester Road Wanchai HONG KONG Tel: 852/5/73.37.83 Fax: 852/5/72.75.35 Tlx: 74545	Mr. D. McKenna Director and General manager	Mr. D. F. L. Turner Vice-Chairperson
Central-European International Bank Ltd. P.O. Box 170 H-1364 Budapest HUNGARY Tel: 36/1/118.83.77 Fax: 36/1/138.22.73 36/1/118.94.15 Tlx: 226104	Mrs. M. Költö Deputy General Manager Direct Tel: 36/1/118.87.28	Mr. G. Zderborski General manager
Merkantil Bank Jozsef Attila utca 24 H-Budapest V. HUNGARY Tel: 36/1/118.26.88 Fax: 36/1/117.23.31 Tlx: 202579	Mr. L. Hamori Manager	Mr. A. Kolossvary Director Direct Tel: 36/1/117.22.70

Appendix 11 (*continued1*)

Company	General manager	Chairperson
International Factors (Ireland) Ltd. Hume House, Ballsbridge IRL-Dublin 4 IRELAND Tel: 353/1/68.97.77 Fax: 353/1/60.28.29 Tlx: 93846	Mr. P. MacCanna Managing Director	Mr. J. G. Collins

IFITALIA-International Factors Italia S.p.A.
P.O. Box 1517
I-20100 Milano
ITALY
 	
Tel: 39/2/67.781
Fax: 39/2/65.30.32
    39/2/677.83.05
    (International Dept.)
Tlx: 312104/314122
	Mr. T. Musso
	Managing Director
		Mr. P. Sciume

Credit Factoring International S.p.A. Via dell'Annunciata, 2 L-20121 Milano ITALY Tel: 39/2/659.62.41 > 5 Fax: 39/2/653.329 Tlx: 321596	Mr. L. Ricci Manager	Dr. V. Loconsole Managing Director
Sanwa Business Credit Corporation Palace Building 5th Floor 1-1-1 Marunouchi, Chiyoda-ku Tokyo 100 JAPAN Tel: 81/3/211.72.81 Fax: 81/33/214.58.30 Tlx: 02226162	Mr. K. Suzuki Manager International Department	Mr. Kanenobu Tanaka

Appendix 11 (*continued*)

Company	General manager	Chairperson
Daihan Investment & Finance Corporation 54-1 KA, Myung-Dong, Chung-Ku Seoul KOREA Tel: 82/2/77.19.00.00 Fax: 82/2/754.81.84 Tlx: 26765	Mr. Byung-Jae Ko	Mr. Jong-Man Lee President
Bando Investment & Finance Corporation 36-14, 4-KA, Chungang-Dong Chung-Ku Pusan KOREA Tel: 82/2/463.71.81 82/2/463.88.71 Fax: 82/2/752.14.37	Mr. Jong-Dae Kim	Mr. Kang-Pyo Kong
Koryo Investment & Finance Corporation 6, 2 GA, Ulchi-Ro Jung-Ku Seoul KOREA Tel: 82/2/754.50.00 82/2/754.34.72 Fax: 82/2/754.23.75	Mr. Sang-Chan Kim President	Mr. Sang-Chan Kim President
SamSam Investment & Finance Corporation 199-63, 2-KA, Ulchi-Ro Chung-Ku Seoul KOREA Tel: 82/2/754.33.11 Fax: 82/2/754.67.10	Mr. Yong-Ki Kim Director	Mr. Seung-Shik Kim

Appendix 11 (*continued*)

Company	General manager	Chairperson
Maroc Factoring 243 Boulevard Mohammed V Casablanca MAROC Tel: 212/2/30.20.08 Fax: 212/2/30.62.77 Tlx: 21079	Mr. A. Nadifi Manager	Mr. A. Jouahri P.D.G. B.M.C.E. - Banque Marocaine du Commerce Extérieur 140 Avenue Hassane II Casablanca 01 MAROC Tel: 212/2/27.20.49 Fax: 212/2/22.01.23
Factoring Comermex S.A. de C.V. Servicios Financieros Multiples Bd M. Avila Camacho 1, 6to Piso Col. Polanco M-C.P. 11560 Mexico MEXICO Tel: 52/5/395.93.77 Fax: 52/5/557.48.48	Mr. Manuel F. De la Rosa Director General	
IFN Factors P.O. Box 604 NL-3000 AP Rotterdam THE NETHERLANDS Tel: 31/10/402.33.44 Fax: 31/10/414.81.05 Tlx: 21387	Mr. J. Van Kooij	Mr. H. J. Rutgers
Factoring Finans P.O. Box 2424 Solli N-0202 Oslo 2 NORWAY Tel: 47/2/43.10.00 Fax: 47/2/44.18.44 Tlx: 19316	Mr. O. Alsaker Director	Mr. O. Alsaker Director
International Factors Portugal S.A. Apartado 21161 P-1129 Lisboa Codes PORTUGAL Tel: 351/1/87.40.21 >6 Fax: 351/1/87.40.28 Tlx: 18336	Mr. J. de Sousa Uva Chairperson and Managing Director	Mr. J. de Sousa Uva Chairperson and Managing Director

Appendix 11 (*continued*)

Company	General manager	Chairperson
International Factors (Singapore) Ltd. 460 Alexandra Road 18-00 PSA Building Singapore 0511 REPUBLIC OF SINGAPORE Tel: 65/2/70.77.11 Fax: 65/2/72.71.83 Tlx: 21524	Mr. K. S. Foo Managing Director	Mr. H. R. Hochstadt
International Factors Espanola S.A. Paseo de la Castellana 32/4a E-28046 Madrid SPAIN Tel: 34/91/431.21.70-(22.96) 34/91/431.22.65-(21.30) Fax: 34/91/576.66.51 Tlx: 49554	Mr. J. A. Montes Direct Tel: 34/1/537.79.10 Mrs. I. Santos International Manager Direct Tel: 34/1/431.21.30	Mr. J. R. Jouve Jimémez
BBV Factoring S.A. Lagasca, 88 - planta 2 E-28001 Madrid SPAIN Tel: 34/1/374.48.80 Fax: 34/1/578.18.11 Tlx: 49923	Mr. J. Perez Calot	Mr. Rafael Accosta

Caixa Factoring S.A.
Avda. Diagonal,
615 - planta 3a
E-08028 Barcelona
SPAIN
Tel: 34/3/410.99.44
    34/3/321.17.67
    34/3/322.30.07
Fax: 34/3/405.27.94
Tlx: 97530
	Mr. J. Soley Sans
	Managing Director and
	Chairperson
	Madrid
	Tel: 34/91/577.39.52
	Fax: 34/1/577.38.13
		Mr. J. Soley Sans
		Managing Director &
		Chairperson

Banesto Factoring S.A. Cardenal Marcelo Spinola s/n Bloque F4 4e piso E-MADRID Tel: 34/1/302.95.04 Fax: 34/1/766.96.36	Mr. J. L. Gonzalez Contreras Managing Director	Mr. J. Banon Seijas

Appendix 11 (*continued*)

Company	General manager	Chairperson
Crédit Lyonnais Ibérica de Factoring S.A. Pza Pablo Ruiz Picasso s/n Torre Picasso - planta 28 E-28020 Madrid SPAIN Tel: 34/1/556.06.74 Fax: 34/18556.41.36	Mr. C. Rico	Mr. G. de Jacquelot
Svenska Finans, AB S:Eriksgatan 117 S-10635 Stockholm SWEDEN Tel: 46/8/788.62.36 46/8/788.60.00 Fax: 46/8/33.36.88 46/8/30.23.41 Tlx: 17744	Mr. M. Persson Executive Vice-President	Mr. B. Gustafson
Factors AG Bäckerstrasse 40 CH-8026 Zurich SWITZERLAND Tel: 41/1/242.16.70 Fax: 41/1/291.03.39 Tlx: 812538	Mr. K. Schaer Manager	Dr. R. Fankhauser President of Factors AG c/o Finalba AG Loewenstrasse, 29 CH-8021 Zürich SWITZERLAND Tel: 41/1/214.81.11 Fax: 41/1/212.16.60 Tlx: 812795
International Factors Ltd P.O. Nox 240 GB-Brighton BN1 3WX ENGLAND Tel: 44/273/21.211 Fax: 44/273/77.15.01 Tlx: 87382	Mr. T. G. Hutson Managing Director	Mr. D. Pirrie Chairperson Lloyds Bank PLC (documents to be sent via Mr. T. Hutson)

Appendix 11 (*continued*)

Company	General manager	Chairperson
BancBoston Financial Company Factoring Division P.O. Box 1816 Boston, MA 02105 USA Tel: 1/617/929.48.88 Fax: 1/617/929.48.90 Tlx: 4996527	Mr. H. Wilson Assistant Vice President Mr. G. E. Romeo, SVP BancBoston Financial Co. 2 Pennsylvania Plaza New York, NY 100001 USA Tel: 1/212/613.30.01 Fax: 1/212/613.30.63 Tlx: 4974216 Mr. L. Fronhöffer Direct Tel: 1/212/613.30.26	Mr. B. J. Bowden President
Republic Factors Corporation 452 Fifth Avenue New York, N.Y. 10018 UNITED STATES OF AMERICA Tel: 1/212/525.52.00 Fax: 1/212/525.50.22	Mr. S. Langer	Mrs. D. Sarachik Executive Vice President

Source: International Factors Group S.C.

Index

Abtretungsverbot, 187
Accountants, 42, 73, 79, 133
Accounting:
   audited Accounts, 73, 99, 120, 122
   client, 21, 61–75
   sales ledger, 5, 12, 14, 22, 53, 67, 69, 121
Accounting Standards Committee, 74–75
After-sales service, 55
Agreement, factoring, 63–65, 164–165
Alex Lawrie Factors Ltd, 114, 135, 188
Anglo Factoring Ltd., 8
Aluminium Industry Vaasen BV *v* Romalpa Aluminium Ltd, 58
Assignment of debt, 20, 60–63
Association of British Factors and Discounters (ABDF), 10, 11, 15, 85, 87, 93, 95, 126, 127, 137, 149–157
   bad debts, 46
   Certificate in Factoring, 150–151
   Chairperson, 149, 153
   Code of Conduct, 148
   Diploma in Factoring, 151
   Education Committee, 149
   Legislative Committee, 149
   members entry fee, 148
   public relations, 117, 149, 151–154, 195, 196
   Public Relations Committee, 149
   statistics, 150
   structure and activities, 149, 150
   training, 150
   Vice-Chairman, 149
Association of Invoice Factors, 16, 84, 156

Bad debts, 46
Balance sheet, 53
Banks, clearing, 3, 9, 10, 15, 54, 79, 194–201
   branch managers, 118–119, 133
   and factoring management, 10, 89
   influence on marketing, 118, 198–201
   as shareholders, 108–116, 196–201
   sterling lending, 84
   waivers on charges, 62
Bannock, Graham and Partners, 131–133
Bank of Credit and Commerce International (BCCI), 136
Barclays Bank, 9, 16
Barclays Commercial Services, 81, 178
Batchelor, Charles, 117, 202
Belgium, 178
Birmingham, 193
Biscoe, Peter, 8
Black, Philip, 178
Bland, Leslie, 153
Bought ledger, 121
Bowden (UK) Ltd *v* Scottish Timber Products, 58
British Airways, 146
British Bankers Association, 84, 119
British Telecom, 105, 106
BS: 5750, 143
Burson Marsteller, 28, 95, 129
Business finance, 124
Business Marketing Services Ltd, 95, 129
Business Plan, 77, 142

Calais, 193
Capital equipment, 55, 162
Carmichael, R S & Co, 185
Case studies, 76–83
Cash collection, 5, 24–25, 28, 51
   and exports, 167–168
   and invoice discounting clients, 94
Cash flow forecasts, 88, 92, 99, 122
   and communication, 141
Castle Corregated Ltd., 82
CBI, 134
Century Ltd., 119, 153
Century Link, 106–107

INDEX

Chambers of Commerce, 191
CHAPS, 34
Civil War, American, 8
City of London, 159–160, 200
Client accounting, 20, 21, 69–73
Clients, factoring, 4, 84–97, 129
  commercial sectors from, 9
  criteria for selection of, 19
  communications with, 104–107
  duration factoring arrangements, 12
  education of, in factors system, 20
  failure, 12, 194
  fraud by, 12, 48, 50
  losses, 194–195
  risks, 47, 100
  performance of, 100
  satisfaction with service, 95–96
Client relations function, 53, 98–107
Client executive, 21, 100, 103
Close Bros Group plc, 82
Closed User Group, 105
Computing, 9, 12
Consultants, use of, 141
Contra trading, 56, 125
Contract terms, 58, 91
Costs of factoring, 40–44, 175
Credit cards, 9
Credit:
  assessment, 23
  concentrations, 18, 52
  control and advice, 22–24
  insurers, 18
  lines, 91
  nature of, 18
  risk-exports, 163
Credit Factoring International Ltd, 169
Credit notes, 20, 100, 102
Currency, foreign, 166
Customer:
  base, 54, 100
  complaints, 143, 144
  factors accounts with, 20
  relations and factoring, 19, 92
  statements, 28
  trading style, 20

Dai Ichi Kango Bank, 185

Daily Telegraph, The, 152
Dearle *v* Hall, 59
Debt(s):
  assignment of, 20, 51, 60–63
  collection, 19, 24–25, 28, 51, 167–168
  credit protection, 19
  dilution of, 52
  quality, 53
De Lage Landen, 178
Department of Overseas Trade, 161
Department of Trade and Industry, 160
Dependable Packs Ltd, 00
Discounts for prompt payment, 52
Disputes, trade, 26, 50, 52, 100, 101, 120

Economy, British, 4, 12, 190–193, 194–195
Enterprise culture, The, 5
Electronic communication, 23, 104–106, 140
Employment, general, 5
Equity gap, 4–5
Equity investment, 77–78, 142
Equitable assignment, 61
Euro-currencies, 160
Exfinco, 171–172
Export Credit Guarantee Department, 161–162, 171, 176, 178, 189, 201
Export factors, 163, 167, 173–174
Export Factoring, 13, 162–170, 201
  and failure to grow, 187, 192
  (*see also* Factoring)

Factoring:
  agency, 35–36
  agreement:
    breadth and scope of, 49, 63–65
    export business, 164–165
  bulk, 35–36
  checklist, choosing your factor, 86–80, 96–97
  costs, 37–38
  commencement procedures, 19–20
  credit protection, 19–20
  definitions, 1–2
  direct export, 169–170

244

INDEX

export, 37, 162–170, 133–176, 201
financial facility, 2, 28, 69–71, 79–80, 88, 99–101
comparison with banking, 118
finance charges, 39
history, 7–10
international, 176–193
maturity, 36–37
myths, 124
non-recourse, 19–29
recourse, 29–32, 101
security, 53–54, 59–66
(*see also* Factors; Factors Chain International)
Factors:
bank-owned, 108–110
early, 7
growth and profitability, 110–112
independent, 3
knowledge of small-medium sized business, 14
locations, 114
market shares, 108
marketing, 117–147
ownership, 108
people in industry, 3, 112–116, 122
(*see also* Factoring; Factors Chain International)
Factors Chain International, 158, 168, 170, 177, 179–181, 192
Factel, 104–105
Factflow, 105
Far East, 178
Feiner, Irwin, 102
Financial institutions, 134, 159
Financial Times, The, 117, 152, 202
Fixed and floating charges, 60, 61, 76
Fraud, 12, 48, 50, 99, 102–103, 194
'Fresh air' invoices, 102
Foreign collections, 91
France, 178, 183
Frankfurt, 159
Fuji Bank, 85, 182

Germany, 138, 186–187
Government, HM, 5, 198
'Green' issues, 154

Growth, corporate, 4, 53, 110
Guardian, The, 152

H & H Factors, 115, 119
Hardy Lennox *v* Graham Puttick, 58
Haywards Heath, 114
Heller International, 182–183
Helstan case, 62
Hill Samuel Commercial Finance, 139–140, 172–173
HM Customs & Excise, 191
Holland, 178
Humphries, Ken, 82

IBM Personal Computers, 105
Import Factor, 163, 167–168
Independent, The, 52
Information flows, 141
International factoring, 158–193
International Factors Ltd, 104–105, 182, 188
International Factors Group, 181–182
Investors in People, 144–145
Insolvency/receivership, 52–53
Institute of Export, 191
Invoices:
as eviden of debt, 20
factoring legend, 20
schedules of, 20, 163
Invoice Discounting:
and credit protection, 3
definition, 1–2, 32–36
factoring, relationship with, 16
information, client, 33
funding limits, 94
exports, 170–172
growth, 47
prepayments, 33
providers, of service, 33
procedures, 32, 33, 94
risks to discounter, 32, 51, 54–55

Japan, 186

Kennedy Administration, 9
Kiev, 193

245

INDEX

Law of Property Act, 1925, 61
Leasing, 9
Lender of last resort, 1, 9, 53
Letter of credit, 160
Levitt, Theodore, 135
Liquidation, 60
Lombard NatWest Commercial Services, 105–106, 169, 188

Maastrict Treaty, The, 192
Management buy-outs, 34–35
Manufacturing industry, 14, 84, 201
Marketing, 10, 108–109, 117–147
Maturity factoring, 36–37, 71, 73
Maturity period, 71–73
McKinley Tariffs, 8
Medium-sized companies, 00
Mexico, 159
Microcomputing, 12, 106
Middle East, 189
Mixed messages, 126–128
Money Lenders Acts, 60

National Commercial Finance Association, 185
NCM Holdings, 190
Negotiations for factoring, 91, 92, 119–120
New start businesses, 54
New York, 8, 159
Notice of Assignment, 20, 166

Observer, The, 201
Oelbermann, Dommerick & Co, 8
Ottowa, 187
Overdraft, bank, 2, 9, 15, 76, 77, 78, 79, 199
Owner-managers, 4

Packaged lending, 139–140
Packaging and paper, 82
Page, Arthur, 81
Page, Tony, 80–83
Page, AE Industrial Holdings Ltd, 80–83
Parliament, Members of, 134
PAYE, 121

Payment availability, 69–71
Personal guarantees, 65
Pilgrim Fathers, the, 8
Plant and machinery, 139
Potential factoring users, 129–130
Pre-invoicing, 48
Prices, 93
Prime Minister, British, 192
Product development, 137–139
Products related to factoring, 12
Prohibition of assignment, 60
Public Relations, 133, 151–153

Quotation for factoring, 120–121

Rabobank, Group, 178
Radcliffe Committee, 159–160
Receivership, 50, 51–52
Recourse factoring, 29–32
Recourse *v* Non-Recourse 90–91
Reservation of Title (Romalpa), 58, 125
Retentions, 57, 125
Risks:
    client, 47–59
    customer, 45–46
Royal Bank of Scotland, 16, 196
Roy Scot Factors, 16

Sales ledger:
    accounting, 67, 69, 74
    administration, 5, 12, 14, 22, 121
    characteristics, 53
    and credit protection, 2, 13
Salespeople, 78, 91, 133, 155, 191
Salespitch, 91, 135
Sale or return, 57
Sales terms, 18, 19, 163
Schedule of Offer, 20
Seasonal business, 56
Security, 59–66
Security Pacific Business Finance (Europe) Ltd, 82
Service charge, 38, 39, 42
Single European Market, 166, 177
South America, 159, 181
South Korea, 159
Spain, 159

SP Business Finance (Europe) Ltd, 82
Staff cost, 145
Stock finance, 139
Survey of new business, 52, 121–122

Technology, 140
Termination of factoring, 64, 91
Textile trade, 7, 186
Thatcher, Mrs Margaret, 5, 11
Times, The, 159
Tokyo, 159
Total Quality Management (TQM), 143–144
Trade credit, 18
Trading style, 20
Training and Enterprise Councils (TEC), 140, 145
Training in small business, 86
TSB Group, 139

Turkey, 188

Unidroit, 187
Unfactorable business, 55–59, 120
USA, 8, 158, 166, 184–186
Uniform Commercial Code, in USA, 60

Value Added Tax (VAT), 121
Venture capital, 5, 142, 160, 177–178
Viewdata, 105

Waiver from banks, 64
Warranties, 64
Welsh Development Agency, 171–172
Weakness, financial, 53–55
Withnall, Tony, 82
Wilson Committee, and equity gap, 4–5
Wilson, Sir Harold, 173

XYZ Limited, case study, 76–80